PRENTICE-HALL FOUNDATIONS OF FINANCE SERIES

PRENTICE-HALL FOUNDATIONS OF FINANCE SERIES

Ezra Solomon, *Editor*

Finance as a
Dynamic Process

Edwin J. Elton

Martin J. Gruber

New York University

PRENTICE-HALL, INC., Englewood Cliffs, New Jersey

Library of Congress Cataloging in Publication Data

ELTON, EDWIN J
   Finance as a dynamic process.

   (Prentice-Hall foundations of finance series)
   Includes bibliographies.
   1.–Corporations—Finance.   I.–Gruber, Martin J., 1937–   joint author.   II.–Title.
HG4011.E4–1975   658.1′5   74-14899
ISBN 0-13-314690-1
ISBN 0-13-314682-0   (pbk.)

© 1975 by Prentice-Hall, Inc., Englewood Cliffs, N.J.

Printed in the United States of America

10 9 8 7 6 5 4 3 2 1

PRENTICE-HALL INTERNATIONAL, INC., *London*

PRENTICE-HALL OF AUSTRALIA, PTY. LTD., *Sydney*

PRENTICE-HALL OF CANADA, LTD., *Toronto*

PRENTICE-HALL OF JAPAN, INC., *Tokyo*

PRENTICE-HALL OF INDIA PRIVATE LTD., *New Delhi*

TO

Jonathan and Stacey

AND TO

Annette, John, Kathryn, and Ned

Editor's Note

The subject matter of financial management is in the process of rapid change. A growing analytical content, virtually nonexistent ten years ago, has displaced the earlier descriptive treatment as the center of emphasis in the field.

These developments have created problems for both teachers and students. On the one hand, recent and current thinking, which is addressed to basic questions that cut across traditional divisions of the subject matter, do not fit neatly into the older structure of academic courses and texts in corporate finance. On the other hand, the new developments have not yet stabilized and as a result have not yet reached the degree of certainty, lucidity, and freedom from controversy that would permit all of them to be captured within a single, straightforward treatment at the textbook level. Indeed, given the present rate of change, it will be years before such a development can be expected.

One solution to the problem, which the present Foundations of Finance Series tries to provide, is to cover the major components of the subject through short independent studies. These individual essays provide a vehicle through which the writer can concentrate on a single sequence of ideas and thus communicate some of the excitement of current thinking and controversy. For the teacher and student, the separate self-contained books provide a flexible up-to-date survey of current thinking on each subarea covered and at the same time permit maximum flexibility in course and curriculum design.

EZRA SOLOMON

Contents

Preface

Most of the analytical work in the field of corporation finance and investments has been based on static one-period analysis. The impact of current decisions on future decisions or the interrelationship of current decisions with future decisions has rarely been considered. However, in recent years an increased awareness of the multiperiod nature of financial decisions has led to the establishment of a growing literature on multiperiod financial models. Unfortunately, the literature that has appeared is so mathematically complex that it is often inaccessible to students (and sometimes to teachers) of finance. The problem has been complicated by the fact that authors often use very different terminology and model construction when studying variations of the same problem. Because of this, we have undertaken to write a monograph to synthesize and extend the use of multiperiod models in finance. In doing so, we have assumed no knowledge on the part of the reader other than acquaintance with algebra and the rudiments of statistics. The book is completely self-contained with respect to the development of multiperiod models. We hope that this monograph will both make multiperiod financial models more accessible and encourage more research in what we consider one of the most exciting areas of finance.

The material in the monograph has been used as the basis for both MBA and Ph.D. finance seminars at New York University. However, we realize that at many universities, all the material found in this book will not be contained in one course. For this reason we have tried to make each chapter of this book reasonably self-contained. In Chapter 1 we present the basis of multiperiod models through a number of examples. We believe that after studying Chapter 1 the reader can proceed to any other chapter in the book which interests him.

Although this book is intended for students of finance, we have been gratified by the reception it has received from our colleagues in operations research. Several of them have used chapters from this book as a source of OR applications for their students, as well as a source of ideas for their own research.

This book was completed while the authors were Senior Research Fellows at the International Institute of Management in Berlin, Germany. We would like to thank IIM for providing us with the financial resources and environment that allowed us to bring this project to fruition. Chapter 9 is based for the large part on the first section of a paper which we jointly authored with Zvi Lieber of Tel Aviv University. We would like to thank him for permission to use the analysis as part of this book. A large number of people have provided us with helpful comments during the preparation of this manuscript. We would like to thank in particular Alex Robichek of Stanford University, Ram Rao of the University of Rochester, Paul Kleindorfer of the University of Pennsylvania, Zvi Lieber of Tel Aviv University, Peter Jennergren of IIM, Manfred Padberg of IIM, Yvo Dirickx of IIM, Mike Kennan of New York University, Bill Carleton of Dartmouth, Lee Wakeman of IIM, and Ed Jurgenson of IIM. Stella Lochner, Lee Sillman, and Beverly With have cheerfully typed the manuscript. We have fortunately been blessed with secretaries who somehow turn our hen scratches into polished professional English. Anyone familiar with either of the authors knows what a difficult task that is. Finally, we would like to thank Dr. Watson who first demonstrated to us a utility function for which myopic consumption decisions are always optimal.

EDWIN J. ELTON
MARTIN J. GRUBER

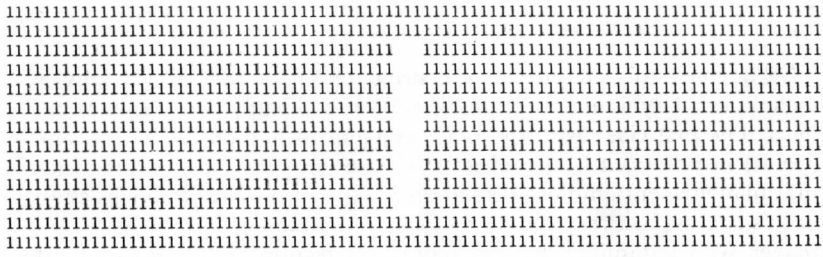

Introduction to Multi-Period Analysis

Until recently, almost all the literature in finance has been concerned with static single-period models. Yet almost all financial decisions are multiperiod in nature. Ignoring the multiperiod nature of financial decisions can, as will become very clear as the reader proceeds through this monograph, lead to nonoptimal decisions. This growing realization has led in recent years to an increased emphasis on the development of multiperiod models in finance. The literature which is evolving in this field has been inaccessible to many people because of its mathematical complexity and because of the absence of a standard terminology or methodology.

The purpose of this monograph is to synthesize and extend the insight that has been gained into financial problems by recognizing and exploiting their multiperiod structure. To make this work available to a wider audience we shall assume no knowledge of multiperiod modeling on the part of the reader and shall present the terminology and techniques of multiperiod modeling in the context of financial applications.

Most of the insights into multiperiod financial problems have been obtained from dynamic programming formulations. Furthermore, multiperiod solutions employing other types of models can often be formulated as dynamic programming problems. Because of the importance of dynamic programming to the understanding of multiperiod models, we have devoted this chapter to the presentation of the terminology and techniques of dynamic programming. We shall study two classes of problems. The first class assumes that management acts on the basis of single (point) estimates of future events. The second type of analysis assumes that management employs probabilistic estimates. The problems studied in this chapter are very simplified forms of real finance problems, and the reader who is familiar with dynamic programming is advised to skip directly to Chapter 2.

In the remaining chapters of this book we shall analyze major financial problems where multiperiod models has been successfully applied. All the latter chapters place less emphasis on numerical calculations and the solution to specific problems and more emphasis on the insights and policy implications that can be gained through constructing and studying multiperiod representations of financial problems.

A. Decision Making with Point Estimates

The purpose of this section is to acquaint the reader with the basic dynamic programming models which can be used to solve problems where all variables are known with certainty or where management elects to make decisions on the basis of point estimates. The necessary models will first be presented in the context of solving a simplified bond-refunding problem.[1] Using a simple example, the traditional capital budgeting approach to the bond-refunding problem will be compared with a solution employing complete enumeration as well as with the three fundamental models of dynamic programming (forward optimization, backward optimization, and the single-equation model).[2] Following this, the application of recursive optimization to the equipment replacement problem will be briefly demonstrated.[3]

1. The Bond-Refunding Decision—A Simple Example

Most corporate bonds contain a provision which allows the issuer to call the bonds before maturity upon repayment of principal plus a premium. This provision raises a series of problems for the financial manager. First, given that the firm has outstanding callable bonds, should it call them today, and if so, with bonds of what maturity should it replace them? Second, what is the cost of following an optimum refunding policy over time? While there are a multitude of factors affecting the optimum timing and value of a call, the factor which has been singled out for special attention is the interest savings that can accrue to the firm

---

[1] A solution to a more realistic bond-refunding problem is presented in Chapter 2.

[2] The single-equation model is usually called the equipment replacement model.

[3] This problem is studied more fully in Chapter 7.

through the execution of a call.[4] It is to this problem that we shall address our attention.

When a firm refunds a bond it incurs a fixed charge equal to the call premium on the old bond plus the cost of floating a new bond. The refunding itself results in a change in future interest payments equal to the difference in interest payments between the old and the new bonds. Most attempts to determine the optimum timing and/or value of a call have solved this problem as a standard capital budgeting decision [5, 6, 22, 23].[5] One form of this solution is to refund in any period if the present value of the interest savings over the life of the outstanding bond exceeds the cost of calling the old bond and floating the new bond.[6] A second form involves refunding in that period where the difference between the present value of the interest savings over the life of the original bond and the cost of calling the old bond and floating the new bond is a maximum. For the reasons discussed below, either solution is likely to lead to wrong decisions.

If the firm views debt as a permanent component of its capital structure (or at least as a component with a life beyond that of its presently outstanding bonds), the firm might well wish to refund bonds when the present-value calculation outlined above is negative. This might happen if interest rates in future periods were expected to be even higher than they are at the time a decision is being made. The present-value calculation can also lead to incorrect solutions because it ignores the option of repetitive refunding. The opportunity to refund repetitively over time is what causes the bond-refunding decision to be a perfect example of a recursive relationship which is amenable to solution via dynamic programming.[7]

To better understand the multiperiod character of the refunding decision and to gain insight into the dynamic programming formulation let us construct a simple refunding problem.[8]

1. Management will maintain a constant level of debt in its capital structure for 5 years after which it will have no debt. This will be referred to as a 5-year time horizon.

---

[4] These reasons include the desire to change a firm's capital structure and maintain flexibility. For a more detailed discussion of additional reasons for employing a call provision, see Bibliography References [18] and [23].

[5] The exceptions to this are Elton and Gruber [8, 9], Weingartner [21], and Kalyman [14]. The recursive nature of the bond-refunding problem was first recognized by Weingartner [21].

[6] This solution has been advocated by Weston and Brigham [22]. Another proposal [5] resembles it except that it uses the present value of interest savings over the life of the new bond. This, too, can lead to incorrect decisions.

[7] For additional discussion of the value of the call premium, see Elton and Gruber [9].

[8] The refunding problem has been kept simple so that diagrammatic as well as analytic presentations are feasible. More realistic (and more complex) examples will be discussed in Chapter 2.

2. Management will issue only callable bonds in $100 denominations and with a maturity of 3 years.
3. Management is indifferent to the timing of cash flows.
4. Flotation expenses on the new debt involve a fixed charge of $2.
5. The cost of calling the old debt is $2 if it is 1 year old and $1 if it is 2 years old. This applies at each decision point as well as at the horizon.
6. Management is willing to base its decision on the point estimates of future interest rates shown in Table 1-1.
7. The firm currently has a 3-year bond outstanding with a coupon rate of 5% and 1 year remaining to maturity.

TABLE 1-1

Time	Interest Rate (%)
−2	5
−1	5
0	4
1	5
2	5
3	7
4	7

a. COMPLETE ENUMERATION AND THE CAPITAL BUDGETING DECISION

With these assumptions, the problem facing management can be represented by the decision tree shown in Figure 1-1. At each of five points management has to make a decision as to whether to keep or refund its outstanding bonds.

If we were to follow the tree diagram, we could calculate the cost of any decision. For example, an initial decision to keep the outstanding bond involves a one-period cost of $5, the interest payment on that bond. If instead the firm decided to refund, the cost would be $1 for calling a 2-year-old bond, plus $2 for floating the new bond, plus the $4 interest payment on the new bond. One period later the firm again faces a decision. Assuming that it had initially refunded, then the cost of the two alternatives would be

1. Keep; $4 interest payment.
2. Refund; $2 call penalty, $2 flotation expense, and $5 interest payment.

In this manner, we could trace out the costs of all feasible decision patterns for the five decision periods. We have done this in Figure 1-1. If we had the option of keeping or refunding at each decision point, we would need $\sum_{i=1}^{5} 2^i + 2^5$ or 94 calculations to trace out all paths. However, since we cannot keep a bond once it has reached maturity, some of the branches of the decision tree can immediately be eliminated. Strategies including more than two successive keeps are infeasible

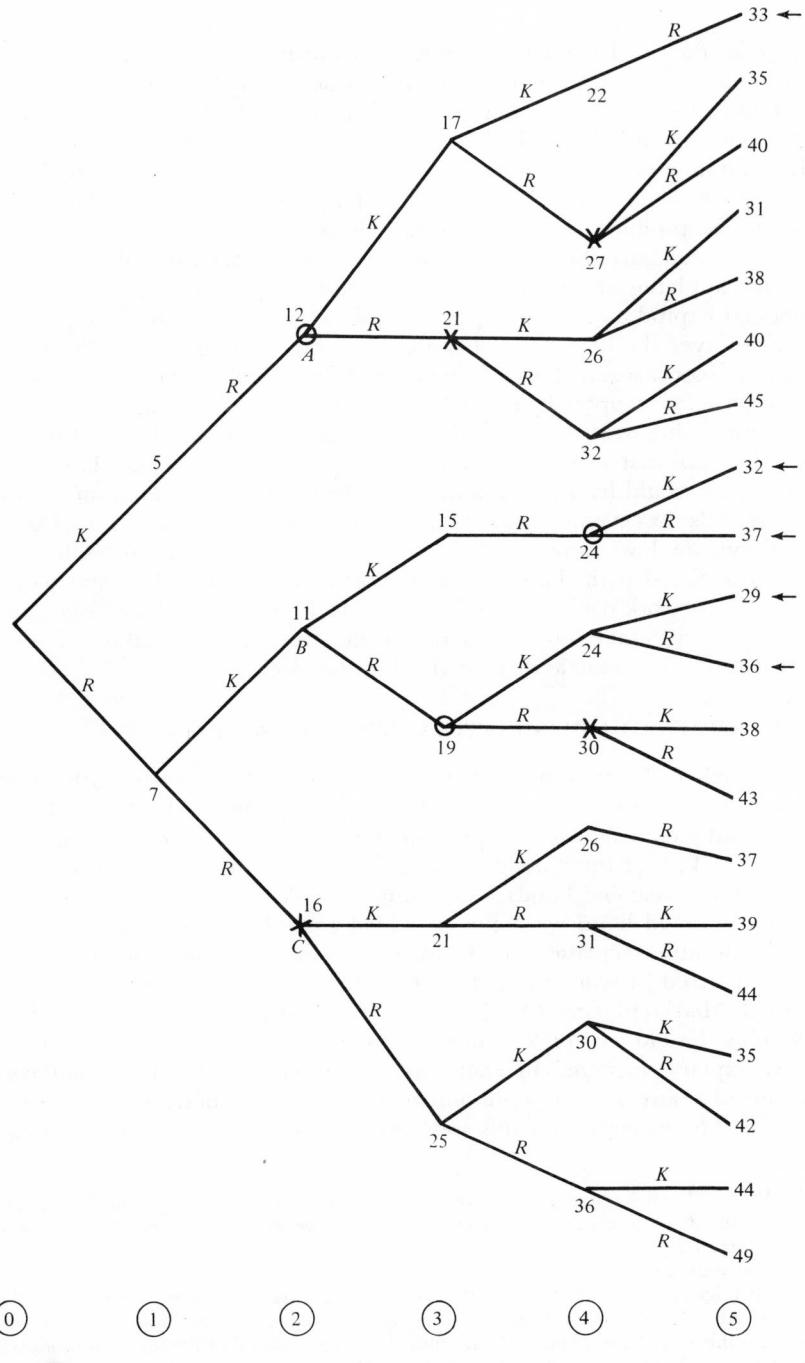

Figure 1-1

5

because they call for a bond to remain outstanding past its maturity.[9] Eliminating all infeasible branches leaves us with 62 calculations.

Figure 1-1 represents a complete enumeration of all possible sequences of decisions which the firm can pursue over its 5-year time horizon. Examination of this decision tree shows that the lowest cost management can incur is $29 and this cost is associated with a sequence of decisions: refund-keep-refund-keep-keep (R-K-R-K-K).

Let us compare this strategy with the strategy which would be arrived at by applying the standard capital budgeting technique. The most popular capital budgeting approach leads to refunding only if the interest savings over the life of the outstanding bond are larger than the transaction costs associated with refunding.[10] If we call initially, we would replace a $5 coupon bond with a $4 coupon bond, resulting in a $1 interest saving over the life of the outstanding bond. But this call results in $1 in call cost and $2 in flotation cost or a total cost of $3. Thus, this approach would lead to an initial keep decision. Examination of Figure 1-1 reveals that even if optimum decisions were made after an initial keep decision, the lowest cost the firm could incur is $31 rather than the $29 cost associated with the optimum decision. The standard capital budgeting framework has led to an incorrect decision. It has done so because it has failed to take into consideration the effect of the initial decision on the options available and the costs of future decisions.[11]

b. FORWARD OPTIMIZATION—TWO-EQUATION FORMS

A further examination of Figure 1-1 reveals that certain paths need not be followed to conclusion or that certain strategies dominate others. For example, as shown in Figure 1-1 the firm has three nodes at decision point 2. Two of these nodes (A and C) involve the decision to keep or replace a 1-year-old bond. Examining node A we see that if we replace this 1-year-old bond we incur an added cost of $9 ($2 in call penalty, $2 in flotation expense, and $5 in interest expense) plus the old cost of $12 incurred in reaching node A or a total of $21. Examining node C reveals that replacing this 1-year-old bond involves an added cost of $9 plus the old cost of $16 incurred in reaching node C. Note that the new expense incurred in each case is the same. The additional cost incurred at any point depends only on the age of the bond and the decision made. The generality of this statement can be seen by tracing through

----

[9] When a bond is refunded it is 1 year old at the end of the refund period. It becomes 2 years old at the end of the first keep period and 3 years old at the end of the second. Therefore, a 3-year-old bond would be designated by refund, keep, and keep.

[10] See footnote 6.

[11] It might appear that traditional analysis will always produce correct results if the life of the original bond coincides exactly with management's time horizon. However, even in this case the possibility of multiple refundings means that the solutions produced by traditional analysis can be incorrect.

the seven decision paths which emanate from node A and comparing them with the parallel decisions emanating from node C. Each of the seven pairs of costs differ by $4, the difference in cost at time 2.

The previous discussion can be summarized into a principle that will lead to a considerable saving in computation time. The optimum pattern of decisions leading to a particular state is independent of the decisions to be made after that state is reached.[12] In the example cited above there were two ways to reach the position (state) of having a 1-year-old bond outstanding at time 2. The minimum cost of obtaining this state is $12 (node A) and the higher-cost path leading to node C can be ignored in all future decisions.

Let us apply this principle to the decision at time 2. At this point we have two ways of ending up with a 1-year-old bond, one with a cost of $21 and one costing $19. Since either path has the same future costs, we eliminate the $21 path. This elimination is noted by the X in Figure 1-1. Note that we could not eliminate all paths which lead to a 2-year-old bond and to a 3-year-old bond at the next decision since future costs would be different. In short, at any point we can eliminate all paths but one path, resulting in a 1-year-old bond at the next decision point, one path resulting in a 2-year-old bond, and one path resulting in a 3-year-old bond. Using the previously stated principle (which is the fundamental theorem of dynamic programming) we are able to reduce the calculations from 62 to 24.[13]

As the reader might suspect, the previous problem can be solved analytically rather than as a tree diagram. To do so, let us define some notation. Let

1. $f_t(j)$ be the cost of having a bond of age j outstanding when t periods have elapsed if an optimum policy were followed.
2. R_t be the interest rate at time t.
3. $C(j)$ be the call penalty associated with calling a bond of age j.
4. F be the flotation expense.

The cost of following any policy before a decision is made at time zero can be denoted by f_0. This is equal to zero since current decisions cannot affect previously incurred costs. If we start at time zero with a 2-year-old bond containing a coupon rate of 5 %, we can make one of two decisions: Keep the bond for another period or refund now. If we keep the bond, we incur an interest cost of $5. Therefore, $f_1(3)$, the cost of making a decision at time zero to have a 3-year bond outstanding at the end of the first year, is R_{-2} or $5.

---

[12] A state is defined by specifying the value of the variables which affect costs in subsequent periods. In this example, the only variable that affects future costs is the age of the bond.

[13] Alternative paths which can be compared at decision points 3 and 4 are noted by Xs and 0s in Figure 1-1, with the Xs representing those which can be eliminated.

If the bond is refunded, the firm incurs a cost of buying back the old bond ($1), the cost of floating a new bond ($2), and the interest cost on the new bond ($4):

$$f_1(1) = C(2) + F + R_0 = \$1 + \$2 + \$4 = \$7$$

The next period we have three choices. First, we can keep the 1-year-old bond, which involves an interest cost of $4 plus the cost of having a 1-year-old bond at this point ($7). Therefore, $f_2(2) = R_0 + f_1(1) = \$4 + \$7 = \$11$. Since we could refund the 1-year-old bond or the 3-year-old bond, we have two possible values for $f_2(1)$:

$$f_2(1) = \min \begin{bmatrix} C(1) + F + R_1 + f_1(1) = 2 + 2 + 5 + 7 = \$16 \\ C(3) + F + R_1 + f_1(3) = 0 + 2 + 5 + 5 = \$12 \end{bmatrix} = \$12$$

Notice that there are two ways we can get to the position of having a 1-year-old bond outstanding at the end of the second decision period. Since the optimum way to get to the position $f_2(1)$ is not affected by where we go from there, we can eliminate the more expensive of these from further consideration. The reader should not find this surprising, since this decision corresponds to the choice discussed earlier between nodes A and C in Figure 1-1.

We can proceed with this analysis using the general formulas

$$f_0(j) = 0, \quad j = 1, 2, 3$$
$$f_t(3) = R_{t-3} + f_{t-1}(2)$$
$$f_t(2) = R_{t-2} + f_{t-1}(1)$$
$$f_t(1) = \min_{j=1,2,3} [C(j) + F + R_{t-1} + f_{t-1}(j)]$$

These formulas can be used to generate the numbers in Table 1-2. An examination of Table 1-2 reveals the optimum policy for the firm to follow. The bottom row of the table shows that the least costly policy involves a cost of $29, which is associated with the retirement of a 3-year-old bond at the horizon (having a 3-year-old bond outstanding at $t = 5$). Thus, the last two decisions were K-K. To have a 3-year-old bond outstanding at time period 5, a 1-year-old bond had to be outstanding at $t = 3$. An examination of $f_3(1)$ shows that the optimum way in which to have a 1-year-old bond outstanding at $t = 3$ is to have replaced a 2-year-old bond (cost $19). The existence of a 2-year-old bond at time period 2 (when it is replaced) indicates that the initial outstanding bond was replaced at time period 0. The optimal path is R-K-R-K-K, the minimum cost is $29, and both the policy path and the policy cost are identical to that found by tracing through the entire decision tree of Figure 1-1. However, the number of calculations have been cut from 62 to 24. Finally, the five decisions made at period 5 are

TABLE 1-2

t	Age of Replaced Bond			$f_t(1),$ Minimum of Replaced	$f_t(2),$ $R_{t-2}+f_{t-1}(1)=$	$f_t(3),$ $R_{t-3}+f_{t-1}(2)=$
	$1,$ $F+C(1)+R_{t-1}$ $+f_{t-1}(1)=$	$2,$ $F+C(2)+R_{t-1}$ $+f_{t-1}(2)=$	$3,$ $F+C(3)+R_{t-1}$ $+f_{t-1}(3)=$			
1		$\boxed{2+1+4+0=7}$		7	$\boxed{4+7=11}$	$5+0=5$
2	$2+2+5+7=16$	$\boxed{2+1+5+11=19}$	$2+0+5+5=12$	12	$5+12=17$	$4+11=15$
3	$2+2+5+12=21$	$2+1+7+17=27$	$2+0+7+15=24$	19	$\boxed{5+19=24}$	$5+17=22$
4	$2+2+7+19=30$	$2+1+7+24=34$	$2+0+7+22=31$	24	$7+24=31$	$\boxed{5+24=29}$
5	$2+2+7+24=35$			31		
5+ (call penalty)	$35+2=37$	$34+2=36$	$31+2=33$		$31+1=32$	$\boxed{29+0=29}$

$\boxed{}$ indicates optimum decision path.

9

the same decisions indicated by arrows in Figure 1-1, and the optimum of $29 is identical.

c. BACKWARD OPTIMIZATION—TWO-EQUATION FORM

There is a second approach which can be used to solve the refunding decision via dynamic programming. Recursive optimization in a backward direction can be employed rather than recursive optimization in a forward direction. The theory of optimization proposed earlier can be restated: The optimum way of getting from a particular state to an end point is not a function of the path taken to that state. In fact, the two theorems can be put together to yield a general theorem of recursive optimization: The optimum path between any two states is neither a function of how one gets to the first state nor where one goes from the second. Let us write out the process of backward optimization letting $f_t(j)$ be the minimum cost of maintaining debt from period t until the horizon given that at time t the firm has a bond j years of age outstanding. Once again we can assume that the cost of decisions outside the period under consideration is zero. However, the firm would incur a call penalty at the horizon if the bond does not mature then. Therefore,

$$f_5(3) = 0 \qquad f_5(2) = 1 \qquad f_5(1) = 2$$

If the firm had a 1-year-old bond in the previous period and replaced it, the firm would incur a call penalty, a flotation expense, an interest payment, plus the costs of having this bond at the horizon, or

$$C(1) + F + R_4 + f_5(1) = 2 + 2 + 7 + 2 = 13$$

On the other hand, if it kept the bond, the firm would incur the interest expense of the bond plus the cost of having a 2-year-old bond at the horizon, or

$$R_3 + f_5(2) = 7 + 1 = 8$$

Since it is cheaper to keep the bond, we have

$$f_4(1) = 8$$

In other words, if the firm ends up with a 1-year-old bond at period 4, it knows that it is cheaper to keep it to the horizon. Whether or not it is optimum to have a 1-year-old bond in period 4 is another matter, which cannot be answered until we calculate the values for the earlier periods 0, 1, 2, and 3.

In a similar manner we can calculate

$$f_4(2) = \min \begin{bmatrix} \text{Keep:} & R_2 + f_5(3) = 5 + 0 = 5 \\ \text{Refund:} & \\ & C(2) + F + R_4 + f_5(1) = 1 + 2 + 7 + 2 = 12 \end{bmatrix} = 5$$

$f_4(3) = \text{Refund:} \quad F + R_4 + f_5(1) = 2 + 7 + 2 = 11$

$f_4(3)$ did not involve a choice because we have assumed that we must replace a 3-year-old bond. The remaining calculations are in Table 1-3 and the general equations are

For $t = T$,

$$f_t(j) = C(j)$$

For all $t < T$,

$$f_t(j) = \min \begin{bmatrix} \text{Keep:} & R_{t-j} + f_{t+1}(j+1) \\ \text{Replace:} & C(j) + F + R_t + f_{t+1}(1) \end{bmatrix},$$
$$t = 4, 3, 2, 1, 0; j = 1, 2, 3$$

where the keep option is not available for a 3-year-old bond ($j = 3$).

The bottom part of Table 1-3 lists the values for $f_0(1)$, $f_0(2)$, and $f_0(3)$, which are the results for all initial strategies. Since we have assumed that management initially had a 2-year-old bond outstanding, the only feasible choice available is to keep or refund this bond [i.e., $f_0(1)$ and $f_0(3)$ are unavailable]. Examination of Table 1-3 shows that this bond should be replaced at zero, and, in fact, the firm should follow the same policy (R-K-R-K-K) and incur the same costs ($\$29$) that were optimum when the problem was solved by forward recursion. An examination of Table 1-3 also shows that if we eliminate all calculations that were not needed to obtain $f_0(2)$, we would have 20 calculations, so that in this case working the problem backward was more efficient. Note also that $f_0(1)$, $f_0(2)$, and $f_0(3)$ are not the same. This indicates that the starting conditions are important in determining both the optimum policy and its associated costs.

d. BACKWARD OPTIMIZATION—ONE-EQUATION FORM

Before leaving this simple example we would like to solve it one final way. This solution technique, while conceptually more difficult, is computationally much simpler and will be the way that will be used to solve the more realistic bond-refunding problems analyzed in Chapter 2.

Instead of stating the problem as "Should the firm keep or refund a j-year-old bond in period t?" we could reformulate it as "Given that the

TABLE 1-3

t	$f_t(1)$ Keep, $R_{t-1} + f_{t+1}(2)$	$f_t(1)$ Replace, $F + C(1) + R_t + f_{t+1}(1)$	$f_t(1)$ Minimum	$f_t(2)$ Keep, $R_{t-2} + f_{t+1}(3)$	$f_t(2)$ Replace, $F + C(2) + R_t + f_{t+1}(1)$	$f_t(2)$ Minimum	$f_t(3)$ Replace, $F + C(3) + R_t + f_{t+1}(1)$	$f_t(3)$ Minimum
4	$7 + 1 = 8$	$2 + 2 + 7 + 2 = 13$	K-8	$5 + 0 = 5$	$2 + 1 + 7 + 2 = 12$	K-5	$2 + 0 + 7 + 2 = 11$	R-11
3	$5 + 5 = 10$	$2 + 2 + 7 + 8 = 19$	K-10	$5 + 11 = 16$	$2 + 1 + 7 + 8 = 18$	K-16	$2 + 0 + 7 + 8 = 17$	R-17
2	$5 + 16 = 21$	$2 + 2 + 5 + 10 = 19$	R-19	$4 + 17 = 21$	$2 + 1 + 5 + 10 = 18$	R-18	$2 + 0 + 5 + 10 = 17$	R-17
1	$4 + 18 = 22$	$2 + 2 + 5 + 19 = 28$	K-22	$5 + 17 = 22$	$2 + 1 + 5 + 19 = 27$	K-22	$2 + 0 + 5 + 19 = 26$	R-26
0	$5 + 22 = 27$	$2 + 2 + 7 + 22 = 30$	K-27	$5 + 26 = 31$	$2 + 1 + 4 + 22 = 29$	R-29	$2 + 0 + 4 + 22 = 28$	R-28

⟍⟍ indicates that this option is infeasible given the initial conditions of the problem.

▭ indicates an optimum decision path.

firm floats a bond in period t, when should it refund again?" Making a parallel change in notation we can let f_t equal the minimum cost of maintaining debt from period t until the horizon given that the firm floats debt in period t. If the firm knew f_t for every period but the current period, it could then calculate the optimum time to refund a bond of any given age in the current period.

The optimum time to refund a brand new bond acquired in period 4 is of course at the horizon when it must be refunded. The cost involved is $2 in flotation to acquire the new bond, $2 in call penalty at the horizon, plus the $7 interest charge, or

$$f_4 = \$2 + \$2 + \$7 = \$11$$

The optimum time to refund a brand new bond acquired in period 3 is either at period 4 or the horizon. If the firm calls at the horizon, it incurs a cost of $2 to float the new bond at period 3, $1 in call penalty, and two interest payments of $7 each. On the other hand, if it calls in period 4, it incurs $2 to float the new bond, $2 in call penalty, one interest payment of $7, and the cost of the optimum policy from period 4 to the horizon. The firm should choose the least expensive and so

$$f_3 = \min \begin{bmatrix} F + C(2) + 2R_3 = 2 + 1 + 14 = \$17 \\ F + C(1) + R_3 + f_4 = 2 + 2 + 7 + 11 = \$22 \end{bmatrix} = 17$$

The other calculations are shown in Table 1-4. The general form is

For $t = T$, $f_t = 0$

For all $t < T$, $f_t = \min_{k=1,\ldots,(3,T-t)} F + C(k) + kR_t + f_{t+k}$

where

1. $(3, T - t)$ means the minimum of 3 years or the number of years to the horizon $(T - t)$.
2. Other symbols as before.

TABLE 1-4   Values for $F + C(k) + kR_t + f_{t+k}$

t	f_t	$k = 1$	$k = 2$	$k = 3$
4	11	$2 + 2 + 7 + 0 = 11$		
3	17	$2 + 2 + 7 + 11 = 22$	$2 + 1 + 14 + 0 = 17$	
2	17	$2 + 2 + 5 + 17 = 26$	$2 + 1 + 10 + 11 = 24$	$\boxed{2 + 0 + 15 + 0 = 17}$
1	26	$2 + 2 + 5 + 17 = 26$	$2 + 1 + 10 + 17 = 30$	$2 + 0 + 15 + 11 = 28$
0	28	$2 + 2 + 4 + 26 = 34$	$\boxed{2 + 1 + 8 + 17 = 28}$	$2 + 0 + 12 + 17 = 31$

$$f_{\text{decision}} = \min \begin{bmatrix} 1 + 28 \\ 5 + 26 \end{bmatrix} = 29$$

$\boxed{}$ indicates an optimum decision path.

Note that the computational efficiency in this method arises from the fact that in computing any f_t all f_{t+k} will already have been calculated. For example, in calculating the costs for f_1 one option is to float debt again at time 2, but the optimal policy to follow from 2 on (f_2) will already have been calculated. The single equation presented above can be used to find the cost of floating a new bond at time 0, 1, 2, etc. However, it does not incorporate the option of not refunding a bond which is outstanding at time period 0. To take this into consideration, we must define a new term f_{decision} which represents the cost of maintaining debt until the horizon given the possibility of not refunding at time 0.

Since we assumed that the firm has a 2-year-old bond outstanding at time 0 the firm has two options at time 0. It has the option of refunding the 2-year-old bond immediately, incurring costs of $C(1) + f_0$ or $\$1 + \$28 = \$29$. The second option is to let the outstanding bond mature, incurring costs of $R_{-2} + f_1(1)$ or $\$5 + \$26 = \$31$. The first option is the more profitable one.

In general f_{decision} can be expressed as[14]

If $j_0 = 0$, $f_{\text{decision}} = f_0$

If $j_0 \neq 0$, $f_{\text{decision}} = \displaystyle\min_{k=0,\ldots,3-j_0} [f_k + C(j_0 + k) + B]$,

$$
\begin{cases}
B = 0, & \text{if } k = 0 \\
B = \displaystyle\sum_{i=1}^{k} R_{-j_0} & \text{if } k \neq 0
\end{cases}
$$

where j_0 is the age of the outstanding bond at time 0.

Table 1-4 demonstrates the optimal set of decisions to make, as well as the minimum cost. f_{decision} shows that the 2-year-old bond should be replaced and a new bond floated at time 0. Examination of the row $t = 0$ shows that the bond should be allowed to remain outstanding for 2 years. This means that a new bond must be floated at $t = 2$. Examination of this row reveals that the bond should be left outstanding for 3 years. Once again we reach an optimum policy path of R-K-R-K-K at a minimum cost of $\$29$. However, the number of calculations have been radically reduced from 62 using complete enumeration, to 24 working forward and comparing keep versus refund, to 20 working backward, and finally to 14 working backward and asking when to refund (the one-equation form of the dynamic programming problem).

2. Equipment Replacement Decision

A firm is often faced with a decision on the optimal time to replace a piece of equipment. If the service performed by the machine is deemed desirable beyond the life of the potential replacement machine, one

---

[14] Of course j_0 could also equal 3.

faces a multiperiod problem analogous to the refunding problem just analyzed.

To set up the dynamic programming solution let[15]

1. f_t be the minimum cost from t to the horizon given that a replacement takes place at time t.
2. I be the capital cost (investment) of a machine.
3. $C_{t,j}$ be the cost of operating a machine j years of age which was originally purchased in year t.
4. N be the maximum number of years for which a machine can perform a service.
5. The discount rate be zero; i.e., management is indifferent as to the timing of cash flows.
6. $[N, (T - t)]$ be the minimum of N and $(T - t)$.

The single-equation recursive optimization for this model is

$$\text{For} \quad t = T, \quad f_t = 0$$

$$\text{For} \quad 0 \leq t < T, \quad f_t = \min_{j=1,\ldots,[N,T-t]}\left[I + \sum_{k=1}^{j} C_{t,k} + f_{t+j}\right]$$

This simply states that the minimum cost policy given replacement in t is found by minimizing the sum of the cost of purchasing a machine, the operating costs until the next replacement, and the cost of following an optimal policy from the time of the next replacement until the horizon. The analogy between this solution and the one-equation solution to the bond replacement problem is easy to see. I (the cost of purchasing a piece of equipment) is analogous to F, the cost of floating new debt.

$$\sum_{k=1}^{j} C_{t,k} \quad \text{(the cost of running the machine for } j \text{ years)}$$

is analogous to kR_t, the cost of paying interest for k years. Subscripts have been added to allow the cost of running the machine to be a function of both the year in which the machine was purchased and the age of the machine.

Once again, an equation for starting conditions (the fact that the company might have an existing machine at the time of the first decision) is needed. If j_0 is the age of the machine in use at the time of the first decision, then

$$f_{\text{decision}} = \min_{j=0,\ldots,N-j_0}\left[\sum_{k=0}^{j} C_{-j_0, j_0+k} + f_{t+j}\right].$$

---

[15] This is a very simple form of the equipment replacement problem. For a more realistic treatment of this problem, see Chapter 7.

Let us illustrate the use of this model with a simple problem. Assume that management

1. Requires the services of a type of equipment for 14 years.
2. Currently has a machine 2 years old which will cost $2900 per year to operate.
3. Estimates the maximum life of a machine as 5 years.
4. Estimates the capital cost of new equipment to be $2250 at any time.
5. Estimates the cost of operating a machine as shown in Table 1-5.

TABLE 1-5

Initial Time of Purchase	Operating Cost Per Year ($)
0	2400
1	2100
2	1800
3	1500
4	1300
5	1100
6	900
7	700
8	600
9	500
10	500
11	500
12	500
13	500

The results of applying the recursive equations presented above are shown in Table 1-6. The second column gives the minimum cost. Once the minimum cost from t to the horizon is known for all t, the initial replacement can be analyzed. If the machine is replaced now, the cost over 15 years is $25,350. If it is replaced next year, the cost is 1 year's operating cost, $2900, plus the minimum cost ($22,050) from period 1 to the horizon given replacement in period 1, or $24,950. If it is replaced in period 2, the cost is 2($2900) + $19,050 = $24,850. And finally, replacement in period 3 costs 3($2900) + $16,450 = $25,150. The optimum course of action is to replace the initial machine at period 2 and then replace again at periods 5 and 9. This is shown by the encircled figures in Table 1-6.

B. Decision Making Under Risk

In the last section of this chapter we assumed that management made decisions as if they were operating in a certain world. In this section we shall assume that management estimates one or more decision parameters probabilistically. The necessary modifications in the dynamic programming formulation will be introduced within the context of the bond-refunding problem and the investment-consumption problem.

TABLE 1-6

$$f_t = \min_{j=1,\ldots,[N,T-t]} \left[I + \sum_{k=1}^{j} C(t, k) + f_{t+j} \right]$$

t	f_t	$k=1$	$k=2$
14			
13	2,750	$\boxed{2250+500+0=2750}$	
12	3,250	$2250+500+2750=5500$	$\boxed{2250+1000=3250}$
11	3,750	$2250+500+3250=6000$	$2250+1000+2750=6000$
10	4,250	$2250+500+3750=6500$	$2250+1000+3250=6500$
9	4,750	$2250+500+4250=7000$	$2250+1000+3750=7000$
8	7,600	$\boxed{2250+600+4750=7600}$	$2250+1200+4250=7700$
7	8,400	$2250+700+7600=10,550$	$\boxed{2250+1400+4750=8400}$
6	9,700	$2250+900+8400=11,550$	$2250+1800+7600=11,650$
5	11,400	$2250+1100+9700=13,050$	$2250+2200+8400=12,850$
4	13,500	$2250+1300+11,400=14,950$	$2250+2600+9700=14,550$
3	16,450	$2250+1500+13,500=17,250$	$2250+3000+11,400=16,650$
2	19,050	$2250+1800+16,450=20,500$	$2250+3600+13,500=19,350$
1	22,050	$2250+2100+19,050=23,400$	$2250+4200+16,450=22,900$
0	25,350	$2250+2400+22,050=26,700$	$2250+4800+19,050=26,100$

t	$k=3$	$k=4$	$k=5$
11	$\boxed{2250+1500=3750}$		
10	$2250+1500+2750=6500$	$\boxed{2250+2000=4250}$	
9	$2250+1500+3250=7000$	$2250+2000+2750=7000$	$\left(2250+2500=4750\right)$
8	$2250+1800+3750=7800$	$2250+2400+3250=7900$	$2250+3000+2750=8000$
7	$2250+2100+4250=8600$	$2250+2800+3750=8800$	$2250+3500+3250=9000$
6	$\boxed{2250+2700+4750=9700}$	$2250+3600+4250=10,100$	$2250+4500+3750=10,500$
5	$2250+3300+7600=13,150$	$\left(2250+4400+4750=11,400\right)$	$2250+5500+4250=12,000$
4	$2250+3900+8400=14,550$	$2250+5200+7600=15,050$	$\boxed{2250+6500+4750=13,500}$
3	$\boxed{2250+4500+9700=16,450}$	$2250+6000+8400=16,650$	$2250+7500+7600=17,350$
2	$\left(2250+5400+11,400=19,050\right)$	$2250+7200+9700=19,150$	$2250+9000+8400=19,650$
1	$\boxed{2250+6300+13,500=22,050}$	$\boxed{2250+8400+11,400=22,050}$	$2250+10,500+9700=22,450$
0	$2250+7200+16,450=25,900$	$\boxed{2250+9600+13,500=25,350}$	$2250+12,000+11,400=25,650$

▭ designates an optimum decision at each t.

⬭ designates an optimum course of action.

1. Bond Refunding Under Risk

Let us return to the two-equation backward optimization models employed in the last section. Once again we shall use it to solve the same simple example. The only change in the example is that we now assume that management bases its decision on probabilistic forecasts of future interest rates as shown in Table 1-7.[16] Since the interest rate is a random

TABLE 1-7

Time	Interest Rates[a]	
−2	5	
−1	5	
0	4	
1	2	8
2	4	6
3	5	9
4	5	9

[a] In each future period the two possible interest rates are assumed equally likely.

variable, we need to define some new notation. Let

1. R_t^* = a particular value for the interest rate at time t. R_t^* is a random variable.
2. $P(R_t^*)$ = the probability of outcome R_t^*.

When single-valued, deterministic forecasts of interest rates were employed, knowing the age of a bond at a particular time uniquely determined the coupon rate on that bond. In our earlier example (Table 1-1), a 3-year-old bond outstanding at time 4 must have a coupon rate of 5%, the interest rate which prevailed when it was issued. However, when probabilistic forecasts are introduced, specifying the age of a bond at a particular point in time no longer uniquely determines the coupon rate on that bond. For example, a 3-year-old bond outstanding at time period 4 could have an interest payment of $2 or $8 depending on the interest rate which prevailed when it was issued. Since future costs depend on both the age of the outstanding debt at a point in time and the cost of maintaining that debt (interest cost), both variables must be retained. In addition, the cost of maintaining debt from time t to the horizon can depend on the interest rate which prevails at t. For example, at time t, the interest rate can either be 5% or 9% and costs may well be different depending on which occurs. Therefore, the state variable becomes $f_t(j, R_{t-j}^*, R_t^*)$ = the minimum cost of maintaining debt from time t until the horizon given that at time t the prevailing interest rate is R_t^*, that the bond is j years old, and that the bond was originally floated

---

[16] This problem has been analyzed by Elton and Gruber [8, 9] and Kalyman [14].

at an interest rate of R^*_{t-j}; the backward recursive relationship is

$$f_t(j, R^*_{t-j}, R^*_t) = \min \begin{bmatrix} \text{Keep:} \\ R^*_{t-j} + \sum_{\text{all } R^*_{t+1}} f_{t+1}(j+1, R^*_{t-j}, R^*_{t+1})P(R^*_{t+1}) \\ \text{Refund:} \quad C(j) + F + R^*_t \\ + \sum_{\text{all } R^*_{t+1}} f_{t+1}(1, R^*_t, R^*_{t+1})P(R^*_{t+1}) \end{bmatrix}$$

Notice that the variables on the right-hand side are almost the same as they were in the certainty case. The only difference is that in addition to solving one problem for each possible age of the outstanding bond we must solve one for each possible coupon rate on the outstanding bond and each possible current interest rate.[17] Formally, the difference between the risk case and the certainty case solved earlier is that the certainty case computes the cost of an optimum policy based on expected interest rates, while the risk case computes expected costs of following an optimum policy for each possible interest rate. The optimum course of action may depend on which interest rates occur. For example, if a low interest rate prevails in t, it may be advantageous to not refund for many periods. With a high interest rate it may be optimum to refund quickly. Since the risk case allows differential treatment for high and low interest rates, it must never lead to higher costs, and if in any period the ability to have differential policies is used, it will lead to lower costs.[18]

These points can be illustrated by solving the simple example under discussion. Note that the only change in the example from the example solved in Section A is to assume that management bases its decision on the full probability distribution of future interest rates rather than on the expected value. Since the expected interest rate in each future period is exactly the same, any differences in the analysis and answers are solely due to incorporation of more information about the distribution of future interest rates into the analysis.

Employing the recursive relationship under risk we can derive the values in Table 1-8. Examining Table 1-8 we can easily find the optimum policy for the firm to follow in this example. The optimum initial decision (time 0) for the firm to make is to refund the outstanding bond. From period 1 on, the decisions diverge according to which interest rates occur. Let us examine the correct sequence of decisions for an interest rate of 2% at time 1. Looking at row $t = 1$ and column $R_t = L$ we shall see that the optimal decision given that we have a 1-year-old bond outstanding

---

[17] The reader should note that while the introduction of risk has meant only a slight increase in the conceptual difficulty of the problem, it has meant a major increase in computational difficulty. The incorporation of risk has caused us to expand our state space from one variable to three variables. Accordingly, one set of computations is needed for each value which each of the three variables can take on.

[18] These are, of course, expected costs; bad forecasts can lead to higher actual costs.

TABLE 1-8

t	$j=1$				$j=2$				$j=3$			
	$R_{t-1}=L$ [a]		$R_{t-1}=H$ [b]		$R_{t-2}=L$		$R_{t-2}=H$		$R_{t-3}=L$		$R_{t-3}=H$	
	$R_t=L$	$R_t=H$	$R_t=L$	$R_t=H$	$R_t=L$	$R_t=H$	$R_t=L$	$R_t=H$	$R_t=L$	$R_t=H$	$R_t=L$	$R_t=H$
4	K-6	K-6	K-10	K-10	K-4	K-4	K-6	K-6	R-9	R-13	R-9	R-13
3	K-8	K-8	K-12	K-12	K-13	K-13	K-14	K-19	R-13[c]	R-21[c]	c	c
2	K-15	K-15	K-16	R-22	R-15[c]	R-21 or K-21[c]	c	c	R-19[c]	R-29[c]	c	c
1	R-21[c]	c	K-22[c]	c								
0					R-28½[e]							

[a] L indicates that the interest rate is at the lowest of its two possible values.
[b] H indicates that the interest rate is at the highest of its two possible values.
[c] This bond was issued at time 0 so that R_{t-j} is known with certainty.
[d] — indicates that the specified bond cannot exist because of the starting conditions of the problem.
[e] There is only one possible state at time 0 for the starting conditions are fully specified.

(we refunded at 0) is to refund the bond. Now we have a 1-year-old bond outstanding at time 2 with a value of $R_{t-1} = R_L$. The optimum decision regardless of interest rates in period 2 is to keep. Similarly, regardless of the level of interest rates we keep in 3 and refund in 4.

We can trace out the decision path emanating from the 8% interest rate in period 1 in a parallel fashion. An optimal set of decisions if the interest rate is 8% in the second period is R-K-R-K-K.[19]

As discussed earlier, the risk formulation leads to lower expected costs. In this example, the expected costs are $28.50 ($28\frac{1}{2}$) rather than $29. This half-dollar difference occurs because of the differential policy allowed by the risk case. In particular, in the certainty case a 1-year-old bond was always kept in period 2 since the expected cost was $22 as of period 1. Under risk there is a differential policy in period 1. If the interest rate is 8%, it does not pay to refund and the expected cost is $22. If the interest rate is 2%, it pays to refund and the expected cost is $21. The differential policy under risk produces the $1 saving in period 1 if the interest rate is 2%. Since the probability of the 2% interest rate occurring is .50, this produces the half-dollar expected saving in the initial period. Once again, the difference between the certainty and risk cases is that the risk case produces a series of policies where the course of action to be taken is specified in terms of which interest rates occur in the future, while the certainty case produces a completely predetermined set of decisions.

2. Portfolio Example

Every investor faces decisions on the composition of the portfolio of assets he will hold over time and the division of his wealth between consumption and investment at any moment in time. The multiperiod nature of the consumption investment decision is obvious. The solution to this problem is rather complex (see Chapter 5). However, we shall now treat a *very* simplified form of this problem as another example of decision making under risk.

Assume that an investor wishes to devise an investment strategy which maximizes his utility of consumption over 3 years. Let his utility function for consumption in the three periods be given by

$$U(C_1, C_2, C_3) = \sum_{t=1}^{3} U(C_t) = \sum_{i=1}^{3} (C_i)^{1/2}$$

where

1. $U(C_t)$ is the one-period utility function in period t.
2. C_t is consumption in t.

---

[19] The reader should note that in period 2 for a bond of age 2 if an interest rate of 6% occurs, both the refund and the keep decision lead to the same costs. If this set of conditions occur, the path R-K-K-R-K is as good but no better than the path R-K-R-K-K.

The above is an additively separable utility function. It is additively separable since the multiperiod utility function shown on the left-hand side of the above expression can be written as the sum of one-period utility functions. The additively separable utility function is the most frequently investigated multiperiod utility function.

To continue the example, assume that an investor has only one possible investment—a risky asset which is either unchanged, or doubles, or triples in price, each event being equally likely. Further assume that he has \$2 at time 0 and that his only source of income for time periods 1 and 2 is his investment portfolio.

Define the following additional symbols:

1. W_t is wealth in period t.
2. X_t is the amount invested in the risky asset at time t.
3. r is 1 plus the return on the risky asset in each period.
4. $E(\ )$ is the expected value operator.
5. $f_t(W_t)$ is the utility of wealth in period t given that an optimal investment policy is followed from period t to the horizon.

In the final period he will consume all available wealth, since utility increases with increased consumption and no value is given to unconsumed wealth. Therefore,

$$f_3(W_3) = C_3^{1/2} = W_3^{1/2} \qquad (1)$$

In earlier periods the investor has a choice between current consumption or investment for increased consumption in later periods. For any given amount of wealth the decision maker chooses the strategy which leads to maximum utility. This choice is expressed as

$$f_t(W_t) = \max_{C_t} [C_t^{1/2} + E[f(W_{t+1})]], \qquad t = 1, 2$$

$f_t(W_t)$ is the utility from an optimum consumption path from period $t + 1$ to the horizon. To complete the dynamic programming formulation we need to state a relationship between consumption in period t and wealth in period $t + 1$. The amount of money we have available in $t + 1$ is the amount we have invested in the risky asset times the return on risky asset, or

$$W_{t+1} = X_t r \qquad (2)$$

However, there are limits to the size of X_t. X_t plus the consumption in t must equal the amount available (i.e., wealth) in t. Therefore,

$$W_t = X_t + C_t \qquad (3)$$

Substituting equation (3) into equation (2) we have

$$W_{t+1} = (W_t - C_t)r$$

The three equations (1), (2), and (3) can be used to solve the portfolio problem. Since $W_0 = \$2$, the maximum consumption in period 3 occurs when the investor puts all his funds in the risky investment and it triples in value each period. In this case, wealth in period 2 would be \$6 and in period 3 it would be \$18. Therefore, the limits for wealth in period 3 are zero and \$18.

Table 1-9 shows the calculations needed to solve this simple problem. In period 3 the calculations are straightforward and given by equation (1). For example, $f_3(6) = \sqrt{6} = 2.45$. In periods 1 and 2 we use equation (2). For example, if $W_2 = 4$, we have five possible investment plans. We can consume \$4 and invest \$0 or \$3 investing \$1 or \$2 investing \$2 or \$1 investing \$3 or \$0 investing \$4. These alternatives along with the outcomes from the investment are shown in the first three columns under $i = 2$. The third column shows the expected utility from period 2 to the horizon given each of these consumption-investment plans. For example, in period 2 if we consume \$2 and invest \$2, the expected utility is given by equation (2) and is $\sqrt{2} + \frac{1}{3}f_3(2) + \frac{1}{3}f_3(4) + \frac{1}{3}f_3(6) = \sqrt{2} + \frac{1}{3}(1.41 + 2 + 2.45) = 3.36$. Notice that for period 1 we only have to consider those decisions involving an initial wealth of \$2. The optimum course of action is to consume \$0 in period 1 and invest \$2. If the investment yields \$2, the optimum course of action is to consume \$1 and invest \$1. If the investment yields \$4, the optimum course of action is to consume \$1 and invest \$3. Finally, if the investment yields \$6, the investor consumes \$2 and invests \$4. All remaining wealth is, of course, consumed in period 3.

Conclusion

In this chapter the reader has been introduced to the basic models of dynamic programming both in the certainty case and under risk. Simple examples and numerical calculations were used to illustrate these models. In the remaining chapters in this book we shall use the methods of recursive optimization to gain insight into several important problems in finance. The problems discussed are much more realistic than those presented for illustrative purposes in this chapter. Emphasis will be placed on the rich insights and policy implications of dynamic programming formulations rather than on the numeric solution to particular problems.

Bibliography

[1] Beckmann, M., *Dynamic Programming of Economic Decisions* (Springer-Verlag, Inc., New York, New York), 1968.

[2] Bellman, Richard, "Equipment Replacement Policy," *Journal of the Society for Industrial and Applied Mathematics*, *3*, No. 3, Sept. 1955, pp. 133–136.

TABLE 1-9

		i=1					i=2		i=3
Wealth	C_1	$W_0 - C_1$	W_1	$f_1(W_1)$	C_2	$W_1 - C_2$	W_2	$f_2(W_2)$	$f_3(W_3)$
1					1	0	0	$1 + 0 = 1$	1
					0	1	1, 2, 3	$0 + \frac{1}{3}(1 + 1.41 + 1.73) = 1.38$	
2	2	0	0	$1.41 + 0 = 1.41$	2	0	0	$1.41 + 0 = 1.41$	1.41
	1	1	1, 2, 3	$1 + \frac{1}{3}(1.38 + 2.38 + 2.95) = 3.24$	1	1	1, 2, 3	$1 + \frac{1}{3}(1 + 1.41 + 1.73) = 2.38$	
	0	2	2, 4, 6	$0 + \frac{1}{3}(2.38 + 3.39 + 4.17) = 3.31$	0	2	2, 4, 6	$0 + \frac{1}{3}(1.41 + 2.00 + 2.45) = 1.95$	
3					3	0	0	$1.73 + 0 = 1.73$	1.73
					2	1	1, 2, 3	$1.41 + \frac{1}{3}(1 + 1.41 + 1.73) = 2.79$	
					1	2	2, 4, 6	$1 + \frac{1}{3}(1.41 + 2.00 + 2.45) = 2.95$	
					0	3	3, 6, 9	$0 + \frac{1}{3}(1.73 + 2.45 + 3) = 2.39$	
4					4	0	0	$2 + 0 = 2$	2.00
					3	1	1, 2, 3	$1.73 + \frac{1}{3}(1 + 1.41 + 1.73) = 3.11$	
					2	2	2, 4, 6	$1.41 + \frac{1}{3}(1.41 + 2 + 2.45) = 3.36$	
					1	3	3, 6, 9	$1 + \frac{1}{3}(1.73 + 2.45 + 3) = 3.39$	
					0	4	4, 8, 12	$0 + \frac{1}{3}(2 + 2.83 + 3.46) = 2.76$	
5					5	0	0	$2.24 + 0 = 2.24$	2.24
					4	1	1, 2, 3	$2 + \frac{1}{3}(1 + 1.41 + 1.73) = 3.38$	
					3	2	2, 4, 6	$1.73 + \frac{1}{3}(1.41 + 2 + 2.45) = 3.68$	

	$i = 1$				$i = 2$				$i = 3,$
Wealth	C_1	$W_0 - C_1$	W_1	$f_1(W_1)$	C_2	$W_1 - C_2$	W_2	$f_2(W_2)$	$f_3(W_3)$
6					2	3	3, 6, 9	$1.41 + \frac{1}{3}(1.73 + 2.45 + 3) = 3.80$	2.45
					1	4	4, 8, 12	$1 + \frac{1}{3}(2 + 2.83 + 3.46) = 3.76$	
					0	5	5, 10, 15	$0 + \frac{1}{3}(2.24 + 3.16 + 3.87) = 3.07$	
					6	0	0	$2.45 + 0 = 2.45$	
					5	1	1, 2, 3	$2.24 + \frac{1}{3}(1 + 1.41 + 1.73) = 3.62$	
					4	2	2, 4, 6	$2 + \frac{1}{3}(1.41 + 2 + 2.45) = 3.95$	
					3	3	3, 6, 9	$1.73 + \frac{1}{3}(1.73 + 2.45 + 3) = 4.02$	
					2	4	4, 8, 12	$1.41 + \frac{1}{3}(2 + 2.83 + 3.46) = 4.17$	
					1	5	5, 10, 15	$1 + \frac{1}{3}(2.24 + 3.16 + 3.87) = 4.07$	
					0	6	6, 12, 18	$0 + \frac{1}{3}(2.45 + 3.46 + 4.24) = 3.38$	
7									2.65
8									2.83
9									3.00
10									3.16
11									3.32
12									3.46
13									3.61
14									3.74
15									3.87
16									4.00
17									4.12
18									4.36

[3] Bellman, Richard, *Dynamic Programming* (Princeton University Press, Princeton, N.J.), 1957.

[4] Bellman, Richard and S. E. Dreyfus, *Applied Dynamic Programming* (Princeton University Press, Princeton, N.J.), 1962.

[5] Bowlin, Oswald, "The Refunding Decision," *Journal of Finance, XXI*, March 1966, pp. 55–68.

[6] Cohen, Jerome, and Sidney Robbins, *The Financial Manager: Basic Aspects of Financial Administration* (Harper & Row, Publishers, New York), 1966.

[7] Crockett, Jean, "A Technical Note on the Value of a Call Privilege," in Bibliographical Reference [10].

[8] Elton, Edwin J., and Martin J. Gruber, "Dynamic Programming Models in Finance," *Journal of Finance*, 26, No. 3, May 1971, pp. 473–505.

[9] Elton, Edwin, J., and Martin J. Gruber, "The Economic Value of the Call Option," *Journal of Finance*, 27, No. 4, Sept. 1972, pp. 891–901.

[10] Hess, Arleigh, and Willis Winn, *The Value of the Call Privilege* (University of Pennsylvania Press, Philadelphia), 1962.

[11] Hickman, W. B., *Corporate Bonds: Quality and Investment Performance*, Occasional Paper 59 (National Bureau of Economic Research, New York), 1959.

[12] Howard, Ronald, *Dynamic Programming and Markov Processes* (The M.I.T. Press, Cambridge, Mass.), 1960.

[13] Jen, Frank, and James Wert, "The Effects of Call Risk on Corporate Bond Yields," *Journal of Finance, XXII*, Dec. 1967, pp. 637–652.

[14] Kalyman, Basil A., "The Bond Refunding Problem with Stochastic Interest Rates," *Management Science*, 18, No. 3, Nov. 1971, pp. 171–184.

[15] Kolodny, Richard, "Corporate Borrowing Decisions and the Evaluation of Interest Rate Forecasts," unpublished Ph.D. Dissertation (New York University, New York), 1972.

[16] Myers, Stewart, Discussion of Bibliographical Reference [9], *Journal of Finance*, 26, No. 3, May 1971, pp. 538–539.

[17] Pye, Gordon, "Markov Model of the Term Structure," *Quarterly Journal of Economics, LXXX*, No. 1, Feb. 1966, pp. 60–72.

[18] Pye, Gordon, "The Value of Call Deferment on a Bond: Some Empirical Results," *Journal of Finance, XXII*, Dec. 1967, pp. 623–636.

[19] Van Horne, James C., *Financial Management and Policy* (Prentice-Hall, Inc., Englewood Cliffs, N.J.), 1969.

[20] Wagner, Harvey, *Principals of Operations Research* (Prentice-Hall, Inc., Englewood Cliffs, N.J.), 1969.

[21] Weingartner, H. Martin, "Optimal Timing of Bond Refunding," *Management Science*, 13, No. 7, March 1967, pp. 511–524.

[22] Weston, Fred, and Eugene Brigham, *Managerial Finance* (Holt, Rinehart and Winston, Inc., New York), 1969.

[23] Winn, Willis, and Arleigh Hess, "The Value of the Call Privilege," *Journal of Finance, XIV*, May 1959, pp. 182–195.

The Bond-Refunding Decision

In this chapter we shall examine a more realistic formulation of the bond-refunding problem than that examined in Chapter 1. Many firms issue bonds with a call provision. The firm then has to decide when to call outstanding bonds. There are many factors affecting the optimum timing of a call. The factor which has been singled out for special attention is the interest saving that can accrue to the firm through the execution of the call. In this chapter we shall examine the firm's decision problem when interest savings are the main motivation for the call.

The chapter is divided into three sections. In the first section we shall discuss the various costs involved in the bond-refunding decision. In the second and third sections we shall present several solutions to the bond-refunding decision. These solutions differ from each other in terms of the type or amount of information which management is assumed to use and the time horizon over which management is assumed to plan. In particular, in Section B we shall assume that management bases its decisions on point estimates of future interest rates, while in Section C we shall examine models which assume that management makes decisions based on estimates of the entire probability distribution of future events. In both sections we shall deal with both the case of finite and infinite horizons.

27

A. The Costs of Refunding

For the firm to refund its bonds it must incur a cost of calling the outstanding bonds (called a call premium). The call premium is usually stated as a function of the coupon rate on the debt and usually declines as maturity approaches. A typical schedule of call premiums would be for the initial premium to be equal to 1 year's interest and to decline linearly to zero at maturity. At a point in time, the call premium on almost all callable bonds will be a function of the age of the bond, the interest rate at the time it was issued, and the original maturity of the bond.

When a firm sells a bond it incurs flotation charges. These flotation expenses usually vary with the size of the issue and often with the associated interest rate. Since we are holding the size of the issue constant, we shall assume in the rest of this chapter that the only source of variation is the level of interest rates.

In deciding on whether to refund a bond or not the firm must decide on the proper discount rate to use in measuring the value of cash flows which accrue at different points in time. This is a rather complex issue. Several alternatives have been presented in the literature. These include the firm's cost of capital, the rate of interest on the new debt, the rate of interest on the old debt, the rate of interest on debt equal in maturity to the age of the outstanding debt at the time it is refunded, the one-period interest rate, and the riskless rate of interest.[1] The appropriate discount rate for management to use is the one that reflects the degree of risk inherent in the refunding decision. The decision is not a riskless decision because in the real world we would be uncertain about the level of future interest rates and therefore the actual costs of any refunding policy. At the other extreme it should not be the cost of capital, for the risk of interest rate changes should be different from and smaller than the risks associated with the firm's assets.

The risks associated with the cash flows from refunding are the risk that the firm will default on its debt obligation (in which case it will not get the benefit from the refunding decision) and the risk of changes in interest rates. The premium that the market demands for bearing these risks is incorporated in the interest rate itself. That is, the interest rate (yield) that must be offered on callable bonds of any particular maturity is the rate which the market demands for buying that bond given the possible loss from default and changes in interest rates (this includes the loss from a possible call). Thus, we feel that the appropriate discount rate for the stream of cash flows that is generated from the decision to call any bond is the yield that must be offered to sell a bond of equal maturity. However, because the issue of the appropriate discount rate

---

[1] See Bibliography References [5, 6, 7, 8, 9, 10, 15, 17, 18, 19, 21, 23] for expositions of these different points of view.

has been subject to so much controversy, we shall present all solutions in terms of a generalized discount rate for which the reader can substitute that rate which he feels is most appropriate.

In constructing all the models in this section, we shall view the refunding decision as a discrete problem. While a firm could decide to call a bond at any moment in time, the amount of data and level of analysis needed to make a decision make it likely that management considers the decision at specified intervals of time. Since the call premium usually decreases after the coupon payment is due, one logical pattern of decision points is immediately after the payment of a coupon. We shall assume that management follows this time pattern in considering the refunding decision.

B. The Bond-Refunding Problem with Point Estimates of Future Interest Rates

Having discussed some of the costs involved in the refunding decision, let us examine one set of such decisions. We shall initially assume that management makes decisions employing point estimates (expected values) of future variables. Two variations will be discussed. The first assumes that management expects to maintain debt at a certain level for a specified number of years after which it intends to eliminate debt from the firm's capital structure (finite horizon case).[2] While most corporations do borrow on a permanent basis, a substantial minority do retire debt.[3] The second assumes that management wants to minimize the cost of maintaining debt in the firm's capital structure over the indefinite future (infinite horizon case).

1. Fixed Horizon with Point Estimates

Let us start by assuming that management intends to issue bonds of a particular maturity M. However, if the horizon is less than M years away, management will consider issuing either bonds of maturity M or debt instruments with a maturity equal to the number of years remaining until the horizon. Let

m = a variable representing the actual maturity of the firm's bonds
M = a constant representing the standard maturity
R_t^m = the yield on a bond issued at time t with a maturity of m years
$F(R_t^m)$ = the fixed cost of floating a bond carrying an interest rate of R_t^m.

---

[2] We shall use the one-equation form of the dynamic programming solution throughout the rest of this chapter. We demonstrated in Chapter 1 that for a very simple example this involves less computations than the two-equation forms. It also involves less computation for all the cases presented throughout the rest of this chapter.

[3] Hickman found that 41% of the bonds retired in the period 1900–1943 were not refunded. See Bibliography Reference [11], page 13.

$C(k, R_t^m, m)$ = the call premium on a bond k years of age, with an interest rate of R_t^m, and an original maturity of m years

α_t = the discount factor (1 divided by 1 plus the discount rate) used to find the present value, as of time period t of cash flows occurring at time period $t + 1$

T = the fixed horizon at which debt will be retired

f_t = the minimum cost of having debt outstanding from time t until time T given that a new issue is floated at time t

f_{decision} = the minimum cost of having debt outstanding from the initial period until T given the characteristics of any bond that might be outstanding in the initial time period

$\alpha_{t, t+k}$ = the discount factor used to find the present value, as of time period t of cash flows occurring at time $t + k$, $\alpha_{t, t+k} = \prod_{i=t}^{t+k-1} \alpha_i$; note that $\alpha_{t, t} = 1$

The dynamic programming solution to this problem is

$$f_T = 0 \tag{1}$$

For all t such that $T - M < t < T$,

$$f_t = \min_{\substack{m=(T-t) \text{ or } M \\ k=1, 2, \ldots, m}} \left[F(R_t^m) + \sum_{i=1}^{k} \alpha_{t, t+i} R_t^m + \alpha_{t, t+k} C(k, R_t^m, m) + \alpha_{t, t+k} f_{t+k} \right] \tag{2}$$

For all $t \leq T - M$,

$m = M$, and

$$f_t = \min_{k=1, \ldots, m} \left[F(R_t^m) + \sum_{i=1}^{k} \alpha_{t, t+i} R_t^m + \alpha_{t, t+k} C(k, R_t^m, m) + \alpha_{t, t+k} f_{t+k} \right] \tag{3}$$

If j_0 is set equal to the age of the bond at t', then to reach a decision at t', we have

If $j_0 = 0$, $f_{\text{decision}} = f_{t'}$

If $j_0 \neq 0$, $f_{\text{decision}} = \min_{k=0, \ldots, m-j_0} \left[\begin{matrix} \alpha_{t', t'+k} f_{t'+k} + \alpha_{t', t'+k} \\ C(j_0 + k, R_{t'-j_0}^m, m) + B \end{matrix} \right] \tag{4}$

where

$$B = \sum_{i=1}^{k} \alpha_{t', t'+i} R_{-j_0}^m \qquad \text{if } k \neq 0$$

$$B = 0 \qquad \text{if } k = 0$$

Equation (1) simply expresses the fact that from the horizon on (when all debt is eliminated) the firm incurs no debt charges. Equations (2) and (3) represent the minimum cost of maintaining debt from each year prior to the horizon, until the horizon. Both equations involve finding the minimum of the cost associated with issuing a new bond and then calling this bond plus the minimum cost of maintaining debt from the call date until the horizon. For example, to calculate the minimum cost at a point in time 40 years prior to the horizon we would compare (1) the cost of floating a bond and calling it in 1 year plus the cost of the optimum way to raise debt for 39 more years with (2) the cost of floating a bond and calling it in 2 years plus the cost of the optimum way to raise debt for 38 more years. We would do this for all possible call dates up to and including the maturity of the bond. The four costs in both equations (2) and (3) represent the cost of floating the bond, the present value of the interest payments made on the bond until it is called, the present value of the call premium, and the present value of the minimum cost of maintaining debt from the call date to the horizon.

Equations (2) and (3) differ in one respect. Equation (3) considers only bonds of one maturity, while equation (2) allows the firm to float bonds with a maturity equal to either the standard maturity or the time remaining to the end of the horizon.[4] Therefore, in equation (2) the pattern of refunding is optimized with respect to the maturity of the bonds as well as the timing of calls.

Equation (4) incorporates starting conditions into the decision. Although $f_{t'}$ yields the optimum pattern of bond refunding providing no bond is outstanding at time t', it does not necessarily produce the best decisions if an outstanding bond exists. The outstanding bond changes the initial options and costs. For example, if at t' a bond was outstanding with 2 years left to maturity, the firm could call immediately and incur the cost of calling plus $f_{t'}$. On the other hand, it could wait 1 year to refund, incurring the interest cost on the old bond for 1 year, the cost of calling a year later, and $f_{t'+1}$. Similarly, the firm could wait 2 years to call and again change its costs. Equation (4) allows the firm to select the optimum strategy to follow given an outstanding bond with any number of years remaining to maturity.

The previous discussion can be further clarified with an example. Assume that the firm has a 12-year horizon and is willing to base its financing decision on the interest rates shown in Table 2-1 under the columns labeled Expected Value. Further assume that the standard bond maturity is 3 years, the call premiums are as shown in Table 2-2, the flotation expense is $2, and the discount factor (α) is 1.

---

[4] A two-equation solution to the form of the bond-refunding problem just discussed has been presented by Weingartner [21]. However, he did not allow the option of floating bonds of standard maturity just prior to the horizon. As we shall show below, preclusion of this option can lead to nonoptimum decisions. Furthermore, the use of the two-equation rather than a one-equation solution to this problem leads to increased calculations.

TABLE 2-1 Assumed Interest Rates

Time Period	Maturity = 1			Maturity = 2			Maturity = 3			Maturity = 4		
	r_1	r_2	Expected Value	r_1	r_2	Expected Value	r_1	r_2	Expected Value	r_1	r_2	Expected Value
0							4	6	5	4	6	5
1							4	6	5	5	7	6
2							5	7	6	4	8	6
3							5	7	6	4	8	6
4							5	7	6	3	7	5
5							4	6	5	3	7	5
6							4	6	5	3	5	4
7							3	5	4	3	5	4
8							4	6	5	5	7	6
9							4	6	5	4	6	5
10				7	9	8	6	8	7	5	7	6
11	7	9	8				6	8	7	6	8	7

TABLE 2-2 Call Premium

Remaining Years to Maturity	Call Penalty
3	3
2	2
1	1
0	0

Applying equations (1) through (4) yields Table 2-3. If the firm is to replace a bond at the beginning of the last period, then it has the choice of issuing a bond with a 1-year maturity or one with a 3-year maturity. If it issues a 3-year bond, it incurs $2 in flotation expenses plus $7 in interest expense plus $2 for calling at the horizon, or $11. If it issues a 1-year bond, it incurs $2 in flotation expense plus $8 in interest expense, or $10. The least expensive alternative is issuing a 1-year bond and calling at the horizon so that $f_{11} = \$10$. If the firm wants to replace a bond two periods from the horizon, then it has the choice of issuing a 3-year bond and calling the next period, issuing a 3-year bond and calling at the horizon, or issuing a bond with a maturity of 2 years. If it issues a 3-year bond and calls the next period, the firm incurs $2 flotation expense, $7 interest expense, $2 call penalty (at the end of the period), and $10 representing the cost of the least expensive way of financing the last period, or a total cost of $21. For period 10 the least expensive alternative is to issue a 3-year bond and call in two periods, incurring a cost of $17. This becomes f_{10}. The cost of this alternative, as well as the other alternatives, is shown in Table 2-3.

TABLE 2-3 Value for

$$F(R_t^m) + \sum_{i=1}^{k} \alpha_{t,\,t+i} R_t^m + \alpha_{t,\,t+k} C(k, R_t^m, m) + \alpha_{t,\,t+k} f_{t+k}$$

t	f_t	$k=1$	$k=2$	$k=3$	$m=T-t$, $k=1$	$m=T-t$, $k=2$
11	10	$2 + 7 + 2 + 0 = 11$			$2 + 8 + 0 + 0 = 10$	
10	17	$2 + 7 + 2 + 10 = 21$	$2 + 14 + 1 + 0 = 17$			$2 + 16 + 0 + 0 = 18$
9	17	$2 + 5 + 2 + 17 = 26$	$2 + 10 + 1 + 10 = 23$	$2 + 15 + 0 + 0 = 17$		
8	26	$2 + 5 + 2 + 17 = 26$	$2 + 10 + 1 + 17 = 30$	$2 + 15 + 0 + 10 = 27$		
7	28	$2 + 4 + 2 + 26 = 34$	$2 + 8 + 1 + 17 = 28$	$2 + 12 + 0 + 17 = 31$		
6	34	$2 + 5 + 2 + 28 = 37$	$2 + 10 + 1 + 26 = 39$	$2 + 15 + 0 + 17 = 34$		
5	41	$2 + 5 + 2 + 34 = 43$	$2 + 10 + 1 + 28 = 41$	$2 + 15 + 0 + 26 = 43$		
4	48	$2 + 6 + 2 + 41 = 51$	$2 + 12 + 1 + 34 = 49$	$2 + 18 + 0 + 28 = 48$		
3	54	$2 + 6 + 2 + 48 = 58$	$2 + 12 + 1 + 41 = 56$	$2 + 18 + 0 + 34 = 54$		
2	61	$2 + 6 + 2 + 54 = 64$	$2 + 12 + 1 + 48 = 63$	$2 + 18 + 0 + 41 = 61$		
1	65	$2 + 5 + 2 + 61 = 70$	$2 + 10 + 1 + 54 = 67$	$2 + 15 + 0 + 48 = 65$		
0	71	$2 + 5 + 2 + 65 = 74$	$2 + 10 + 1 + 61 = 74$	$2 + 15 + 0 + 54 = 71$		

☐ designates an alternative with a minimum cost for each t.

⬭ designates an alternative with a minimum cost and that is expected to constitute an optimal policy.

33

Having determined the cost of the least expensive method of going from any period where the firm replaces a bond to the horizon, the firm is ready to make a decision. Assume that it currently (time period 0) has a 1-year-old bond outstanding with a coupon rate of 4% and 2 years remaining until it matures. Then, utilizing equation (4) (see Table 2-5), the firm has three possible decisions: replace now, replace in one period, or replace in two periods. If it replaces now, the firm incurs a call penalty of $2 plus the cost of the optimum decision from the current period to the horizon given that a bond is replaced in the current period ($f_0 = $71), or a total cost of $73. If it replaces in the next period, the firm incurs a call penalty of $1, an interest expense of $4, plus the cost of the optimum decision from the next period to the horizon given that a bond is replaced then (which is $f_1 = $65), producing a total cost of $70. Finally, if the firm replaces in two periods, it incurs an interest cost of $8 and a future cost of $61 for a total of $69. Therefore, the firm should replace in period 2. The firm should expect the bond it floats in period 2 to remain outstanding for 3 more years since the minimum value of f_2 ($61) is associated with this decision. As can be seen from Table 2-3, the firm should expect to replace bonds in periods 2, 5, 7, and 9 as well as at the horizon (T).

A question may arise as to whether or not one should consider both the option of issuing a bond that matures at the horizon and the option of issuing a bond of longer maturity and calling at the horizon. If the potential bondholders perfectly anticipate the call at the horizon, then the expected yield on a 3-year callable bond must be the same as the yield on a 2-year bond, and issuing a bond that matured at the horizon would have to involve the same cost to management.[5]

If, on the other hand, the bondholders did not perfectly anticipate the call and the yield curve was downward sloping, then issuing a bond which matures after the horizon, and calling it, could be the least expensive alternative. It would be the least expensive alternative if the interest saving on issuing a bond with a longer maturity (in the example 3 years) is greater than the call penalty. Since it seems unrealistic to assume that potential bondholders can perfectly anticipate the length of management's horizon and thus the timing of the final call, issuing a bond which matures beyond the horizon can be optimum.

It is quite easy to generalize this solution to the case where management will consider floating bonds of more than one maturity.[6] The notation will remain the same as in the previous case except that M will now stand for the set of all maturities that the firm considers issuing and M' will stand for the longest maturity in that set.

---

[5] Yield is being used rather than coupon rate since the callable bond would be retired at a price greater than par.

[6] Once again Weingartner [21] solved a similar problem. The difference between our solution and Weingartner's are enumerated in footnote 4.

Equation (1) remains the same. Equations (2) and (3) generalized for all allowable maturities become for all $t < T$,

$$f_t = \min_{\substack{m \in M \\ \text{and also} \\ m = T-t \\ \text{for } T-t < M' \\ k=1,\ldots,m}} \left[F(R_t^m) + \sum_{i=1}^{k} \alpha_{t,t+1} R_t^m + \alpha_{t,t+k} C(k, R_t^m, m) + \alpha_{t,t+k} f_{t+k} \right] \quad (5)$$

In this equation we are optimizing across all possible maturities as well as all possible call times.

Letting m_0 equal the maturity of the outstanding bond at the time (t') a decision is made, equation (4) becomes

$$\text{If } j_0 = 0, \quad f_{\text{decision}} = f_{t'}.$$

$$\text{If } j_0 \neq 0, \quad f_{\text{decision}} = \min_{k=0,\ldots,m_0-j_0} [\alpha_{t',t'+k} f_{t'+k} +$$

$$\alpha_{t',t'+k} C(j_0 + k, R_{t'}^{m_0-j_0}, m_0) + B] \quad (6)$$

where

$$B = \sum_{i=1}^{k} \alpha_{t',t'+i} R_{t'}^{m_0-j_0} \qquad \text{if } k \neq 0$$

$$B = 0 \qquad \text{if } k = 0$$

These three equations [(1), (5), and (6)] allow the firm to decide on the optimum pattern of bond refunding over a finite horizon as well as the maturity of the bond it should issue at any refunding and the cost of pursuing this policy.[7] As shown below the solution to these equations yields the single decision which should be made at each moment of time.

Let us continue with the previous example. Once again, assume that interest rates are shown in Table 2-1, the call penalty is shown in Table 2-2, the flotation expense is $2, and the discount factor is 1. Table 2-4 shows the calculations leading to an optimum decision. These calculations are analogous to those illustrated in Table 2-3. For example, consider the calculations necessary to select an optimum call time for a bond with a maturity of 4 years issued at time period 6. If the firm refunds in 1 year, then it incurs a flotation expense of $2, an interest cost of $4, a call penalty of $3, and the cost of acting in an optimum fashion from the seventh period to the horizon ($28). This total of $37 is the value shown for $t = 6$, $m = 4$, and $k = 1$ in Table 2-4. If the firm holds the bond for

---

[7] Actually, this decision is only optimum given the type of information management is assumed to use. As we shall see later, if management makes use of the entire distribution of possible interest rates, better decisions might well be made.

TABLE 2-4

$$F(R_t^m) + \sum_{i=1}^{k} \alpha_{t,t+i}R_t^m + \alpha_{t,t+k}C(k, R_t^m, m) + \alpha_{t,t+k}f_{t+k})$$

t	f_t	$m=3$ $k=1$	$k=2$	$k=3$
11	10	2+7+2+0=11		
10	16	2+7+2+10=21	2+14+1+0=17	
9	17	2+5+2+16=25	2+10+1+10=23	[2+15+0+0=17]
8	26	[2+5+2+17=26]	2+10+1+16=29	2+15+0+10=27
7	28	2+4+2+26=34	[2+8+1+17=28]	2+12+0+16=30
6	32	2+5+2+28=37	2+10+1+26=39	2+15+0+17=34
5	39	2+5+2+32=41	2+10+1+28=41	2+15+0+26=43
4	46	2+6+2+39=49	2+12+1+32=47	2+18+0+28=48
3	52	2+6+2+46=56	2+12+1+39=54	[2+18+0+32=52]
2	58	2+6+2+52=62	2+12+1+46=61	2+18+0+39=59
1	63	2+5+2+58=67	2+10+1+52=65	[2+15+0+46=63]
0	68	2+5+2+63=72	2+10+1+58=71	2+15+0+52=69

$m=4$ $k=1$	$k=2$	$k=3$	$k=4$	$m=T-t$
2+7+3+0=12				[2+8+0+0=10]
2+6+3+10=21	[2+12+2+0=16]			2+16+0+0=18
2+5+3+16=26	2+10+2+10=24	2+15+1+0=18		
2+6+3+17=28	2+12+2+16=32	2+18+1+10=31	[2+24+0+0=26]	
2+4+3+26=35	2+8+2+17=29	2+12+1+16=31	[2+16+0+10=28]	
2+4+3+28=37	2+8+2+26=38	[2+12+1+17=32]	2+16+0+16=34	
2+5+3+32=42	2+10+2+28=42	2+15+1+26=44	[2+20+0+17=39]	
2+5+3+39=49	[2+10+2+32=46]	[2+15+1+28=46]	2+20+0+26=48	
2+6+3+46=57	2+12+2+39=55	2+18+1+32=53	2+24+0+28=54	
2+6+3+52=63	2+12+2+46=62	2+18+1+39=60	[2+24+0+32=58]	
2+6+3+58=69	2+12+2+52=68	2+18+1+46=67	2+24+0+39=65	
2+5+3+63=73	2+10+2+58=72	2+15+1+52=70	[2+20+0+46=68]	

[ ] designates an alternative with a minimum cost for each t.

4 years, it incurs a flotation expense of $2, four interest payments of $4 each or $16, no call penalty, and the cost of behaving in an optimum manner from period 10 to the horizon ($16). This is the result from $t = 6$, $m = 4$, and $k = 4$ in Table 2-4.

Recall when we were discussing the fixed maturity case that we assumed that at the time of its first refunding decision the firm had a 4% bond outstanding which matured in 2 years. Employing this same assumption in the variable maturity case means that the firm's optimum decision, as shown in Table 2-5, is to allow this bond to mature in period 2. The

TABLE 2-5 Expected Refunding Cost

Time Bond Refunded	Fixed Maturity Case	Variable Maturity Case
0 for current period	$2 + 0 + 2 + 71 = 75$	$2 + 0 + 2 + 68 = 72$
1 in 1 year	$2 + 4 + 1 + 65 = 72$	$2 + 4 + 1 + 63 = 70$
2 in 2 years	$2 + 8 + 0 + 61 = 71$	$2 + 8 + 0 + 58 = 68$

firm should then (as shown in Table 2-4) issue a 4-year bond and allow it to mature in period 6, issue a 4-year bond and call it in period 9, and issue a 3-year bond which matures at the horizon. Costs are reduced from $71 in the fixed maturity case to $68 in the variable maturity case. Allowing management a choice of maturity cannot increase costs and in general should reduce them.

2. Infinite Horizon with Point Estimates

Up to now we have assumed that management was interested in making decisions over a finite horizon. It is more common for management to plan to have debt remain as a permanent component of the firm's capital structure. In this case management should optimize over an infinite horizon. The solution to an infinite horizon dynamic programming problem is made tenable when all the parameters on which one's decisions depend are assumed to reach a stationary value after some point in time. In this case (as discussed below) all that is necessary is the assumption that expectations as to future interest rates reach a fixed value after some point in time (T).[8] Evidence for this expectation is provided by the fact that almost all yield curves reach a constant level for long maturities.

Employing the same notation as in the previous case with the exception that T now stands for the point in time at which interest rates are expected

---

[8] T now designates the point in time after which interest rates are expected to stabilize, rather than the time after which debt will be eliminated from the firm's capital structure. However, this new definition of T (as will be made clear by the analysis which follows) plays a role analogous to that of a time horizon and makes the solution to the bond-refunding problem tractable.

to stabilize, we can rewrite equation (5) as

For $t \geq T$,

$$f_t = \min_{\substack{m \in M \\ k=1,\ldots,m}} \left[F(R_t^m) + \sum_{i=1}^{k} \alpha_{t,t+i} R_t^m + \alpha_{t,t+k} C(k, R_t^m, m) + \alpha_{t,t+k} f_{t+k} \right] \quad (7)$$

Since interest rates are assumed to be stable after T, it is reasonable to assume that R is invariant with changes in maturity.[9] If R_t^m is constant, then $F(R_t^m)$ and α_t are also constants. We shall use the subscript T to denote all three variables after the horizon. Equation (7) can now be rewritten as

For $t \geq T$, $\quad f_t = \min_{\substack{m \in M \\ k=1,\ldots,m}} \left[F_T + \sum_{i=1}^{k} \alpha_T^i R_T + \alpha_T^k C(k, R_T, m) + \alpha_T^k f_{t+k} \right]$

$$(8)$$

When the interest rate, flotation expenses, and call costs are stationary over time, the optimum policy and the optimal policy cost is stationary over time.[10] This follows since the same sequence of decisions follow period t and period $t + k$. Thus, $f_t = f_{t+k}$, and the recursive relationship can be restated as[11]

For $t \geq T$, $\quad f_t = \min_{\substack{m \in M \\ k=1,\ldots,m}} \left[F_T + \sum_{i=1}^{k} \alpha_T^i R_T + \alpha_T^k C(k, R_T, m) + \alpha_T^k f_t \right]$

Solving for f_t,

$$f_t = \min_{\substack{m \in M \\ k=1,\ldots,m}} \left[\frac{F_T + \alpha_T^k C(k, R_T, m)}{1 - \alpha_T^k} + \frac{\sum_{i=1}^{k} \alpha_T^i R_T}{1 - \alpha_T^k} \right]$$

By employing the formula for the sum of a geometric progression the last term on the right-hand side of the above equation can be simplified and the recursive relationship becomes

For $t \geq T$, $\quad f_t = \min_{\substack{m \in M \\ k=1,\ldots,m}} \left[\frac{F_T + \alpha_T^k C(k, R_T, m)}{1 - \alpha_T^k} + \frac{\alpha_T}{1 - \alpha_T} R_T \right] \quad (9)$

---

[9] Under the expectations theory of interest rates a flat yield curve (or a flat portion of the yield curve) is consistent with equal expected and actual rates on all maturities. Modifications to the following equations to allow interest to be a function of maturity are straightforward.

[10] For proof, see Bibliography References [12] and [20].

[11] An alternative approach to this derivation of equation (9) is to repetitively substitute values for $f_{t+k}, f_{t+2k}, \ldots$ into equation (8) and solve the resulting equation as the sum of a geometric progression.

Examination of equation (9) will allow us to construct an optimum policy for management to pursue for any refunding after year T. Let us for the moment examine equation (9) for a fixed value of m. As k becomes larger the first term of equation (9) becomes smaller. Its numerator becomes smaller since α^k and $C(k, R_T^m, m)$ become smaller and F_T is a constant—the former because a number less than 1 raised to a higher power is a smaller number, and the latter because the call premium falls over the life of a bond. Furthermore, the denominator $(1 - \alpha^k)$ becomes larger as k increases, for α^k becomes smaller. Since the value of the second term in equation (9) is independent of k, equation (9) is minimized if k is made as large as possible.

Since equation (9) is minimized when k is at a maximum, the bond should be allowed to mature. Consequently, the call penalty is zero and can be eliminated from equation (9).

By analogous reasoning we can see that m should be made as large as possible to minimize equation (9).

Defining M' as the longest maturity the firm will issue, we have

$$\text{For } t > T, \qquad f_t = \frac{F_T}{1 - \alpha_T^{M'}} + \frac{\alpha_T}{1 - \alpha_T} R_T \qquad (10)$$

This represents the cost of following the optimum policy of issuing bonds of maximum maturity and never refunding, computed as of the time of the first refunding after T regardless of the time at which this refunding takes place. To compute the cost of refunding before year T one simply employs equations (5) and (6). All we have really had to do to solve the infinite horizon model is to specify a set of ending conditions for equation (5). The optimum decisions for a firm to make will now consist of a specified set of refunding dates and associated specified maturities to some date past T plus a policy of always floating the maximum maturity bond and never calling after that date.

To illustrate the application of the equations assume that $\alpha_T = .8$, $R_T = \$5$, the flotation expense is $\$2$, and the only possible maturities are 3 and 4 years. Then for $t > T$ we have

$$f_t = \frac{2}{1 - (.8)^4} + \frac{.8}{1 - .8}(5) = 24.882$$

Assume that the firm is willing to make explicit forecasts of future interest rates for four periods and that these rates are shown in Table 2-1 (for the time periods 0, 1, 2, and 3). Further assume that the call premium is given in Table 2-2 and that flotation expenses are $\$2$ and that a value of α of .8 is assumed to be appropriate for all periods.

Applying equations (5), (6), and (10) shows that if the firm had 2 years remaining on a bond with a coupon rate of 4%, it would allow the outstanding bond to mature and replace it with a 4-year bond, after which it would always float 4-year bonds and allow them to remain outstanding until maturity. The total expected cost of this policy would be $22.63.

C. The Bond-Refunding Problem Under Risk

Up to this point we have assumed that management, while recognizing that risk was present in the refunding decision, would made the refunding decision on the basis of point estimates (expected values) of future interest rates. Now let us assume that management is willing to employ information about the distribution of future interest rates in making its refunding decision.[12]

1. Finite Horizon Under Risk

We shall again start with the case of decisions over a finite horizon. Let

M = the set of maturities which management considers offering

M' = the maximum maturity management considers offering (the largest element in the set M)

m = a particular maturity (an element of the set M)

R_i^* = a random variable representing the level of the yield curve at a particular point in time;[13] R_i is always expressed in terms of 1-year rates

R^* = a particular level for the yield curve (i.e., one particular R_i^*); R^* is always expressed in terms of a 1-year rate

$f_t(R^*)$ = the minimum cost of having bonds outstanding from period t until the horizon given the occurrence of yield curve R^* at time t

$d_{t+q}(R_t^m, m)$ = the minimum cost of having bonds outstanding from year $t + q$ to the horizon given that a bond of maturity m bearing an interest rate R_t^m is floated in year t and is left outstanding q years or longer

$P_q(R_i^*/R^*)$ = the probability of yield curve R_i^* occurring at time $t + k$[14]

T = the horizon year after which the firm is assumed to have no debt in its capital structure

$[(m - 1), (T - t)]$ = is defined as the minimum of $m - 1$ and $T - t$

All other terms as before

---

[12] This problem has been analyzed by Elton and Gruber [8, 9] and Kalyman [14].

[13] We are assuming that once the level of the yield curve is specified the full yield curve is known. Variations where this is not true are easy to incorporate into the decisions but require enormous amounts of input data.

[14] We are assuming that interest rates follow a Markov process. If the interest rates at $t + 1$ are unrelated to interest rates at t, the conditional probability $P_q(R_i^*/R^*)$ can be replaced by the simple probability $P(R_i^*)$.

We can now write the recursive relationship for the cost of debt to the horizon. Before doing so, let us make one more assumption in the interest of realism and assume that management is willing to sell non-standard maturities (maturities not contained in the set M) as the horizon approaches in order to allow the bonds to mature at the horizon:

For all $t \geq T$ $f_t = 0$

For all $t < T$ and all R^*,

$$f_t(R^*) = \min \ [F(R_t^m) + \alpha_{t+1}R_t^m + \alpha_{t+1}d_{t+k}(R_t^m m)], \tag{11}$$

where the minimization is performed over the following limits

if $M' > T - t$,   then $m \in M$ or $T - t$

if $M' \leq T - t$ $m \in M$

For $q = m$, $d_{t+q}(R_t^m.m) = \sum\limits_{R_i^*} [f_{t+q}(R_i^*)][P_q(R_i^* \mid R^*)],$ (12)

For $q = m - 1, \dots, 1$

$$d_{t+q}(R_t^m, m) = \sum P_q(R_i^* \mid R^*)[f_{t+q}(R_i^*) + C(q, R_t^m, m)]$$
$$+ \ [1 - \sum P_q (R_i^* \mid R^*)][\alpha_{t+q+1}R_t^m + \alpha_{t+q+1}d_{t+q+1}(R_t^m, m)] \tag{13}$$

The summation is done for all cases where

$$f_{t+q}(R_i^*) + C(q, R_t^m, m) < \alpha_{t+q+1}R_t^m + \alpha_{t+q+1}d_{t+q+1}(R_t^m, m)$$

If $j_0 = 0$, $f_{\text{decision}} = f_{t'}(R_{\text{actual}})$

If $j_0 \neq 0$, $f_{\text{decision}} = \min\limits_{k=0,\dots,m_0-j_0} \left[\alpha_{t',t'+k} \sum\limits_{R_i^*} [f_{t'+k}(R_i^*)][P(R_i^* \mid R^*)] \right.$

$$\left. + \ \alpha_{t',t'+k}C(j_0 + k, R_{t'-j_0}^{m_0}, m_0) + B \right] \tag{14}$$

where

$$B = 0 \qquad\qquad\qquad\qquad \text{if } k = 0$$

$$B = \sum\limits_{i=1}^{k} \alpha_{t',t'+i}R_{t'-j_0}^{m_0} \qquad \text{if } k \neq 0$$

Equations (12) and (13) express the minimum expected cost of having debt in the firm's capital structure from time $t + q$ to T given each possible level of interest rates at time t, the maturity of the bond issued at time t, and the minimum time that the bond will be left outstanding (q).

Equation (12) simply computes the expected costs of following an optimum refunding policy from the end of the maximum life of a bond issued at time t until the horizon. Equation (13) computes the same expected cost for all years of the bond's potential life. The latter equation has two terms. The first term represents the expected cost associated with calling the bond in year $t + q$ under those conditions where such a call is profitable. The limits over which the first term is summed ensures that the cost of calling the bond is computed only under these conditions when it is profitable to call. The second term of equation (13) represents the expected cost of maintaining debt from year $t + q$ to T under those conditions when it is not profitable to call the bond in year q. For any time period t a value of equation (12) is computed for all possible levels of interest rates and all possible maturities of bonds issued at t. Equation (11) is then used to minimize the expected cost of any refunding policy between year t and year T, with respect to maturity for each possible level of interest rates at time t. The quantity minimized is simply the sum of the cost of floating a bond at time t, plus the cost of paying interest on the bond for one period, plus the expected cost of the optimal way of financing debt from time $t + 1$ until the horizon.

Equation (14) incorporates starting conditions into the decision. Once again the value of $f_t(R^*)$ arrived at from equation (11) might not produce a minimum cost solution if the firm has a bond outstanding in the initial period. Instead, the option of keeping the outstanding bond for all periods up to its maturity must be considered rather than assuming [as we did in calculating $f_t(R^*)$] that the bond will be refunded at the beginning of t.

These four equations [(11), (12), (13), and (14)] allow the firm to decide on an optimum pattern of bond refunding over a finite horizon, the maturity of the bond it should issue any time it refunds, and the cost of making optimum decisions. In a moment we shall turn to an example of the decision to which this model will lead, but before doing so we might note certain of its properties.

In the previous examples, the decisions produced by the model were deterministic in nature and were of the form "refund in year Y" or "do not refund in year Y." Now, since the level of interest rates is assumed to be a stochastic variable, our decision rules are more complex. The decision will be of the following form: If a bond carries an interest rate of X_1 and is of age X_2 and the level of interest rates is X_3 in year Y, refund.

Let us continue with our previous example. Once again the call premium is given by Table 2-2, the flotation expense is \$2, and the discount factor is assumed to be 1. Table 2-1 shows the possible levels of future interest rates. Taking expected values of the entries in Table 2-1 yields the interest rates used in previous examples. Consequently, any differences in the analysis and answers are due solely to the incorporation of more information about the distribution of future interest rates into the analysis.

Part of the results are shown in Table 2-6. To understand the use of the previous equations let us examine the entries for the high interest rate in period 6. Assume that the firm will issue a 3-year bond. Then the value of equation (12) is $17. This value represents the expected cost to the firm of holding the bond to maturity and following an optimum policy to the horizon. Holding the 3-year bond to maturity means that the firm must issue a new bond in period 9 at whatever interest rate prevails at that time. If the interest rate is low, the expected cost is $14. It it is high, the expected cost is $20. $17 represents the average of these two figures.

Instead of holding the bond to maturity the firm could refund it in an earlier period. Equation (13) is used for this analysis. When the 3-year bond is 2 years old, the firm has two choices: keep the bond for another year, incurring a cost of $6 in interest plus the $17 expected cost from when it matures to the horizon, or refund at the rates that prevail in period 8. If the lower rate prevails, then examination of Table 2-6

TABLE 2-6 $F(R_t^m) + \alpha_t R_t^m + \alpha_t d_{t+1}(R_t^m, m)$

t	R^*	M	$f(R^*)$	d_4	d_3	d_2	d_1	$k = 1$
9	Low	3	14					
		4						
9	High	3	20					
		4						
8	Low	3	22	0	10	14	17	23
		4		0	5	10	15	22
8	High	3	$26\frac{3}{4}$	0	10	$15\frac{1}{2}$	$18\frac{3}{4}$	$26\frac{3}{4}$
		4		0	7	14	19	28
7	Low	3	24	0	16	17	20	25
		4		10	13	16	19	24
7	High	3	30	0	16	18	23	30
		4		10	15	18	23	30
6	Low	3	28	0	17	21	25	$2 + 4 + 25 = 31$
		4		16	17	20	23	$2 + 3 + 23 = 28$
6	High	3	$34\frac{1}{2}$	0	17	23	$27\frac{1}{2}$	$2 + 6 + 27.5 = 35.5$
		4		16	18	23	$27\frac{1}{2}$	$2 + 5 + 27.5 = 34.5$

shows that the firm incurs an expected cost of $22 plus $1 in call penalty. If the high rate prevails, the expected cost is $26.75 ($26\frac{3}{4}$). If the low interest rate occurs in period 8, the firm incurs a cost of $23 whether it refunds or not. If the higher interest rate occurs, the firm should not refund but wait for the next period. Since high interest rates are assumed as likely as low interest rates, the expected cost is an average of the two costs. We have just applied equation (13) to calculate d_2. To calculate d_1 we observe that if the firm keeps the bond the second year it incurs a cost of $6 plus the expected cost from the second year to the horizon, or d_2, or $23 + 6 = \$29$. Refunding a 1-year-old bond involves a call penalty of $2, so that the cost of refunding if low interest rates prevail in period 7 is \$2 + \$24, while with high interest rates it is \$2 + \$30. If low interest rates prevail, the firm should refund since expected costs are less; otherwise it should keep the bond. The expected cost from period 7 to the horizon when a bond is issued in period 6 is an average of the two costs, or \$27.50 ($27\frac{1}{2}$), and is symbolized by d_1. Having applied equation (13) to obtain the ds we are now ready to calculate one candidate for minimum f. Applying equation (11) shows that this is the flotation expenses of \$2 plus interest costs of \$6 plus the optimum from period 8 to the horizon given that the firm refunds in period 6, or d_1, or \$27.50 ($27\frac{1}{2}$). Comparing this with the minimum obtainable from a 4-year bond shows that the 4-year bond is preferable.

Earlier we argued that utilizing information about the distribution of future interest rates rather than basing the decision on expected values should lead to lower cost decisions. To illustrate this in the context of the current example assume that the firm has a 3-year bond outstanding with 2 years remaining to maturity. In this case, the optimum decision is to refund in two periods with a cost of \$65$\frac{465}{512}$. This compares to a cost of \$68 when the firm is assumed to base its decisions on expected values.

As argued earlier, decision rules are more complex when the firm utilizes information about the distribution of future interest rates. However, it is not so complex as might first be expected, since

1. If at a particular moment in time the optimum decision is for the firm to refund at an interest rate R^*, it is also optimum for the firm to refund at an interest rate R, where $R < R^*$.
2. If at a particular moment in time the firm should keep the old bond at an interest rate R^*, it should also keep at a rate R^*, where $R > R^*$.
3. If the percentage change in the call penalty is invariant with the maturity, then the firm should issue the bond with the longest maturity providing the yield curve is flat or downward sloping.

2. Infinite Horizon Under Risk

Let us now extend the analysis of the refunding decision which employs information about the probability distribution of future returns to the case in which management expects to maintain debt in the firm's capital structure into the indefinite future.

Again we shall assume that management has specific expectations about interest rates in each period up to some horizon year T. Now these expectations will be in the form of a group of possible yield curves in each year and of a probability associated with each yield curve in the group (as in the case just discussed).[15] The question remains as to management's expectations about interest rates in the years beyond the horizon. In the earlier cases we assumed that management had an

---

[15] This assumption can be relaxed; see footnote 12.

expected interest rate which would prevail from year T onward. In this case we are going to make a more complex assumption: that management expects interest rates to follow a stable Markov process from the horizon on and will estimate the transition probabilities of this process. The Markov assumption implies that the probability of a particular interest rate existing in period t is a function of the interest rate which existed in period $t - 1$. The Markov assumption is appealing for many reasons. As Pye [18] has shown, it is consistent with data on observed yield curves and with much of the empirical literature on term structure of interest rates. Second, it is a very rich assumption in the sense that the general model presented in terms of the Markov process can be used to solve problems where the assumptions about future interest rates are much simpler. For example, a natural analogy to the expected value case would be to assume that interest rates after year T can take on one of a group of values in each period. This can be handled within the Markov model simply by making all column transition probabilities the same.

Employing the same notation as in the previous case

$$\text{For } t \geq T, \qquad f(R^*) = \min_{m \in M} [F(R^m) + \alpha R^m + \alpha d_q(R^m, m)] \qquad (15)$$

$$\text{For } q = m, \qquad d_q(R^m, m) = \sum_{R_i^*} [f(R_i^*)][P_q(R_i^* \mid R^*)] \qquad (16)$$

$$\text{For } q = m - 1, \ldots, 1, \qquad d_q(R^m, m) = \sum P_q(R_i^* \mid R^*)[f(R_i^*)$$
$$+ C(q, R^m, m)] + [1 - \sum P_q(R_i^* \mid R^*)][\alpha R^m + \alpha d_{q+1}(R^m, m)] \qquad (17)$$

The summation is done for all cases where

$$f(R_i^*) + C(q, R^m, m) < \alpha R^m + \alpha d_{q+1}(R^m, m)$$

These equations represent a generalization of the finite case equations to the infinite case. The subscript t is missing from all variables because given R^* their value should not be a function of the year in which the bond was floated (since we have assumed that interest rates follow a Markov process). That is, given a particular interest rate, in any period (t) after T the occurrence of any interest rate a fixed number of periods later is invariant with t. For the same reasons α should not be affected by t. We can remove the subscript t from $f_t(R^*)$ because we can show that a Markov process will yield a stationary optimum policy over time.

This set of equations can be used to arrive at a set of $f(R^*)$ for any value of R^*. The Markov properties of interest rates have been used to determine equations (15), (16), and (17). The solution to this set of equations is not as obvious as it has been in the previous cases. Appendix I, which follows the Conclusion, uses the Markov properties of interest rates both to simplify the structure of these equations and to show how linear programming can be used to arrive at optimum values for $f(R^*)$.

These values can then be set equal to all $f_t(R^*)$ for $T \leq t \leq T + m - 1$ and a solution arrived at for the refunding decision by the recursive use of equations (11), (12), (13), and (14).

Conclusion

In this chapter we have constructed general models of the bond-refunding problem under the alternative assumption that management acts on point estimates and on probabilistic estimates of future interest rates. We have seen how the inclusion of probabilistic estimates into the refunding decision changes the nature of the optimal refunding policy and leads to a more profitable series of decisions.

Appendix I: The Solution of an Infinite Dynamic Programming Problem with Markov Probabilities

Equations (15), (16), and (17) in Section C can be more explicitly applied to a problem where one-period interest rates follow a Markov process. In particular, both the interest rate for any maturity R^m and the conditional probability of any one-period rate $P_n(R_i^*/R^*)$ can be expressed as functions of the Markov probabilities.

Let

$A_{R_1 R_2}$ = the transition probability that the one-period rate of interest will be R_2 next period given that it is R_1 this period

A = the matrix of transition probabilities of one-period interest rates

A_{R_1} = A row vector of the transition probabilities from a one-period rate of interest R_1 to any other rate

Then from the general properties of a Markov process we know that given that the one-period rate of interest is now R^* the probability distribution of one-period rates n periods later is

$$P_n(R_i^* \mid R^*) = A_{R^*} A^{n-1}$$

Having arrived at the probability distribution of all future one-period rates we can find the expected interest rate for a bond of any maturity simply by taking the expected value of the geometric average of the relevant one-period future rates.

Given R^*, to find the interest rate R^m on a bond with maturity m when there are N possible rates,

$$R^m = \sum_{i(1)=1}^{N} \sum_{i(2)=1}^{N} \cdots \sum_{i(m-1)=1}^{N}$$

$$\left[\left[(1 + R^*) \prod_{k=1}^{m-1} (1 + R_{i(k)}^*) \right]^{1/m} - 1 \right] \left[A_{R^* R_{i(1)}^*} \prod_{k=1}^{m-2} A_{R_{i(k)}^* R_{i(k+1)}^*} \right]$$

Thus, all one needs to know to specify the probability distribution of future interest rates is the transition probability matrix A.

If these transition probabilities are stationary over time (interest rates follow a Markov process), then it has been shown that there is a unique series of policies which will produce minimum costs. While the optimum policy can be found through an iterative solution in policy space, a solution can be found more directly through use of a linear programming algorithm. Any stochastic dynamic programming problem with Markov probabilities has a corresponding linear programming formulation. Equations (15), (16), and (17) in Section C can be transposed to the following linear programming problem:

$$\text{Max} \sum_{i=1}^{N} C_i f(R_i^*)$$

subject to

$$f(R^*) \leq F(R^m) + \sum_{l=1}^{q} \alpha^l R^m + \alpha^q d_q(R_m, m),$$

$$q = m - 1, \ldots, 1 \text{ and for all } m \in M$$

For $q = m$, $\quad d_q(R^m, m) = \sum_{i=1}^{N} [f(R_i^*)][P_q(R_i^* \mid R^*)]$

For $q = m - 1, \ldots, 1$, and for $j = 0, \ldots, N$,

$$d_q(R^m, m) \leq \sum_{i=1}^{j} P_q(R_i^* \mid R^*)[f(R_i^*) + C(q, R^m, m)]$$

$$+ [1 - \sum P_q(R_i^* \mid R^*)][\alpha R^m + \alpha d_{q+1}(R^m, m)]$$

where

$$\sum_{i=1}^{j} P_q(R_i^* \mid R^*) = 0 \qquad \text{for } j = 0$$

Bibliography

[1] Beckmann, M., *Dynamic Programming of Economic Decisions* (Springer-Verlag, Inc., New York, New York), 1968.

[2] Bellman, Richard, "Equipment Replacement Policy," *Journal of the Society for Industrial and Applied Mathematics*, 3, No. 3, Sept. 1955, pp. 133–136.

[3] Bellman, Richard, *Dynamic Programming* (Princeton University Press, Princeton, N.J.), 1957.

[4] Bellman, Richard and S. E. Dreyfus, *Applied Dynamic Programming* (Princeton University Press, Princeton, N.J.), 1962.

[5] Bowlin, Oswald, "The Refunding Decision," *Journal of Finance, XXI*, March 1966, pp. 55–68.

[6] Cohen, Jerome, and Sidney Robbins, *The Financial Manager: Basic Aspects of Financial Administration* (Harper & Row, Publishers, New York), 1966.

[7] Crockett, Jean, "A Technical Note on the Value of a Call Privilege," in Bibliographical Reference [10].

[8] Elton, Edwin J., and Martin J. Gruber, "Dynamic Programming Models in Finance," *Journal of Finance*, 26, No. 3, May 1971, pp. 473–505.

[9] Elton, Edwin, J., and Martin J. Gruber, "The Economic Value of the Call Option," *Journal of Finance*, 27, No. 4, Sept. 1972, pp. 891–901.

[10] Hess, Arleigh, and Willis Winn, *The Value of the Call Privilege* (University of Pennsylvania Press, Philadelphia), 1962.

[11] Hickman, W. B., *Corporate Bonds: Quality and Investment Performance*, Occasional Paper 59 (National Bureau of Economic Research, New York), 1959.

[12] Howard, Ronald, *Dynamic Programming and Markov Processes* (The M.I.T. Press, Cambridge, Mass.), 1960.

[13] Jen, Frank, and James Wert, "The Effects of Call Risk on Corporate Bond Yields," *Journal of Finance*, XXII, Dec. 1967, pp. 637–652.

[14] Kalyman, Basil A., "The Bond Refunding Problem with Stochastic Interest Rates," *Management Science*, 18, No. 3, Nov. 1971, pp. 171–184.

[15] Kolodny, Richard, "Corporate Borrowing Decisions and the Evaluation of Interest Rate Forecasts," unpublished Ph.D. Dissertation (New York University, New York), 1972.

[16] Myers, Stewart, Discussion of Bibliographical Reference [9], *Journal of Finance*, 26, No. 3, May 1971, pp. 538–539.

[17] Pye, Gordon, "Markov Model of the Term Structure," *Quarterly Journal of Economics*, LXXX, No. 1, Feb. 1966, pp. 60–72.

[18] Pye, Gordon, "The Value of Call Deferment on a Bond: Some Empirical Results," *Journal of Finance*, XXII, Dec. 1967, pp. 623–636.

[19] Van Horne, James C., *Financial Management and Policy* (Prentice-Hall, Inc., Englewood Cliffs, N.J.), 1969.

[20] Wagner, Harvey, *Principals of Operations Research* (Prentice-Hall, Inc., Englewood Cliffs, N.J.), 1969.

[21] Weingartner, H. Martin, "Optimal Timing of Bond Refunding," *Management Science*, 13, No. 7, March 1967, pp. 511–524.

[22] Weston, Fred, and Eugene Brigham, *Managerial Finance* (Holt, Rinehart and Winston, Inc., New York), 1969.

[23] Winn, Willis, and Arleigh Hess, "The Value of the Call Privilege," *Journal of Finance*, XIV, May 1959, pp. 182–195.

The Cash Balance Problem

ONE function of the financial officer of a firm is to decide on the optimal amount of cash (or demand deposits) to keep on hand in order to meet the needs of his firm. This function can be interpreted so widely as to include all decisions about sources and uses of funds by the firm. Indeed, the cash position is affected by all decisions to raise or spend funds, and the availability of cash, in turn, affects these decisions.

However, almost all research in this area has been devoted to a much more constrained form of the cash management problem. Most authors have dealt with the optimum allocation of liquid assets between cash and marketable securities. The decision maker is seen as determining this allocation in order to maximize the revenues from the marketable security portfolio less both the transaction costs from changing the size of this portfolio and the cost of running out of cash. Furthermore, the decision maker is assumed to have no control over inflows and outflows from the pool of liquid assets.[1] Rather these are assumed to be exogenously determined usually by a stochastic process.

This form of the cash management problem, which is called the cash balance problem, is a realistic description of a type of problem faced by most firms. For example, it captures the nature of the problem faced by

---

[1] Alternative assumptions have been examined by Robichek *et al.* [13] and Orgler [12].

the financial officer of an industrial corporation who has the job of managing the company's day-to-day cash position given that the financing and investment decisions are either determined by others or fixed over a reasonable period of time.[2] It also captures the problem, faced by the treasurer, of many types of financial intermediaries (e.g., mutual funds, pension funds, college endowment funds, and insurance companies). In each case the inflows and outflows of cash are beyond the control of the decision maker. In each case the decision maker must decide how much of the liquid assets to hold in cash to meet transaction demands and how much to place in the institution's portfolio of securities. For example, the cash demand faced by the treasurer of a mutual fund is largely determined by the net of redemptions, new contributions, and inflows from investments. Although he may affect the inflows from new investments, it is reasonable to assume that the other net cash flows to the firm are beyond his control.

In this chapter we shall present a generalized dynamic programming solution to the cash balance problem just discussed. We shall then make a series of simplifying assumptions. Each of these assumptions will allow us to derive one or more models currently available in the literature.

A. The Optimum Allocation Between Cash and Marketable Securities—General Solution

The cash balance problem involves the decision on the optimal level of cash with which to start each period (j) given (1) an initial cash position (i), (2) a set of transfer costs, (3) understock and holding costs, and (4) a density function for stochastic changes in cash flows. The solution to this problem is similar to a dynamic programming solution to the inventory problem in that both involve the balancing of understock, holding, and transaction costs so as to minimize the present value of expected future costs. However, there are major differences in that (1) stochastic changes in the level of cash can be positive or negative, and (2) the manager can either increase or decrease the amount of inventory (cash) at the start of each period.

---

[2] One might argue that the scope of this problem could be extended by redefining the problem as the transference of funds between earning assets and a pool of cash. However, the structure of the problem becomes much more complex because:

1. Earning assets cannot be treated as homogeneous either with respect to return or risk.
2. The investment in earning assets is not continuous.
3. To make this problem at all realistic, one also has to consider alternative sources of funds and the problems of estimating the costs of alternative sources.

In short, this becomes a dynamic programming model of the optimal behavior of the firm. While the construction of such a model is desirable, given the present state of knowledge, it is not feasible.

We can represent the transfer costs of changing the cash level of the firm from i to j as

$$\text{Transfer costs } T(i,j) = \begin{bmatrix} T_u + t_u(j-i) & \text{if } j > i \\ 0 & \text{if } j = i \\ T_d + t_d(i-j) & \text{if } j < i \end{bmatrix} \qquad (1)$$

In this expression, T_u and T_d represent, respectively, any fixed costs involved in increasing or decreasing the level of the cash balance, while t_u and t_d represent the marginal costs per dollar of change.

Holding and understock costs can be assumed to be a function of the level of cash at the beginning or the end of each period, or they can be assumed to be a function of some intermediate or average cash position during the period. It is difficult to choose among these assumptions, and in fact the best choice depends on the circumstances facing the firm.[3] Fortunately, the choice of assumption does not affect the type of analysis or conclusions contained in this book, though it will affect the numerical calculations for any problem. To make the analysis generally useful, we shall define the costs associated with the level of cash $L(j)$ (holding and understock costs) in two different ways: first in terms of beginning cash balance levels, and then in terms of ending cash balance levels. For both these cases let

1. $h(\ )$ be the function that represents the opportunity cost associated with having a positive cash balance of any size.
2. $u(\ )$ be the function that represents the understock costs associated with having a negative cash balance of any size.

At this point we have made no assumption as to the functional form of $h(\ )$ and $u(\ )$.

If we assume that the argument of these functions is the cash level at the beginning of the period (immediately after a decision is made on the level of cash), then

$$L(j) = \begin{bmatrix} u(j) & \text{if } j < 0 \\ 0 & \text{if } j = 0 \\ h(j) & \text{if } j > 0 \end{bmatrix} \qquad (2)$$

To define $L(j)$ when costs depend on the cash balance with which we end a period, we must describe the distribution of changes in the cash balance. We shall treat exogenous changes in the cash account as an independently distributed random variable with a density function $P(e)$.[4]

---

[3] Alternative assumptions have been made in articles discussing the cash management problem. See Bibliography References [5], [6], [8], and [12].

[4] In solving any problem, management will often treat e as a discrete variable with finite bounds. While all the analysis in this chapter could be performed by treating e as a discrete variable with finite bounds without a change in results, the analysis is facilitated by treating e as a continuous variable.

With this definition expected understock costs will be

$$\int_j^\infty u(e - j)P(e)\, de$$

The expected opportunity cost of having too much cash is

$$\int_{-\infty}^j h(j - e)P(e)\, de$$

Finally, the cost associated with starting a period with a level of cash, j, is the sum of these costs, or[5]

$$L(j) = \int_{-\infty}^j h(j - e)P(e)\, de + \int_j^\infty u(e - j)P(e)\, de \qquad (3)$$

The analysis contained in the remainder of this chapter is appropriate under either of these definitions of $L(j)$, equation (2) or (3), unless an exception is explicitly noted.

The recursive relationship representing the optimal cash management problem can now easily be constructed. The optimal cash balance to move to j given any starting cash balance i at time t is going to be that value which minimizes the sum of

1. The transfer cost of going from a cash balance of i to one of j or $T(i,j)$.
2. The holding-understock cost which is associated with a cash balance of j or $L(j)$.
3. The present value of the expected minimum cost of managing cash from period $t + 1$ until the horizon given a move to state j at time t.[6]

If we let

α = the appropriate discount factor
$f_t(i)$ = the minimum expected cost of managing cash from period t until the horizon given that the opening cash balance is i in period t

then the recursive relationship becomes

$$f_t(i) = \min_j \left[T(i,j) + L(j) + \alpha \int_{-\infty}^\infty f_{t+1}(j - e)\, P(e)\, de \right] \qquad (4)$$

---

[5] The firm may be operating under constraints (e.g., need for compensating balances) which make the switch from holding to understock costs occur at some positive cash position m rather than at a zero cash balance. Under this assumption, equation (3) becomes

$$L(j) = \int_{-\infty}^{j-m} h[(j - m) - e]\, P(e)\, de + \int_{j-m}^\infty u[e - (j - m)]\, P(e)\, de$$

[6] We are numbering periods forward in time. The horizon is period T, the period before the horizon is period $T - 1$, etc.

This relationship can be used to solve any cash balance problem. However, the special structure of many cash balance problems allows us to employ this relationship both to define the form of an optimal cash balance policy and to simplify the calculations needed to reach such a policy. Furthermore, knowing the form of the optimum cash balance policy is often more important than the numeric solution to a particular problem.

B. Exploiting Special Structure

Our ability to deduce the form of the optimum policy from the dynamic programming formulation depends on the special structure of the components of the dynamic programming equation. If these cost components are convex or concave functions, we can gain insights into the problem. In particular, we can simplify the solution to the cash management problem because $L(j)$ can reasonably be assumed to be a convex function of j. The function $L(j)$ is convex if holding costs increase at least proportionately (or faster) with increases in cash balances for positive cash balances, if understock costs increase at least proportionately with decreases in cash balances for negative cash balances, and if $h(0) = u(0) = 0$.[7] The actual composition of holding and understock costs is consistent with the convexity of $L(j)$. Holding costs are the interest foregone by holding cash rather than marketable securities. These should be directly proportional to the size of the cash balance. Understock costs are costs associated with the delay and embarrassment caused by an inability to promptly meet obligations. These should increase more than proportionately with the size of the obligation. Finally, note that $L(j)$ has a finite minimum equal to or greater than zero, the cost of having the cash balance of zero.

Once the convexity of $L(j)$ is accepted, one can proceed to derive the optimum form of the cash balance policy. We shall start by studying the case where the fixed component of transactions costs is assumed equal to zero.[8] Then we shall study cases where the fixed component has a positive value.

1. Variable Costs but No Fixed Costs

The assumption that the fixed cost per transaction approaches zero seems to be a reasonable assumption for the cash balance problem of many firms. For example, a mutual fund in transferring funds from cash

---

[7] The convexity of $L(j)$ under the assumptions stated in the text can be seen by examining equations (2) and (3).

[8] The cash management problem was originally formulated as a dynamic programming problem by Eppen and Fama [6]. They analyzed the case of fixed transaction costs equal to zero and assumed that h and u in equation (2) were linear functions with an intercept of zero. We shall present the case where h and u are general convex functions. While our proofs will be more complex than those presented by Eppen and Fama [6], they are more general and represent the framework which can be used to study other dynamic programming problems with convex cost structures.

to its portfolio will incur a transaction cost on purchase or sale which is roughly proportional to the amount of funds involved. There are some fixed costs involved in writing a check and processing the paper work, but these should be negligible compared to the variable component.[9]

If we accept the fixed component in the transaction cost as being equal to zero, equation (4) can be rewritten as

$$
f_t(i) = \min \begin{bmatrix} \min_{j>i} \left[t_u(j-i) + L(j) + \alpha \int_{-\infty}^{\infty} f_{t+1}(j-e)\, P(e)\, de \right] \\[2ex] L(i) + \alpha \int_{-\infty}^{\infty} f_{t+1}(i-e)\, P(e)\, de \\[2ex] \min_{i>j} \left[t_d(i-j) + L(j) + \alpha \int_{-\infty}^{\infty} f_{t+1}(j-e)\, P(e)\, de \right] \end{bmatrix} \tag{5}
$$

a. OPTIMAL POLICY FOR THE FINAL DECISION PERIOD

For the last decision point, equation (5) can be rewritten as[10]

$$
f_{T-1}(i) = \min \begin{bmatrix} -t_u \cdot i + \min_{j>i} \left[t_u \cdot j + L(j) \right] \\[2ex] L(i) \\[2ex] t_d \cdot i + \min_{i>j} \left[-t_d \cdot j + L(j) \right] \end{bmatrix} \tag{6}
$$

Consider the upper part of the recursive relationship.

Since $L(j)$ is a convex function with a finite minimum and $t_u \cdot j$ is a linear function of j, their sum is a convex function of j. Therefore, there is a minimum which can be denoted by D_{T-1} such that[11]

$$
\min_j \left[t_u \cdot j + L(j) \right] = t_u \cdot D_{T-1} + L(D_{T-1}) \tag{7}
$$

Furthermore, by the properties of convexity a local optimum value of D_{T-1} is also a global optimum.

---

[9] To the extent that these functions are performed by employees with slack time, they are not a real cost of the decision.

[10] The final decision period is $T - 1$ and $f_T = 0$.

[11] While this function will usually have a unique minimum, it is possible that it has a minimum value over a range of i. If this occurs, D_{T-1} should be defined as the lowest value of i for which the equality holds. In this case all the results stated below still hold. The proofs would *remain* valid except that some of the inequalities of the greater-than form would have to be replaced with inequalities of the equal-to-or-greater-than form. In the proofs involving upper limits if a minimum value occurs over a range of i, U_{T-1} should be defined as the biggest value of i for which the minimization equality holds. In addition, the reader should note that it is possible for D_{T-1} to be equal to $-\infty$ and for U_{T-1} to be equal to $+\infty$.

Assume that $i \geq D_{T-1}$. Values of j greater than i do not contain D_{T-1}, and i is closer to D_{T-1} than any value of j. Since we are assuming convex functions, we have

$$\min_{j > i} [t_u \cdot j + L(j)] > t_u \cdot i + L(i)$$

Rearranging terms,

$$-t_u \cdot i + \min_{j > i} [t_u \cdot j + L(j)] > L(i)$$

The left-hand side of this expression is the same as the top choice in equation (6). Since $L(i)$ is smaller, the middle choice is preferable to the top choice, and we have the following: If $i \geq D_{T-1}$, then do not raise the level of the cash balance.

Assume that $i < D_{T-1}$. If we examine all j greater than i, setting $j = D_{T-1}$ is one possible choice. Since $t_u \cdot D_{T-1} + L(D_{T-1}) < t_u \cdot i + L(i)$, then $-t_u \cdot i + t_u \cdot D_{T-1} + L(D_{T-1}) < L(i)$, and the top choice in equation (6) is preferred, and we have the following: If $i < D_{T-1}$, set $j = D_{T-1}$. By an analogous argument it can be shown that

$$\min_{j} [-t_d \cdot j + L(j)] = -t_d \cdot U_{T-1} + L(U_{T-1})$$

and the optimal policy becomes[12]

For $i \leq U_{T-1}$,   do not lower the level of cash

For $i > U_{T-1}$,   set $j = U_{T-1}$ and therefore $f_{T-1}(i)$

$$= t_d(i - U_{T-1}) + L(U_{T-1})$$

A general policy can now be stated for time $T - 1$. If the cash position is below D_{T-1}, sell enough securities to bring the cash position up to D_{T-1}. If the cash position is above U_{T-1}, buy enough securities to restore the cash position to U_{T-1}. If it is between these two limits, take no action. Notice that we can state the optimal policy independently of the starting position of cash. D_{T-1} and U_{T-1} are not functions of i.

Before leaving this section, it is worthwhile examining diagrammatically why this is so. We shall do so for U_{T-1}. Consider Figure 3-1, which is constructed assuming that the firm has a positive cash position at time $T - 1$ and that holding and understock costs are given by equation (2). The minimum cannot lie to the right of i since both holding and transfer costs are increasing. The minimum must lie at i or to the left of i. If the marginal transaction cost is larger than the marginal savings from decreasing holding costs at the point i, then the minimum lies at i.

---

[12] For this policy to be optimum it is necessary that $U_{T-1} \geq D_{T-1}$. In a later section we shall prove that $U_{T-1} \geq 0$ and $D_{T-1} \leq 0$. Therefore, $U_{T-1} \geq D_{T-1}$.

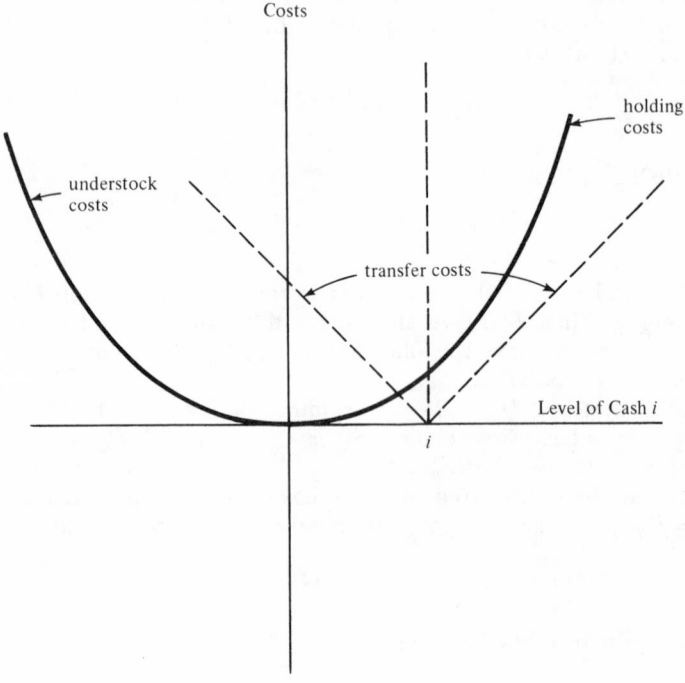

Figure 3-1

If this condition is not met, it lies to the left of i at that point where the marginal cost of decreasing cash is exactly equal to the marginal savings in holding cost. The transfer costs have a constant slope throughout. Changing the location of i by one unit does not change the size of the increase in transaction costs for a unit decrease in the cash level j. Therefore, the j for which the slope of the holding costs is the same as the slope of the transaction costs is not a function of i, and there is a unique value for U_{T-1}. An analogous argument (with i to the left of zero) could be used to show the existence of the minimum D_{T-1}.

The costs involved in following the optimum policy are a function of i. They can be presented as

$$f_{T-1}(i) = \begin{bmatrix} t_u(D_{T-1} - i) + L(D_{T-1}) & \text{if } i < D_{T-1} \\ L(i) & \text{if } D_{T-1} \leq i \leq U_{T-1} \\ t_d(i - U_{T-1}) + L(U_{T-1}) & \text{if } i > U_{T-1} \end{bmatrix} \quad (8)$$

A diagrammatic representation of the cost of the optimum policy is presented in Figure 3-2.

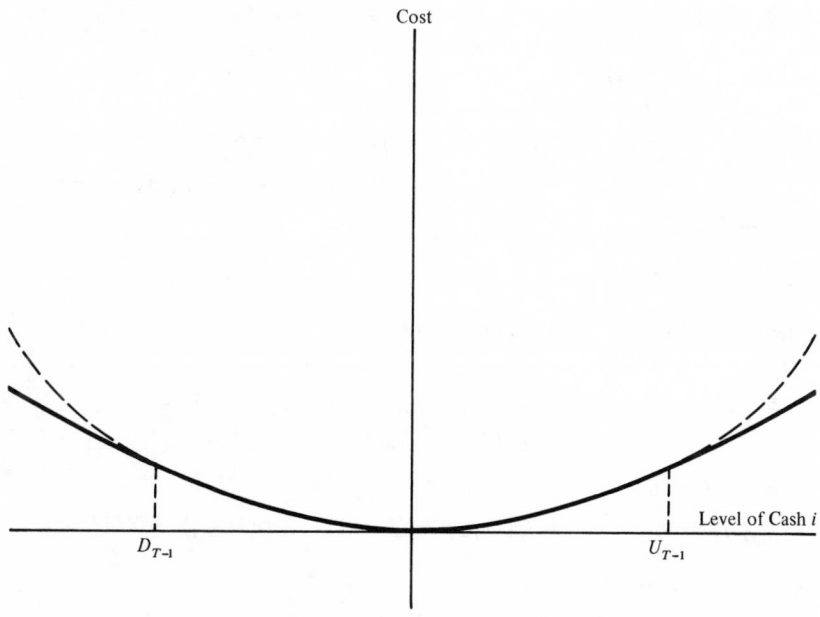

Figure 3-2

b. OPTIMAL POLICY FOR EARLIER DECISION PERIODS

We have now formulated an optimum policy for the last decision period. To extend this analysis to earlier periods we must be able to make statements about the form of $f_{T-1}(i)$. As we shall show below, if $f_{T-1}(i)$ is a convex function, we can arrive at optimum policies for all periods. The reader who is willing to accept the convexity of $f_{T-1}(i)$ can skip to the next section.

The Convexity of f_{T-1} (i)

A function $f(i)$ is convex if

$$f^*(i) = f(i+1) + f(i-1) - 2f(i) \geq 0 \qquad (9)$$

for all values of i. Below, we shall show that $f_{T-1}(i)$ is convex for all values of i by employing equations (7), (8), and (9).

Equation (8) consists of three separate functional forms. To show convexity, it is necessary to show that each functional form is convex and that convexity is maintained across each intersection of the functions. We shall examine six sections of the function $f_{T-1}(i)$: the region below

D_{T-1}, the region between D_{T-1} and U_{T-1}, the region above U_{T-1}, and the regions in the neighborhood of U_{T-1} and D_{T-1} (for $U_{T-1} \neq D_{T-1}$ and $U_{T-1} = D_{T-1}$).

1. $i + 1 < D_{T-1}$:

$$f^*_{T-1}(i) = t_u[D_{T-1} - (i + 1)] + L(D_{T-1}) + t_u[D_{T-1} - (i - 1)]$$
$$+ L(D_{T-1}) - 2[t_u(D_{T-1} - i) + L(D_{T-1})] = 0$$

2. $U_{T-1} \geq i + 1$ and $i - 1 \geq D_{T-1}$:

$$f^*_{T-1}(i) = L(i + 1) + L(i - 1) - 2L(i) \geq 0$$

This holds since $L(\ )$ is a convex function.

3. $i - 1 > U_{T-1}$:

$$f^*_{T-1}(i) = t_d[(i + 1) - U_{T-1}] + L(U_{T-1}) + t_d[(i - 1) - U_{T-1}]$$
$$+ L(U_{T-1}) - 2[t_d(i - U_{T-1}) + L(U_{T-1})] = 0$$

4. $i = D_{T-1}$:

$$f^*_{T-1}(i) = L(i + 1) + t_u[D_{T-1} - (i - 1)] + L(D_{T-1}) - 2L(D_{T-1})$$

Since $i = D_{T-1}$, we have

$$f^*_{T-1}(i) = L(i + 1) + t_u - L(i)$$

Adding and subtracting $t_u \cdot i$ we have

$$f^*_{T-1}(i) = L(i + 1) + t_u(i + 1) - L(i) - t_u(i)$$

This is greater than zero since $D_{t-1} = i$ and since by the definition of D_{t-1} in equation (7)

$$L(j) + t_u(j) \geq L(D_{T-1}) + t_u(D_{T-1})$$

and one possible value for j is $i + 1$.

5. $i = U_{T-1}$:

$$f^*_{T-1}(i) = t_d[(i + 1) - U_{T-1}] + L(U_{T-1}) + L(i - 1) - 2L(U_{T-1})$$

Since $i = U_{T-1}$,

$$f^*_{T-1}(i) = t_d + L(i - 1) - L(i)$$

Subtracting and adding $t_d \cdot i$ we have

$$f^*_{T-1}(i) = -t_d(i - 1) + L(i - 1) - [-t_d(i) + L(i)]$$

This is greater than zero since $U_{t-1} = i$ and since by definition of U_{T-1}

$$-t_d(j) + L(j) \geq -t_d U_{T-1} + L(U_{T-1})$$

and one possible value for j is $i - 1$.

6. $i = D_{T-1} = U_{T-1}$:

$$f^*_{T-1}(i) = t_u[D_{T-1} - (i-1)] + L(D_{T-1})$$
$$+ t_d[(i+1) - U_{T-1}] + L(U_{T-1}) - 2L(i)$$

Since $i = D_{T-1} = U_{T-1}$,

$$f^*_{T-1}(i) = t_u + t_d > 0$$

The expression $\int_{-\infty}^{\infty} f_{T-1}(j - e)\, P(e)\, de$ is also convex because the sum of convex functions is a convex function and integration, a summation operation, preserves convexity.

Equation (5) can now be rewritten to define f_{T-2} as

$$f_{T-2}(i) = \min \begin{bmatrix} -t_u \cdot i + \min_{j > i} [t_u \cdot j + L(j) \\ \qquad + \alpha \int_{-\infty}^{\infty} f_{T-1}(j - e)\, P(e)\, de] \\[2ex] L(i) + \alpha \int_{-\infty}^{\infty} f_{T-1}(i - e)\, P(e)\, de \\[2ex] t_d \cdot i + \min_{i > j} [-t_d \cdot j + L(j) \\ \qquad + \alpha \int_{-\infty}^{\infty} f_{T-1}(j - e)\, P(e)\, de] \end{bmatrix} \qquad (10)$$

Consider the top expression in equation (10). Since $L(j)$ is a convex function of j, $t_u \cdot j$ is a linear function of j and $\int_{-\infty} f_{T-1}(j - e)\, P(e)\, de$ is a convex function of j, their sum is a convex function of j. Therefore, there is a minimum which can be denoted by D_{T-2} such that

$$\min_j \left[t_u \cdot j + L(j) + \alpha \int_{-\infty}^{\infty} f_{T-1}(j - e)\, P(e)\, de \right]$$
$$= t_u \cdot D_{T-2} + L(D_{T-2}) + \alpha \int_{-\infty}^{\infty} f_{T-1}(D_{T-2} - e)\, P(e)\, de$$

Since D_{T-2} is a global optimum for this function, one can proceed directly paralleling the steps of the proof in Section B, #1a to show that the optimum policy for period $T - 2$ is described as

$$\begin{aligned} \text{If } i < D_{T-2}, &\qquad j = D_{T-2} \\ \text{If } D_{T-2} \le i \le U_{T-2}, &\qquad j = i \\ \text{If } U_{T-2} < i, &\qquad j = U_{T-2} \end{aligned}$$

Diagrammatically the reasons are identical to the reasons in period $T - 1$. What is necessary is to combine Figures 3-1 and 3-2.[13] This produces a diagram with the same structure as Figure 3-1, and an analogous argument follows. One can then proceed by paralleling the steps in the proof of convexity of $f_{T-1}(i)$ to show that $f_{T-2}(i)$ is also convex.

This procedure can then be repeated for periods $T - 3$, $T - 4$, $T - 5$, etc., to show that for any periods the costs of following the policy can be represented as

$$f_t(i) = \begin{bmatrix} t_u(D_t - i) + L(D_t) \\ \quad + \alpha \int_{-\infty}^{\infty} f_{t+1}(D_t - e)\, P(e)\, de \qquad \text{for } i < D_t \\[2ex] L(i) + \alpha \int_{-\infty}^{\infty} f_{t+1}(i - e)\, P(e)\, de \qquad \text{for } D_t \le i \le U_t \\[2ex] t_d(i - U_t) + L(U_t) \\ \quad + \alpha \int_{-\infty}^{\infty} f_{t+1}(U_t - e)\, P(e)\, de \qquad \text{for } U_t < i \end{bmatrix} \qquad (11)$$

and that the optimum policy can be represented as

$$\text{If } i < D_t, \qquad j = D_t$$
$$\text{If } D_t \le i \le U_t, \quad j = i$$
$$\text{If } U_t < i, \qquad j = U_t$$

We have now exploited the cost structure of the cash balance problem to define the form of an optimum cash management policy. Note that as shown in equation (11) this policy can be stated to hold *regardless* of the cash balance of the firm at any moment in time. The limits U_t and D_t are not affected by the cash balance at any time. The independence of U_t and D_t from i leads to a vast reduction in calculations since

1. U_t and D_t need be determined only once in any period. Furthermore, that determination is simplified by the fact that the functions are convex and each possesses a minimum.
2. Once U_t and D_t are determined, $f_t(i)$ is a simple linear function of i for $i < D_t$ and $i > U_t$ [see equation (11)].

Before leaving this section we shall show how the form of the recursive relationship can be used to define an optimal policy in more detail. In

[13] Actually a smoother Figure 3-2, since the recursive relationship averages sections of Figure 3-2.

particular, we shall show that if $L(j)$ is defined as in equation (2), D_t must be nonpositive and U_t must be nonnegative for all t.[14] U_t is the value of i for which a decrease in the beginning cash balance is no longer profitable. Consider Figure 3-3. If i is zero, a decrease in cash leads to both an increase in transaction costs and an increase in the costs associated with the level of cash. Hence, a decrease in cash below zero is unprofitable. Consider a positive i (such as i' in Figure 3-3). In this case, it will pay to decrease cash if the decrease in holding-understock costs is greater than the increase in transfer costs. This will be true as long as the slope of the holding-understock cost curve is greater than minus the slope of the transfer costs case. Since the slope of the holding and understock cost curve will generally decline as i approaches 0, the equality will normally occur with positive U_{t-1}.[15] As shown above, it can never occur below zero since both transfer costs and holding-understock costs increase in this region.

Up to this point we have assumed that the fixed cost component of

---

[14] This can also be shown analytically. Given any level of cash, the marginal cost of increasing the cash balance by one unit [see equation (5)] is

$$t_u + \Delta L(i) + \alpha \Delta \int_{-\infty}^{\infty} f_{t+1}(i - e)\, P(e)\, de$$

where Δ represents the value of the term which follows it evaluated at $i + 1$ minus the value of the term evaluated at i. For the increase in cash balance to be profitable, this expression must be no larger than zero. Or rearranging terms,

$$\Delta L(i) + \alpha \Delta \int_{-\infty}^{\infty} f_{t+1}(i - e)\, P(e)\, de \leq -t_u$$

The second term can be evaluated from equation (11):

$$\Delta f_{t+1}(i) = \begin{bmatrix} -t_u & \text{for } i < D_t \\ \Delta L(i) + \alpha \Delta \int_{-\infty}^{\infty} f_{t+2}(i - e)\, P(e)\, de & \text{for } D_t \leq i \leq U_t \\ t_d & \text{for } i > U_t \end{bmatrix}$$

Since we have established that $f_{t+1}(i)$ is convex, $\Delta f_{t+1}(i)$ is monotone nondecreasing with a minimum value of $-t_u$. Since $\Delta f_{t+1}(i) \geq -t_u$ for any i, then $\Delta \int_{-\infty}^{\infty} f_{t+1}(i - e)\, P(e)\, de$ must be greater or equal to $-t_u$. Furthermore, since α is a number smaller than 1, $\alpha \Delta \int_{-\infty}^{\infty} f_{t+1}(i - e)\, P(e)\, de \geq -t_u$. Therefore, for the left-hand side of equation (12) to be less than or equal to $-t_u$, $\Delta L(i)$ must be negative or equal to zero. From equation (12) this can happen only if i is less than or equal to zero. Thus, it will not pay to raise the level of cash if the level of cash is above zero and $D_t \leq 0$. If we had employed equation (3) as the definition of $L(j)$, then an upper limit on D_t could be established as that value of i for which $\Delta L(i)$ first became negative.

[15] Figure 3-3 is of course technically valid only in period $T - 1$. However, as argued earlier, a representation of the decision in earlier periods has the same form.

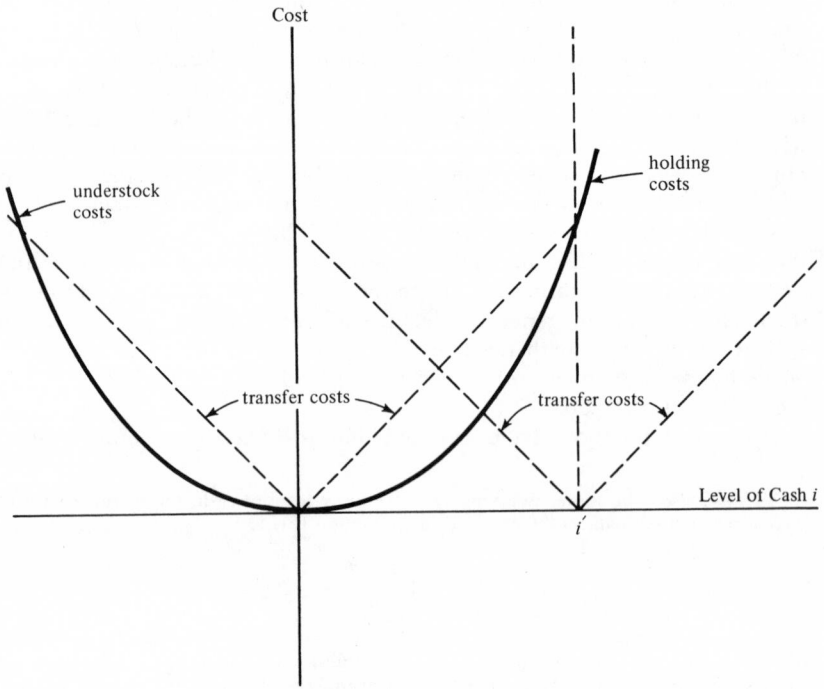

Figure 3-3

transaction costs was equal to zero. While we believe this is a reasonable assumption for many cash management problems, in the next section we shall briefly explore the form of optimum policies when fixed costs are present.

2. Optimum Policies with Variable and Fixed Transaction Costs

The fixed component of transaction costs is likely to be small relative to the variable component. However, these costs are often positive since any transaction in securities involves a certain amount of a financial officer's time, plus clerical costs (e.g., cost of entering the transactions on the books and recording receipts).

Let us take the simplest case where a fixed cost is present on one side of the transaction but not on the other.[16] In particular, let us assume that there is a fixed cost T_u of selling securities. Then, for the last period,

---

[16] The case where there is a fixed cost on one side of a transaction in securities but not on the other has been analyzed by Girges [8]. Parts of the analysis in the text draw upon this work.

equation (4) can be written as

$$f_{T-1}(i) = \min \begin{bmatrix} T_u - t_u \cdot i + \min_{j > i} [t_u \cdot j + L(j)] \\ L(i) \\ t_d \cdot i + \min_{i > j} [-t_d \cdot j + L(j)] \end{bmatrix}$$

Consider the top part of the recursive relationship. From the convexity of $t_u \cdot j + L(j)$ there is a minimum which can be denoted by D_{T-1} such that

$$\min_{j} [t_u \cdot j + L(j)] = t_u \cdot D_{T-1} + L(D_{T-1})$$

Now suppose that $i \geq D_{T-1}$. Values of $j > i \geq D_{T-1}$ do not contain D_{T-1}. Since we are assuming convex functions, the minimum occurs at the feasible value nearest D_{T-1} or i. Therefore,

$$\min_{j > i} [t_u \cdot j + L(j)] > t_u \cdot i + L(i)$$

Rearranging terms,

$$-t_u \cdot i + \min_{j > i} [t_u \cdot j + L(j)] > L(i)$$

Adding T_u to the left-hand side would not change the inequality. With this addition the left-hand side of the inequality is identical to the top of the recursive relationship, and the right-hand side is the same as the middle part. The implication of the inequality is that if the level of cash balance is greater than D_{T-1}, do not raise it.

Now suppose that $i < D_{T-1}$. Then D_{T-1} is a feasible choice, and the minimum cost is less than or equal to the cost at an arbitrary level i, or

$$\min_{j > i} [t_u \cdot j + L(j)] < t_u \cdot i + L(i)$$

Rearranging terms,

$$-t_u \cdot i + \min_{j > i} [t_u \cdot j + L(j)] < L(i)$$

The inequality is the same as the top and middle of the recursive relationship with the addition of T_u to the left-hand side. The addition of T_u to the left-hand side may or may not reverse the inequality.

Let d_{T-1} be the smallest value of i that reverses the inequality. That is, d_{T-1} is the smallest value of i for which

$$T_u - t_u \cdot i + \min_{j > i} [t_u \cdot j + L(j)] > L(i)$$

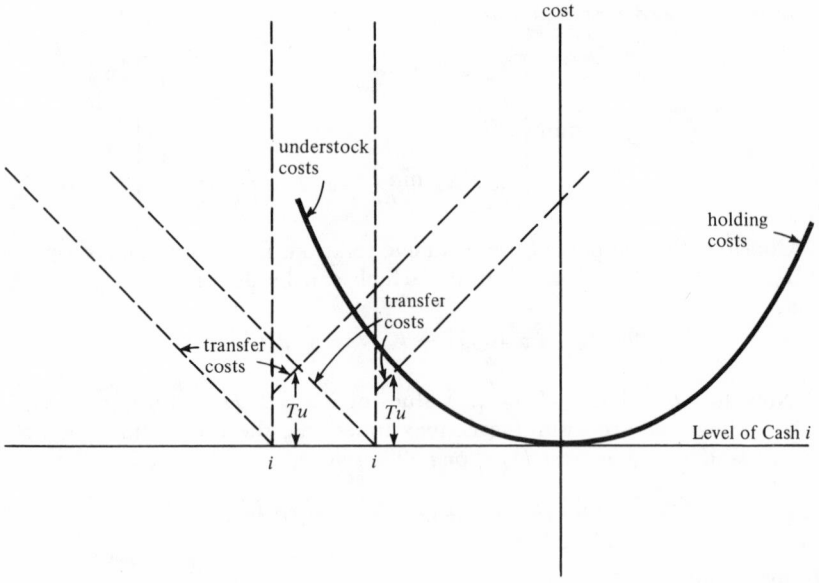

Figure 3-4

Then we have the following: If $i \geq d_{T-1}$, do not raise the cash balance and $j = i$.[17] If $i < d_{T-1}$, then the inequality is retained and the optimal policy is to raise the level of cash to the value D_{T-1}, a value which minimizes the top part of the recursive relationship.[18]

The proof for an upper limit on the cash balance is exactly the same as in Section B, #1, and the optimum last-period policy can be stated as

$$\text{If } i < d_{T-1}, \qquad\qquad \text{set } j = D_{T-1}$$

$$\text{If } d_{T-1} \leq i < U_{T-1}, \qquad \text{set } j = i$$

$$\text{If } U_{T-1} \leq i, \qquad\qquad \text{set } j = U_{T-1}$$

The reason for this is easy to see diagrammatically. Consider Figure 3-4. As in the case of no fixed costs, if you increase the cash level (j), you increase it until the marginal increase in transaction costs exactly balances the marginal decrease in out-of-stock costs. Since transaction costs are a linear function, the marginal transaction cost at any j is a constant, independent of the location of i. Hence, if you increase j, it is always to

---

[17] Because of the convexity of $t_u \cdot i + L(i)$, increasing i makes the difference between the left- and right-hand sides smaller.

[18] By contrasting this proof with the discussion in Section A, #1 the reader can see how the presence of a fixed cost has modified the analysis.

the same level. However, with a fixed cost it may not pay to increase j even if i is to the left of the optimum j (which we call D_t). In particular, the reduction in out-of-stock costs must be larger than the increase in transaction costs by the amount of fixed costs for it to be profitable to change the cash levels.

The cost of following this policy can be stated as

$$
f_{T-1}(i) = \begin{bmatrix} T_u + t_u(D_{T-1} - i) + L(D_{T-1}) & \text{for } i < d_{T-1} \\ L(i) & \text{for } d_{T-1} \le i < U_{T-1} \\ t_d(i - U_{T-1}) + L(U_{T-1}) & \text{for } U_{T-1} \le i \end{bmatrix}
$$

A diagrammatic presentation of the cost of following this policy is shown by the solid lines in Figure 3-5.

Comparing Figure 3-2 with Figure 3-5 reveals that the only difference is that when fixed costs are present, cash balances should be increased only if these fixed costs are covered. Notice that the presence of fixed costs means that $f_{T-1}(i)$ is no longer a convex function. While it is convex in the region $d_{T-1} \le i \le \infty$, it is not convex over all possible

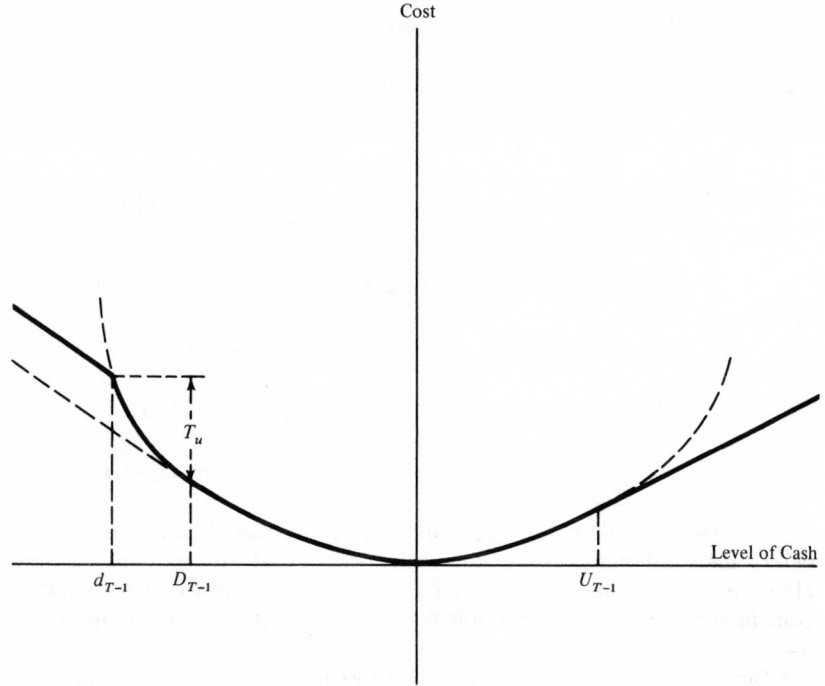

Figure 3-5

values of i.[19] The fact that $f_{T-1}(i)$ is not a simple convex function complicates the analysis for earlier periods. In particular, $f_t(i)$ for $t < T - 1$ can have a local minimum such that a simple policy such as that discussed earlier in this chapter is no longer optimal.

For example, the costs associated with alternative cash balances might look like those in Figure 3-6.

Part of the optimal policy is the same as that found for decisions in period $T - 1$. Using the same methodology as that first employed and defining d_t, D_t, and U_t as we have done earlier it can easily be shown that if the cash balance is below d_t, raise it to D_t. If it is above U_t, lower it to U_t. However, the solution in the range d_t to U_t now depends on the particular problem under investigation. In general, all we can say is that for $d_t < i < U_t$, the optimal j is a function of i [represented by $j = g(i)$] and that $d_t \leq j \leq i$. Notice in Figure 3-6 that costs may be decreased by lowering the cash balance at levels below U_t (e.g., if $i = z$ in Figure 3-6, it will pay to lower the cash balance to D_t).

The optimal policy for any period can be defined as[20]

$$\text{If } i < d_t, \qquad j = D_t$$
$$\text{If } d_t \leq i < U_t, \qquad j = g(i), \text{ where } d_t \leq g_t(i) \leq i$$
$$\text{If } U_t \leq i \qquad j = U_t$$

and the associated optimum cost can be found by

$$f_t(i) = \begin{bmatrix} T_u + t_u(D_t - i) + L(D_t) \\ \quad + \alpha \int_{-\infty}^{\infty} f_{t+1}(D_t - e)\,P(e)\,de \qquad \text{for } i < d_t \\[2em] t_d(i - g_t(i)) + L(g_t(i)) + \alpha \int_{-\infty}^{\infty} f_{t+1}(g_t(i) - e)\,P(e)\,de \\ \qquad\qquad\qquad\qquad\qquad \text{for } d_t \leq i < U_t \\[2em] t_d(i - U_t) + L(U_t) + \alpha \int_{-\infty}^{\infty} f_{t+1}(U_t - e)\,P(e)\,de \\ \qquad\qquad\qquad\qquad\qquad \text{for } U_t \leq i \end{bmatrix}$$

In this case, unlike the previous case, the optimal policy cannot be determined independently of the cash balance i at any moment in time. However, computations can be facilitated by a procedure directly analogous to that described in Section A except that after determining D_t one

---

[19] The curve $f_{T-1}(i)$ is actually a right-hand K-convex function of i. For a discussion of the properties of right-hand K-convex functions, see Wagner [17] and Girges [8].

[20] For a rigorous proof, see Girges [8].

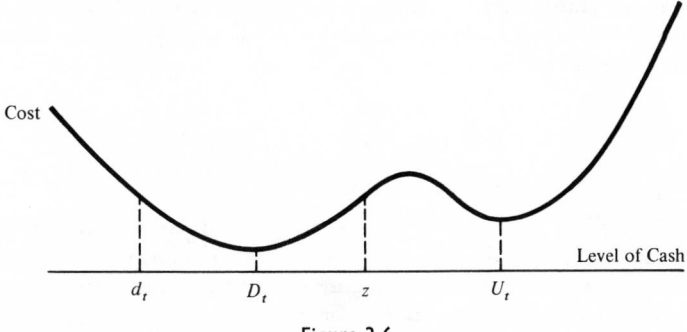

Figure 3-6

tries alternative values of d_t progressively smaller than D_t until

$$T_u + t_u(D_t - d_t) + L(D_t) + \alpha \int_{-\infty}^{\infty} f_{t+1}(D_t - e)\, P(e)\, de$$

$$\leq L(d_t) + \alpha \int_{-\infty}^{\infty} f_{t+1}(d_t - e)\, P(e)\, de$$

However, having done so one must still solve each problem explicitly for the form of the optimal policy to pursue when $d_t \leq i < U_t$.

Directly analogous results can be derived if $T_u = 0$ and $T_d > 0$.[21] In this case, it can be shown that the optimal policy is

$$\begin{aligned}
&\text{If } i < D_t, && j = D_t \\
&\text{If } D_t \leq i \leq u_t, && j = g_t(i), \text{ where } i \leq g_t(i) \leq u_t \\
&\text{If } u_t < i, && j = U_t
\end{aligned}$$

and the associated cost of following that policy is

$$f_t(i) = \begin{bmatrix}
t_u(D_t - i) + L(D_t) \\
\quad + \alpha \int_{-\infty}^{\infty} f_{t+1}(D_t - e)\, P(e)\, de \qquad \text{if } i \leq D_t \\[2mm]
t_u(g_t(i) - i) + L(g_t(i)) \\
\quad + \alpha \int_{-\infty}^{\infty} f_{t+1}(g_t(i - e)\, P(e))\, de \qquad \text{if } D_t < i \leq u_t \\[2mm]
T_d + t_d(i - U_t) + L(U_t) \\
\quad + \alpha \int_{-\infty}^{\infty} f_{t+1}(U_t - e)\, P(e)\, de \qquad \text{if } u_t < i
\end{bmatrix}$$

----

[21] This policy arises from the fact that f_{T-1} is a left-hand K-convex function rather than a simple convex function.

One might think that the methodology presented above could easily be used to derive the optimal policy for $T_u > 0$ and $T_d > 0$ and that the optimal policy would be

$$\text{If } i \le d_t, \qquad\qquad j = D_t$$
$$\text{If } d_t < i \le u_t, \qquad j = g_t(i)$$
$$\text{If } u_t < i, \qquad\qquad j = U_t$$

However, this form of policy is not, in general, optimum. In fact, a policy which determines any type of limits independently of cash balance (i) is not, in general, optimum, because the cost functions are more complex and generally contain both concave and convex regions when T_d and T_u are positive.[22] In this case while some simplification of the optimal policy is possible, it is generally necessary to return to equation (4) for the solution of the cash management problem. In the infinite case, computations can be simplified by employing the linear programming transformation of equation (4) presented in Appendix I of this chapter.

3. Optimal Models with Only Fixed Transaction Costs

A number of cash balance models have been developed under the assumption that the transfer cost per transaction does not vary with the amount of funds transferred. While we believe that this is the least realistic assumption with respect to transaction costs, these models are worth examining for two reasons[23]:

1. They have received a lot of attention in the literature.
2. The authors who have constructed these models have generally *assumed* the form of the optimal policy and simply solved for the parameters of the model. The general dynamic programming model developed earlier in equation (4) can be used to show whether the assumed form of the policy is indeed optimum.

In this section we shall examine three models developed by Baumol [1], Sastry [14], and Miller and Orr [9, 10] which assume that transaction costs are fixed. Each of these models is a continuous time model. However, the discrete dynamic programming model can be used to reproduce the results by allowing the time intervals between each cash level change to be infinitely small.

---

[22] Neave [11] has demonstrated that a simple policy involving decision points which are independent of i is generally nonoptimal when fixed and variable costs are present. The problem arises because the cost functions are not everywhere 0-convex, nor right-hand K-convex, nor left-hand K-convex. Neave [11] has further shown that it is possible to *partially* define a policy in terms of fixed decision points.

[23] The total cost of a transaction should vary with the size of the transaction simply because of the structure of brokerage commissions in effect. The size of these commissions is likely to be quite large relative to the fixed cost of planning and executing a transaction.

a. BAUMOL'S MODEL

The first model for the cash balance problem which treated transaction costs as fixed was developed by Baumol [1].[24]

He assumed that

1. The outflow of cash per period (e) is a positive constant known with certainty.
2. Management is concerned with an infinite horizon.
3. Management will never incur a cash shortage (stockout costs are infinite).
4. The holding cost of cash equals h dollars per dollar of average inventory held during a period.
5. All transactions increase the cash level, and if a transaction takes place, the cost is T_u and is independent of the size of the transaction.

In terms of previously defined symbols we have

$$1.[25] \quad T(i,j) = T_u \qquad \text{if } j > i$$
$$0 \qquad \text{if } j = i$$

$$2. \quad L(j) = \frac{j + (j - e)}{2} \cdot h \qquad \text{if } j \geq e$$

$$\infty \qquad \text{if } j < e$$

$$3. \quad P(e) = 1 \qquad \text{for } e = \bar{e}$$
$$P(e) = 0 \qquad \text{for } e \neq \bar{e}$$

If we now rewrite equation (4) using these new definitions, we have

$$f(i) = \min \left[\begin{array}{ll} \min_j \left[T_u + \dfrac{j + (j - e)}{2} h + \alpha f(j - e) \right] & \text{if } j > i \\[2ex] \dfrac{i + (i - e)}{2} h + \alpha f(i - e) & \text{if } j = i \end{array} \right]$$

The time subscript can be dropped since all costs are assumed to be stable over an infinite horizon.

An examination of the above equation shows that the same problem is being faced repetitively, over an infinite horizon, and that a stationary policy exists. Therefore, letting K be the number of periods between voluntary changes in the cash balance, the recursive relationship can be

---

[24] Tobin [16] developed a similar formulation.

[25] j cannot be less than i under Baumol's assumption.

reformulated to solve the optimum time between transactions, or[26]

$$f_t = \min_K \left[T_u + he \sum_{y=1}^{K} \alpha^y \frac{(2K - 2y + 1)}{2} + \alpha^K f_{t+K} \right]$$

To arrive at the Baumol results we must make the assumption that $\alpha = 1$. Then we can state the recursive relationship in terms of equivalent average return, or[27]

$$f = \min_K \left\{ \frac{T_u + he \sum_{y=1}^{K} [(2K - 2y + 1)/2]}{K} \right\}$$

The terms in braces are convex with repect to K and thus a minimum exists.[28] The presence of a minimum implies that there is an optimum time between reorders or equivalently an optimum order size. Employing the sum of an arithmetic progression and simplifying yields

$$f = \min_K \left[\frac{T_u}{K} + \frac{heK}{2} \right]$$

Differentiating the above formula and setting it equal to zero yields as the optimum time between orders[29]

$$K = \sqrt{\frac{2T_u}{he}}$$

---

[26] Holding costs are based on average inventory and so are equal to

$$h \left[\alpha \frac{Ke + (Ke - e)}{2} + \alpha^2 \frac{(Ke - e) + (Ke - 2e)}{2} + \cdots \right.$$
$$\left. + \alpha^k \frac{e + 0}{2} \right] \quad \text{or} \quad h \sum_{y=1}^{K} \frac{a^y e(2K - 2y + 1)}{2}$$

[27] For a discussion of the properties of equivalent average return, see Wagner [17], pp. 367–370. For α less than 1 and large K this solution is not necessarily optimum.

[28] The convexity of the expression in brackets can be shown by proving that an average of the above expression evaluated at $K + 1$ and $K - 1$ is greater than this expression evaluated at K, that is,

$$\frac{\left(T_u + he \sum_{y=1}^{K+1} \{[2(K + 1) - 2y + 1]/2\} \right)}{2(K + 1)} + \frac{\left(T_u + he \sum_{y=1}^{K-1} \{[2(K - 1) - 2y + 1]/2\} \right)}{2(K - 1)}$$
$$\geq \frac{\left\{ T_u + he \sum_{y=1}^{K} [(2K - 2y + 1)/2] \right\}}{K}$$

simplifying yields

$$\frac{T_u}{K(K - 1)(K + 1)} > 0$$

[29] We have followed Baumol [1] in treating K as a continuous variable.

The optimum order size is ke, or

$$Ke = \sqrt{\frac{2T_u e}{h}}$$

which is Baumol's formula for cash management.

b. SASTRY'S MODEL

Sastry [14] has modified Baumol's model to allow cash shortage at a cost u per average dollar of cash shortage per period. Let K equal the number of periods between transactions and k equal the number of periods for which the firm has a positive cash balance. Then let $K - k$ equal the optimum number of periods for which there is a cash shortage.

$$f_t = \min_{k,K} \left[T_u + h \sum_{y=1}^{k} \frac{\alpha^y e(2k - 2y + 1)}{2} \right.$$
$$\left. + u \sum_{y=1}^{K-k} \alpha^{k+y} \frac{e[2(K-k) - 2y + 1]}{2} + \alpha^K f_{t+K} \right]$$

If we assume that $\alpha = 1$, then for the infinite case this equation can be written in terms of the equivalent average return:

$$f = \min_{K,k} \left\{ \frac{T_u}{K} + \frac{he \sum_{y=1}^{k} [(2k - 2y + 1)/2]}{K} \right.$$
$$\left. + \frac{ue \sum_{=1}^{K-k} [(2(K-k) - 2y + 1)/2]}{K} \right\}$$

Employing the formula for the sum of an arithmetic progression and simplifying,

$$f = \min_{K,k} \left[\frac{T_u}{K} + \frac{hek^2}{2K} + \frac{ue(K-k)^2}{K} \right]$$

Taking the partial derivative of f with respect to K and k, setting the partial derivative equal to zero, and solving yields

$$k = \sqrt{\frac{2T_u}{he}} \sqrt{\frac{u}{h+u}}$$

or the optimum amount of cash to hold immediately after increasing the cash position is

$$ke = \sqrt{\frac{2T_u e}{h}} \sqrt{\frac{u}{h+u}}$$

which is Sastry's result.

c. MILLER AND ORR'S MODEL

Miller and Orr [9, 10] have modified the above analysis by making the demand for cash a stochastic variable (e) which can take on either positive or negative values.[30] They assume, as did the other models in this section, that the time horizon is infinite and that transaction costs, per transaction, are a fixed quantity. In terms of previously defined symbols,

$$L(j) = \frac{j + (j - e)}{2} \qquad \text{if } j > e$$

$$\infty \qquad \text{if } j < e$$

$$T(i,j) = T_u \qquad \text{if } j > i$$

$$0 \qquad \text{if } j = i$$

$$T_d \qquad \text{if } j < i$$

The recursive relationship is

$$f_t(i) = \min \begin{bmatrix} T_d + \min_{j>i} \left[\int_e \frac{j + (j - e)}{2} h\, P(e) + \int_e \alpha f_{t+1}(j - e)\, P(e) \right] \\[2ex] \int_e \frac{i + (i - e)}{2} h\, P(e) + \int_e \alpha f_{t+1}(i - e)\, P(e) \\[2ex] T_u + \min_{i>j} \left[\int_e \frac{j + (j - e)}{2} h\, P(e) + \int_e \alpha f_{t+1}(j - e)\, P(e) \right] \end{bmatrix}$$

Since there is an infinite horizon, the subscript on the f_t can be dropped. Dropping the subscript and letting $\bar{e}$ stand for the expected value of e yield

$$f(i) = \min \begin{bmatrix} T_d + \min_{j>i} \left[\frac{j + (j - \bar{e})}{2} h + \alpha \int_e f(j - e)\, P(e) \right] \\[2ex] \frac{i + (i - \bar{e})}{2} h + \alpha \int_e f(i - e)\, P(e) \\[2ex] T_u + \min_{i>j} \left[\frac{j + (j - \bar{e})}{2} h + \alpha \int_e f(j - e)\, P(e) \right] \end{bmatrix}$$

---

[30] They further specify that the probability distribution of e is symmetrical.

The above is a discrete formulation with respect to time, while Miller and Orr's formulation [9, 10] is continuous. However, by letting the time interval go to zero, the continuous form is approximated. The terms which are to be minimized with respect to j in the top and bottom part of the recursive relationship are identical. This implies that once the fixed charge is incurred, the cash level after the transaction will be identical whether the original cash level was too high or too low. A little reflection shows that this is sensible. There are no variable transaction costs. Once the fixed cost is incurred, any cash level can be selected without further cost. This is true whether T_d or T_u is paid. Consequently, the same decision problem is being faced in both cases, and they must have a common optimum.[31]

Consider that there is an optimum set of decision rules that determine whether to increase or decrease cash. For ease of understanding one could imagine an upper bound that determined when cash is turned into securities, a lower bound that determined when securities were sold, and a common return point. What happens when all three decision points are lowered by a constant amount? The number of transactions and the time between a transaction would be unchanged since these depend only on the shape of the pattern (width of boundaries and location of return point) and the shape is unchanged by a constant decrease. However, holding costs are reduced since the whole channel within which the cash position can move and consequently the average level of cash held has been reduced. Carried to an extreme this implies that the securities should be sold only when the cash level reaches minus infinity. What prevents this from happening is Miller and Orr's assumption [9, 10] that cash cannot be reduced below a certain level, which is determined exogenously. Given this external level specified as the minimum cash balance, the argument presented above shows that cash should be increased only when the minimum is reached.[32] If we let L_B be the externally determined level, then we can state that the lower branch is selected when $i = L_B$.

Up to this point we have used the dynamic programming formulation to show that there is a unique lower bound and that there is a common return point to which the firm moves once a transaction cost is incurred. Why might there be a unique upper bound? First, there must be at least one upper bound, since without one, holding costs can go to infinity. If the return point is fixed, then each unit change in the upper bound leads to the same increase in holding costs. However, transaction costs should decrease at a decreasing rate, since we are going further and further into the tail of the distribution of cash levels. At some point the changes are equal and a unique optimum exists. If the return point is then increased,

---

[31] Miller and Orr [9], p. 419, state that it may not be so if $T_u \neq T_d$. The equality of T_d and T_u is not important; what is important is that there are no variable costs.

[32] Miller and Orr [9] assume that this is true but express concern that such a policy need not be optimal (p. 419). There is no basis for their concern.

holding costs increase linearly, while transaction costs should decrease at a decreasing rate since the distribution of cash levels becomes more centered. Both these processes have the same effect with the result that through such an iterative process a unique minimum could be determined. Given the knowledge of such a unique bound, it could, of course, also be determined by equating the upper and middle part of the recursive relationship.

In short, from the dynamic programming framework we can show that the policy assumed by Miller and Orr [9, 10] does appear to be optimal. Once this form of policy is determined as optimum, Miller and Orr's analysis [9, 10] of the location of the upper bound and return point follows logically.

C. The Cash Balance Problem with Multiple Sources of Funds

Up to this point we have described the cash balance problem as the optimum allocation of a stock of funds between cash and a homogeneous interest-bearing investment. This analysis can be easily extended to take account of alternative investments or alternative sources of funds. Perhaps the most realistic extension is to assume that the financial manager in charge of the company's day-to-day cash position can engage in short-term borrowing as well as the sale and purchase of marketable securities.[33]

To make the problem even more realistic let us assume that (1) the financial officer faces a limit (B'_t) on the amount of short-term debt that he can have outstanding at a point in time (t), and (2) the firm has a limited amount of marketable securities (S) which it can convert to cash. In addition let

B = the dollar value of the company's outstanding short-term loans at a point in time

b = the amount of additional borrowing undertaken at the beginning of a period (b is negative if the debt is repaid)

s = the amount of marketable securities sold at the beginning of a period (s is negative if securities are bought)

S = the dollar value of outstanding marketable securities

Let us assume that the costs of transferring funds (whether through transactions in marketable securities or charges in the debt level) are fixed and variable. Let

$_sT_u$ = the fixed cost of increasing cash by selling securities

$_st_u$ = the variable cost of increasing cash by selling securities

$_sT_d$ = the fixed cost of decreasing cash by buying securities

$_st_d$ = the variable cost of decreasing cash by buying securities

---

[33] We shall assume that the amount of borrowing to meet day-to-day transaction costs is small enough so that we do not have to consider the effects of this borrowing on the overall cost of capital of the firm.

$_bT_u$ = the fixed cost of increasing cash by borrowing
$_bt_u$ = the variable cost of increasing cash by borrowing
$_bT_d$ = the fixed cost of decreasing cash by repaying debt
$_bt_d$ = the variable cost of decreasing cash by repaying debt

Then the cost of all transactions can be represented as

$$T(s, b) = \begin{bmatrix} {}_sT_u + {}_st_u(s) & \text{if } s > 0 \\ {}_sT_d - {}_st_d(s) & \text{if } s < 0 \\ {}_bT_u + {}_bt_u(b) & \text{if } b > 0 \\ {}_bT_d - {}_bt_d(b) & \text{if } b < 0 \end{bmatrix}$$

To facilitate our description of holding and understock costs, let us assume that these costs are functions of the level of cash on hand at the beginning of a period (immediately after a decision is made on changing the level of marketable securities or debt). Furthermore, assume that the cost of short-term borrowing exceeds the return on marketable securities.[34] Let

i = the level of cash prior to the decision on changing the level of marketable securities and debt
$u( )$ = the functional relationship between understock cost and the level of cash on hand
h_1 = the interest rate on short-term debt
h_2 = the opportunity cost of not placing another dollar in marketable securities
$B + b$ = the level of borrowing after the borrowing decision is made
$S - s$ = the level of marketable securities after transactions from the security account

The level of cash immediately after a transaction decision is made is equal to $i + s + b$. The general expression for holding and understock costs can be written as

$$L(i + s + b) = \begin{bmatrix} u(i + s + b) & \text{if } i + s + b \leq 0 \\ h_1(i + s + b) & \text{if } (i + s + b) > 0 \\ & \text{and } i + s + b \leq B + b \\ h_1(B + b) & \text{if } i + s + b > B + b \\ \quad + h_2[i + s - B] & \end{bmatrix}$$

The top expression in the brackets simply represents the understock cost expressed as a function of the negative cash balance. Holding costs are more complex than they have been in previous models. If the firm

---

[34] The problem can easily be formulated under alternative assumptions. This assumption seems reasonable for most corporations.

has a positive level of cash which is less than or equal to the amount of its short-term borrowing, then the opportunity cost of maintaining this cash position is simply the interest payments foregone by not repaying this amount of debt—hence the middle term in brackets. The bottom term represents the opportunity cost of funds when the firm has a cash balance in excess of its outstanding debt. In this case, the opportunity cost is the sum of the interest savings foregone by not paying off outstanding debt plus the return given up by not placing the excess funds in marketable securities.[35]

The optimal policy to follow at any time is going to be a function of the amount of outstanding debt and marketable securities which the company has as well as its starting cash position. This is true because the amount of outstanding debt and marketable securities affect the options open to the company. The cost of following a decision at time t is equal to the sum of the transaction costs, the holding and understock costs, and the minimum costs of managing cash from time $t + 1$ to the horizon. The problem can now be formulated as

For $t = T$, $f_T(i, S, B) = 0$

For $t < T$, $f_t(i, S, B) = \min_{s, b} T(s, b) + L(i + s + b)$

$$+ \alpha \int_{-\infty}^{\infty} f_{t+1}(i + s + b - e, S - s, B + b) \, P(e) \, de$$

subject to

$$B + b \leq B'_{t+1}$$

$$S - s \geq 0$$

The constraints ensure that the upper limit on borrowing is not violated and that the firm does not sell more securities than it has in its portfolio.

An approach similar to that presented above can be employed to extend the cash balance problem to incorporate multiple sources of borrowing and investment in multiple types of securities.

Appendix I: The Linear Programming Model of the Infinite Horizon Cash Management Problem with Markovian Transition Probabilities

Let us consider a general dynamic programming problem of the form

$$f_t(i) = \min_{j} \left[C_{ij} + \alpha \sum_{k} f_{t+1}(k) P(k \mid i, j) \right] \tag{I-1}$$

where

$f_t(i)$ = the minimum cost from period t until the horizon given that we are in state i at time t

---

[35] This statement depends on our assumption that the return the firm earns on its portfolio of securities is less than the cost of borrowed funds.

j = a decision made at time t
C_{ij} = the cost of decision j given that we are in state i
$P(k \mid i,j)$ = the probability of starting the subsequent period in state k given that we started period t in state i and made decision j
α = the appropriate discount factor

If equation (I-1) represents a problem with an infinite horizon, if $\alpha < 1$, and if transition probabilities can be described by a Markov process, then a stationary policy is optimal. That is, the same decision j should be made any time we are in a particular state i.[36] Therefore, the time subscript can be deleted and the optimal policy must satisfy the following extremal equation:

$$f(i) = \min_j \left[C_{ij} + \alpha \sum_k f(k)\, P(k \mid i,j) \right]$$

Let us now define r_k as the probability that the system is in state k at the beginning of the first time period. Let N designate the number of states the system can enter. Then

$$r_k \geq 0 \qquad \text{for } k = 1, 2, \ldots, N$$

$$\sum_{k=1}^{N} r_k = 1$$

Let us further designate J_i as the set of all possible decisions (j) which we can make when in state i.

Then the dynamic programming problem presented in equation (I-1) has been shown to be identical to the following linear programming model:[37] Minimize

$$\sum_{i=1}^{N} \sum_{j \in J_i} C_{ij} X_{ij}$$

subject to

$$\sum_{j \in J_k} X_{kj} - \alpha \sum_{i=1}^{N} \sum_{j \in J_k} X_{ij}\, P(k \mid i,j) = r_k \qquad \text{for } k = 1, 2, \ldots, N$$

$$X_{ij} \geq 0 \qquad \text{for } i = 1, 2, \ldots, N,\ j \in J_i$$

The optimal basic solution will contain one and only one X_{ij} greater than zero for each i. The optimal policy is to make a particular decision j whenever the system is in state i. The expected present cost of following this policy is given by the value of the objective function.

By defining k as equal to $j - e$ and recognizing that there are finite limits on the level of the cash balance and that the cash level changes by

---

[36] For a proof of this statement, see Wagner [17], pp. 747–748.
[37] See Wagner [17] and Ghellinck and Eppen [7].

discrete amounts we can rewrite equation (4) in Section A as

$$f_t(i) = \min_j \left[T(i,j) + L(j) + \alpha \sum_{k=1}^{N} f_{t+1}(k) P(k \mid j) \right] \qquad \text{(I-2)}$$

Let

$$C_{ij} = T(i,j) + L(j)$$

and j represents one of the N states defined as possible for the system. Then equation (4) has the same form as equation (I-1). Utilizing the previous analysis, we can write the linear programming model of the cash management problem as follows:[38] Minimize

$$\sum_{i=1}^{N} \sum_{j=1}^{N} [T(i,j) + L(j)] X_{ij}$$

subject to

$$\sum_{j=1}^{N} X_{kj} - \alpha \sum_{i=1}^{N} \sum_{j=1}^{N} X_{ij} P(k \mid j) = r_k \qquad \text{for } k = 1, 2, \ldots, N$$

$$X_{ij} \geq 0 \qquad \text{for } i = 1, 2, \ldots, N \quad \text{and} \quad j = 1, 2, \ldots, N$$

Bibliography

[1] Baumol, William, "The Transaction's Demand for Cash: An Inventory Theoretic Approach," *Quarterly Journal of Economics, LVI,* Nov. 1952, pp. 545–556.

[2] Beranek, William, *Working Capital Management* (Wadsworth Publishing Company, Inc., Belmont, Calif.), 1968.

[3] Daellenbach, Hans, and Stephen Archer, "The Optimal Bank Liquidity: A Multi-Period Stochastic Model," *Journal of Financial and Quantitative Analysis, IV,* No. 3, Sept. 1969, pp. 329–343.

[4] Elton, Edwin J., and Martin J. Gruber, "Dynamic Programming Applications in Finance," *Journal of Finance, XXVI,* No. 2, May 1971, pp. 473–505.

[5] Eppen, Gary, and Eugene Fama, "Solutions for Cash Balance and Simple Dynamic Portfolio Problems," *Journal of Business, XLI,* Jan. 1969, pp. 94–112.

[6] Eppen, Gary, and Eugene Fama, "Cash Balance and Simple Dynamic Portfolio Problems with Proportional Costs," *International Economic Review,* 10, No. 2, June 1969, pp. 119–133.

[7] Ghellinck, Guy, and Gary Eppen, "Linear Programming Solutions for Separable Markovian Decision Problems," *Management Science, XIII,* Jan. 1967, pp. 371–394.

---

[38] Alternative forms of this problem which allow some savings in computation time can be found in Ghellinck and Eppen [7] and Eppen and Fama [5].

[8] Girges, Nadia, "Optimal Cash Balance Levels," *Management Science*, XV, No. 3, Nov 1968, pp. 130–140.

[9] Miller, Merton, and Daniel Orr, "A Model of the Demand for Money by Firms," *Quarterly Journal of Economics*, 80, No. 3, Aug. 1966, pp. 413–435.

[10] Miller, Merton, and Daniel Orr, "The Demand for Money by Firms: Extensions and Analytical Results," *Journal of Finance*, XXIII, No. 5, Dec. 1968, pp. 735–759.

[11] Neave, Edwin, "The Stochastic Cash Balance Problem with Fixed Costs for Increases and Decreases," *Management Science*, 16, No. 7, March 1970, pp. 472–490.

[12] Orgler, Yair, *Cash Management: Methods and Models* (Wadsworth Publishing Company, Inc., Belmont Calif.), 1970

[13] Robichek, A., D. Teichroew, and R. Jones, "Optimal Short Term Financing Decision," *Management Science*, 12, No. 1, Sept. 1965, pp. 1–36.

[14] Sastry, A. S. Rawa, "The Effect of Credit on Transaction Demand for Cash," *Journal of Finance*, XXV, No. 4, Sept. 1970, pp. 743–760.

[15] Sethi, Suresh, and Gerald Thompson "Applications of Mathematical Control Theory to Finance: Modeling Simple Dynamic Cash Balance Problems," *Journal of Financial and Quantitative Analysis*, 5, Dec. 1970, pp. 381–394.

[16] Tobin, James, "The Interest-Elasticity of Transaction Demand for Cash," *Review of Economics and Statistics*, XXXVIII, No. 3, Aug. 1956, pp. 241–247.

[17] Wagner, Harvey, *Principle of Operations Research* (Prentice-Hall, Inc., Englewood Cliffs, N.J.), 1969.

The Credit-Granting Decision

OPTIMUM policy with respect to the extension of credit has received a great deal of attention in the finance literature. This research has to a great extent been concerned with techniques for discriminating between good and bad credit risks, primarily through the use of multiple discriminant analysis. The approach taken has almost universally been static single-period analysis. In this chapter we shall not review this literature; rather we shall concentrate on the dynamic aspects of the credit-granting decision. Specifically, we shall examine how the repetitive utilization of credit effects the initial credit-granting decision.

This chapter is divided into two sections. In the first section we shall provide a simple example to show the effect of future credit on the profitability of the initial credit decision. In the second section we shall present and discuss the dynamic programming solution to the problem.

A. A Simple Example

Assume that a firm is examining credit extension in the following situation: The selling price of the item is $100. The variable costs associated with the item involve an expenditure of $60. The probability of payment is 50 %, and there is no recoverable value if the customer defaults with his payment. If the firm extends credit, its expected return is $(.50)(\$100) - \$60 = -\$10$. If the firm denies credit, its expected return is $0. Since

$0 is better than $-$ \$10, the optimum course of action would seem to be to deny credit to the class of customers described above.

Now let us examine what happens if we consider the multiperiod nature of the problem. Specifically, let us take into consideration the fact that initial credit experience with a customer modifies our ability to estimate his future repayment behavior. For example, assume that the odds of a customer paying in the second period, given various payment patterns in the initial period, are as shown in Table 4-1. If the firm extends

TABLE 4-1   Probability of Paying in Period 2

Paid in period 1	.90
Did not pay in period 1	.10

credit to those customers who paid in period 1, the expected return is $(.90)(\$100) - (\$60) = \$30$. If it denies credit, it, of course, earns zero. The extension of credit is the more profitable alternative, and the firm earns \$30 in period 2 on those customers who paid in period 1. For those customers who did not pay in period 1, the relevant profits are

1. $(.10)(\$100) - \$60 = -50$ if credit was extended.
2. \$0 if credit was denied.

The optimum policy in this case is to deny credit. Since an equal number of customers are expected to pay and not to pay in period 1, the expected return in period 2 is an average of \$0 and \$30 or \$15. To get this return, the firm had to extend credit in period 1 involving a loss for period 1 of \$10. Therefore, the undiscounted expected return from extending credit in period 1 and following an optimum policy in period 2 is \$5. This is better than the zero profit that resulted from not initially extending credit. Considering outcomes in the second period has changed the optimum first-period decision.

One reason this might have occurred would be because of a change in the probability of payment for the population as a whole in period 2. In period 1 the odds of payment and nonpayment were identical. If in period 2 we increased the odds of payment, such a reversal in decisions could occur. Notice, however, that this is *not* what has occurred. The odds of payment and default in period 2 for the population as a whole are still equal, as the following calculations show. If $P(a_i)$ is the probability of payment in period i, $P(\bar{a}_i)$ is the probability of nonpayment in period i, and $P(a_i/a_j)$ is the probability of payment in period i given payment in j, then we have

1. Probability of payment in period $2 = P(a_2) = P(a_2/a_1) P(a_1) + P(a_2/\bar{a}_1) P(\bar{a}_1) = .9(.5) + (.1)(.5) = .5$.
2. Probability of default in period $2 = P(\bar{a}_2) = P(\bar{a}_2/a_1) P(a_1) + P(\bar{a}_2/\bar{a}_1) P(\bar{a}_1) = (.1)(.5) + (.9)(.5) = .5$.

If the probability of payment has not increased, what then causes the two-period decision to be profitable where the one-period decision was not? The two-period decision is profitable because the decision maker is able to separate the original population of customers into two groups with very different probabilities of payment and for which very different actions are optimal. The extension of credit in the initial period provides information that allows subsequent decisions to be sufficiently improved so as to make the multiperiod extension of credit profitable even when the initial extension was not. The additional information gathered in the second period may well lead to even further improvement and the expected return in subsequent periods may well be even higher.

B. The Dynamic Programming Formulation

The multiperiod aspects of the credit-granting decision can be incorporated in a dynamic programming formulation. The state variable is the probability of payment, and the dynamic programming formulation becomes

For $t = T$, $f_t(P_{t,i}) = 0$

For $t < T$, $f_t(P_{t,i}) = $ max (extend credit, deny credit)

$$= \max [P_{t,i}(\pi + \alpha z_{t+1} f_{t+1}(P_{t+1,i}/\text{payment}))$$

$$- (1 - P_{t,i})(C + \alpha z_{t+1} f_{t+1}(P_{t+1,i}/\text{default})), 0]$$

for all values of i, where

$P_{t,i}$ = the ith possible value for the probability of payment in period t

$f_t(P_{t,i})$ = the expected value of an optimum policy of credit extension from period t to the horizon given that the probability of a payment in period t is $P_{t,i}$

π = the profit from the customer who pays

C = the variable cost of the goods sold

α = the discount factor, i.e., 1 over 1 plus the cost of capital

z_{t+1} = the probability that the customer will still be purchasing items in $t + 1$

$P_{t+1,i}/\text{payment}$ = the revised probability of payment in period $t + 1$ given that the customer paid in period t

$P_{t+1,i}/\text{default}$ = the revised probability of payment in period $t + 1$ given that the customer defaulted in period t

The dynamic programming formulation shows that there are two possibilities in every period; to extend credit or not to extend credit. If the firm denies credit, then it is assumed that the customer does not return or is denied credit in subsequent periods, for a return to the firm of zero.[1] If the customer receives credit, then the firm earns the difference between the expected profit from payment and the expected cost of default. Each of these terms has two parts, the current profit or loss (π or C) and the discounted value of future extensions of credit. This second term is eventually zero. The probability (z_{t+n}) that the customer will still be purchasing items in $t + n$ declines as n increases, eventually falling to zero. z_t declining to zero allows the dynamic programming formulation to have a finite horizon. The horizon year T can be considered to be that year where z_t declines to zero. In practice it is rarely necessary to carry computations this far into the future. Although it is strictly true that terminating before this date could change the initial solution, any change is likely to be small and earlier termination is reasonable.[2]

There is a second application of the recursive relationship. $f_t(P_{t,i})$ gives the present value of an optimum policy from t to the horizon given that the probability of payment is $P_{t,i}$. $f_t(P_{t,i})$ can be used to examine the profitability of techniques to improve the estimates $P_{t,i}$. For example, a credit search or the use of discriminate analysis may lead to a change in the estimate of $P_{t,i}$. Examining $f_t(P_{t,i})$ can show if such a search is profitable.

A number of ways exist for estimating the conditional probabilities in the credit-granting model. Past experience is one possibility. Subjective estimates are a second. In either case, assumptions about the form of the distribution of probabilities can simplify the analysis. Bierman and Hausmann [1] present an example of one such simplification. They assume that Bayesian analysis is appropriate and that the decision maker's feelings about the probability of payment can be represented by a beta distribution. The beta distribution has two parameters, r and N. The probability of payment is equal to the ratio r/N with the absolute size of r and N determining the magnitude of the change in the probability of default or payment as experience is gained. If N is large, then each extension has little effect on the magnitude of the estimated probability of payment. If N is small, then each extension of credit produces a large change in the size of the estimated probability of payment. In particular, if credit is extended N' times with r' payments and the original probability of payment is r/N then the revised probability of payment is[3]

$$\frac{r''}{N''} = \frac{r + r'}{N + N'}$$

---

[1] The customer could, of course, pay cash for the purchase. This is accounted for by making the profit the incremental expected profit from credit sales rather than that from cash sales.

[2] Since z_t declines to zero for large t, the value of the recursive relationship is zero for large t. This relationship can be used to define ending conditions.

[3] This assumes that each extension involves the same amount of credit.

For example, if the probability of payment is assumed to be .50 and N is assumed to be 2, then if the customer pays, the new probability of payment would be $\frac{2}{3}$ and if he defaults the probability of payment would be $\frac{1}{3}$. If P is assumed to be .50 and N is assumed to be 50, then payment would mean a new probability of payment of $\frac{26}{51}$, while default means a new estimate of the probability of payment equal to $\frac{25}{51}$.

The assumptions of Bierman and Hausmann [1] concerning probability revision leads to the following dynamic programming formulation:

For $t = T$, $f_t = 0$

For $t < T$, $f_t(r, N) = $ max (extend credit, deny credit)

$$= \max \left[\frac{r}{N} (\pi + \alpha z_{t+1} f_{t+1}(r + 1, N + 1)) \right.$$

$$\left. - \left(1 - \frac{r}{N}\right)(C + \alpha z_{t+1} f_{t+1}(r, N + 1)), 0 \right]$$

where

1. $f_t(r, N)$ is the expected value of an optimum policy from period t to the horizon given the parameters r and N.
2. Other terms as before.

Many firms will not continue to extend credit to a customer who has failed to pay a previous debt. In this case, the model presented above can be restated as

$$f_t(r, N) = \max \left[\frac{r}{N}(\pi + \alpha z_{t+1} f_{t+1}(r + 1, N + 1)) - \left(1 - \frac{r}{N}\right)C, 0 \right]$$

Note that the recursive term f_{t+1} can be dropped from the term representing the expected revenues from defaulted credit. This is done since no future sales will be made to those customers, and thus they will contribute no future profits to the firm.

Conclusion

In this chapter we have presented a simple example to illustrate how the multiperiod nature of credit extension affects the initial decision to extend credit. A dynamic programming solution to the multiperiod problem was then presented.

Bibliography

[1] Bierman, H., and W. Hausmann, "The Credit Granting Decision," *Management Science*, 16, No. 8, April 1970, pp. B519–B532.
[2] Elton, Edwin, J., and Martin J. Gruber, "Dynamic Models in Finance," *Journal of Finance*, 26, No. 3, May 1970, pp. 473–505.

```
555555555555555555555555555555555555555555555555555555555555555555555555555555555
555555555555555555555555555555555555555555555555555555555555555555555555555555555
5555555555555555555555555555555555555    5555555555    5555555555555555555555555555555555
55555555555555555555555555555555555555    5555555555    5555555555555555555555555555555555
55555555555555555555555555555555555555555    555555555    5555555555555555555555555555555555
555555555555555555555555555555555555555555    5555555    5555555555555555555555555555555555
5555555555555555555555555555555555555555555555    55555    5555555555555555555555555555555555
55555555555555555555555555555555555555555555555    555    5555555555555555555555555555555555
555555555555555555555555555555555555555555555555    5    5555555555555555555555555555555555
5555555555555555555555555555555555555555555555555    5555555555555555555555555555555555555
55555555555555555555555555555555555555555555555555    5555555555555555555555555555555555555
555555555555555555555555555555555555555555555555555555555555555555555555555555555555
555555555555555555555555555555555555555555555555555555555555555555555555555555555
```

MultiPeriod Portfolio Analysis

Almost all portfolio theory is concerned with the one-period portfolio problem. Yet most portfolio problems are multiperiod. Individuals normally invest money with the expectation that they will maintain an investment portfolio over a number of years. The portfolio is often intended to provide income as well as saving for retirement or for a specific purchase such as a home. The portfolio problem faced by most institutions is also multiperiod in nature. Pension funds, mutual funds, and trust departments of banks make decisions as if they intend to maintain a portfolio for a number of periods. Although most portfolio literature is still concerned with the single-decision portfolio problem, a growing amount of attention is being directed toward the multiperiod problem.

Multiperiod portfolio theory can be conveniently divided into two parts on the basis of the objective function which has been assumed. One problem which has received attention is the portfolio problem that results from the following criterion: Maximize the utility of terminal wealth. A second multiperiod portfolio problem results from the following criterion: Maximize the utility of multiperiod consumption. If no additional assumptions are made about the form of the multiperiod consumption function (the general case), this criterion leads to only sparse conclusions and implications. However, for a constrained form of this criterion, when utility functions are assumed separable, the implications of the model are more numerous. This chapter is divided into two sections corresponding to the two objective functions discussed earlier. In each section, we shall present the model and discuss the implications of the models for multiperiod portfolio theory.

A. Multiperiod Portfolio Theory with the Following Criterion: Maximize the Utility of Terminal Wealth

The simplest form of multiperiod portfolio theory results from the following criterion: Maximize the expected utility of terminal wealth. This problem has been studied by Chen et al. [2], Hagen, [10], Hakansson [15], and Mossin [21]. This criterion function can be stated formally as

$$\text{Maximize} \quad E[u(W_T)] \tag{1}$$

where

1. $u(\ )$ is the utility function.
2. W_T is terminal wealth.

The problem situation is defined as follows. An investor has a known time horizon at which time his wealth is valued according to function (1). At the beginning of each of T periods the investor can reformulate his portfolio utilizing information about previous performance. However, all investment decisions are made with the object of maximizing this function. Finally, transaction costs and taxes are assumed to be zero.

This formulation of the portfolio problem clearly ignores intermediate consumption. Since most investors plan to make periodic withdrawals from a portfolio for consumption and since intermediate consumption decisions are clearly interrelated with portfolio decisions, the conclusions drawn from this objective function are not universally applicable.

Yet the problem is of interest for two reasons:

1. It represents a class of problems that actually exists. The investor setting up a fund for a specific purpose (e.g., to buy a house or take a vacation) can have his behavior described by this model. In addition, many types of trust funds are managed according to the assumptions of this model.
2. It provides both insight into the nature of the multiperiod portfolio problem and a simple framework within which to examine principles that can then be applied to the more complex case of intermediate consumption.

If we let W_t (the state variable) be the value of the investor's portfolio (cash available) at the beginning of t, then we can link periods t and $t + 1$ as follows:[1]

$$W_{t+1} = \sum_{i=2}^{m} \beta_{it} z_{it} + r_t z_{1t} \tag{2}$$

---

[1] It is easy to allow for an exogenous deterministic income. Such an addition adds little to the analysis here. As an example, we include such an addition in Section B, #2.

where

1. β_{it} is 1 plus the return on a dollar investment in asset i at time t, $i = 2, \ldots, m$.
2. r_t is 1 plus the interest rate on a riskless security at time t.[2]
3. z_{it} is the dollars invested in asset i at time t. z_{1t} is the dollars invested in the riskless asset.

Equation (2) states that the cash available at $t + 1$ is equal to the value of the $(m - 1)$ risky investments $\sum_{i=2}^{m} \beta_{it} z_{it}$ and the value of the riskless investment $r_t z_{1t}$.

Clearly, there are restrictions on the total dollars invested. The total dollars invested must equal the dollars available for investment, or

$$W_t = \sum_{i=2}^{m} z_{it} + z_{1t}$$

Solving for z_{1t} and substituting into expression (2) yield

$$W_{t+1} = \sum_{i=2}^{m} (\beta_{it} - r_t) z_{it} + r_t W_t \qquad (3)$$

If we assume that the β_{it} are independently distributed through time (the random walk assumption), we can derive a straightforward recursive relationship. Let $f_t(W_t)$ be the expected utility of following an optimum policy from period t to the horizon T given that W_t dollars are available at t. By definition for $t = T$ we have

$$f_T(W_T) = E(u(W_T)) \qquad (4)$$

For $t = T - 1$ we have

$$f_{T-1}(W_{T-1}) = \max_{z_{iT-1}} E[f_T(W_T)] \qquad (5)$$

where, from equation (3),

$$W_T = \sum_{i=2}^{m} (\beta_{iT-1} - r_{T-1}) z_{iT-1} + r_{T-1} W_{T-1}$$

Examine equation (5). W_T is a random variable. The values it can take on depend on how the W_{T-1} dollars are invested. Each possible set of investments yields a particular distribution of W_T. Each portfolio of investments can be valued in terms of the expected utility of its outcomes. Equation (5) states that the value of W_{T-1} dollars is equal to the expected utility of the investment which has the maximum expected utility of its outcomes.

Having presented the relationship for $T - 1$, it is easy to state it for any t:

$$f_t(W_t) = \max_{z_{it}} E[f_{t+1}(W_{t+1})] \qquad (6)$$

with W_{t+1} defined as in equation (3).

---

[2] The assumption of the existence of a riskless rate of interest is made throughout this chapter and does not affect any of the analysis. It is a conventional assumption, and we have made it here. The reader who wishes can set this term equal to zero.

This equation represents the general dynamic programming formulation that can be used to solve all portfolio problems which have as the criterion maximize the expected utility of terminal wealth and which conform to the problem situation defined earlier.[3] To derive $f_{t+1}(W_{t+1})$ the decision maker must in general solve a portfolio problem for each level of wealth and each period between $t + 1$ and the horizon. The function $f_{t+1}(\ )$ may be thought of as a derived utility function since it represents the utility of any level of wealth in period $t + 1$ derived from a specific utility function for terminal wealth. It is easy to see from equation (6) that the investor behaves in period t as if he were employing a one-period wealth maximization (portfolio) model. The form of the derived utility function need not be of the same form as either the utility function for terminal wealth or commonly accepted one-period utility functions. But the action of the investor, maximizing the utility of one-period wealth, is identical.

We can further restrict the form of the derived utility function if the utility function for terminal wealth is a monotonically increasing strictly concave function of W_T. In this case, the derived utility function would also be concave and monotonically increasing with wealth. The proof of monotonicity is quite simple. An extra dollar of wealth in any period can always be invested in the riskless asset, increasing wealth at the horizon. Since the utility of terminal wealth is an increasing function of W_T and since an increase in wealth in any earlier period increases W_T, all derived utility functions are monotonically increasing with respect to wealth. The proof of concavity involves two parts. First, it is easy to show that if $f_T(W_T)$ is a strictly concave function of W_T, the expected utility function $E[f_T(W_T)]$ is also strictly concave. This follows since the expected value operator is a summation operation and the sum of concave functions is concave. To complete the proof, it is necessary to show that if $E[f_T(W_T)]$ is a strictly concave function, then $f_{T-1}(W_{T-1})$ also has this property, where

$$f_{T-1}(W_{T-1}) = \max_{z_i{_{T-1}}} E[f_T(W_T)] \tag{7}$$

---

[3] The introduction of transaction costs and taxes vastly complicates the analysis and, in general, makes the dynamic programming formulation computationally infeasible. The problem arises because taxes and transaction costs depend on the amount of securities bought and sold. Consequently, to determine the optimum portfolio to buy at time t, as well as the amount of money available for investment (and in the models of Section B for consumption), it is necessary to retain information concerning the amount of each security in the portfolio immediately before the purchase decision. For example, the inclusion of a security in the optimum portfolio may depend on whether it is in the current portfolio, since if it is, then its inclusion saves the taxes and transaction costs that would be incurred otherwise. Thus, in equation (6), the state variable becomes $(Z_{1t-1}, Z_{2t-1}, \ldots, Z_{mt-1})$ rather than W_t, and a dynamic programming problem would have to be solved for each level of each Z_{it-1}. This complication remains even under the assumption of log or power utility functions (made later) since taxes and transaction costs affect the returns from various securities and hence the optimum portfolio.

Define

1. $\hat{W}_T^*$ as the random variable which arises from investing $\hat{W}_{T-1}$ in that set of investments which maximizes $E[f_T(W_T)]$.
2. $\hat{\hat{W}}_T^*$ as the random variable which arises from investing $\hat{\hat{W}}_{T-1}$ in that set of investments which maximizes $E[f_T(W_T)]$.
3. $W_T = a\hat{W}_T^* + (1-a)\hat{\hat{W}}_T^*$ for $0 < a < 1$.

From the concavity of expected utility, we have $E[f_T(W_T)] > aE[f_T(\hat{W}_T^*)] + (1-a)E[f_T(\hat{\hat{W}}_T^*)]$. By the definition of $\hat{W}_T^*$ and $\hat{\hat{W}}_T^*$ and from equation (7), we have $E[f_T(W_T)] > af_{T-1}(\hat{W}_{T-1}) + (1-a)f_{T-1}(\hat{\hat{W}}_{T-1})$.

Let $W_{T-1} = a\hat{W}_{T-1} + (1-a)\hat{\hat{W}}_{T-1}$. One way to allocate W_{T-1} is to place $a\hat{W}_{T-1}$ into that portfolio which is the optimum way to allocate funds when wealth is $\hat{W}_{T-1}$ and $(1-a)\hat{\hat{W}}_{T-1}$ into that portfolio which is the optimum way to allocate funds when wealth is $\hat{\hat{W}}_{T-1}$. From definition 3, this yields the random outcome W_T (i.e., W_T is the random variable $a\hat{W}_T^* + (1-a)\hat{\hat{W}}_T^*$). This need not be the optimum allocation of funds. Therefore,

$$f_{T-1}(W_{T-1}) = \max_{z_{iT}} E[f_T(W_T)]$$

$$f_{T-1}(W_{T-1}) \geq E[f_T(W_T)] \geq af_{T-1}(\hat{W}_{T-1}) + (1-a)f_{T-1}(\hat{\hat{W}}_{T-1})$$

Thus, f_{T-1} is a monotonically increasing strictly concave function of W_{T-1}. Examining the proof shows that it depends only on the original assumption that $f_T(W_T)$ had these properties. Since we have now proved that $f_{T-1}(W_{T-1})$ has the same properties, the proof can be repeated sequentially to derive the same results for all earlier periods.

At this point we can conclude that from a dynamic programming formulation of the multiperiod portfolio problem, one can derive a one-period utility function such that maximization of one-period expected utility is consistent with maximizing the utility of terminal wealth. Furthermore, if the utility function for terminal wealth is concave, the derived utility function will also be concave. However, to arrive at the derived utility function, one generally has to solve portfolio problems in each period for each possible level of wealth. Furthermore, the derived utility function does not necessarily have the same functional form as the utility of terminal wealth.

It would vastly simplify the problem, both conceptually and computationally, if realistic classes of utility functions existed which allowed an optimum set of portfolios to be determined independently of wealth position. In the remainder of this section, we shall derive this class of utility functions and show that they lead to a condition where myopic investment decisions are optimum.

1. Utility Functions Whose Optimum is Independent of Wealth

The optimum proportion of wealth to invest in any asset will be independent of the amount available for investment if the relative ranking of the outcomes of all investment plans is independent of the amount of the investment.[4] If an investor had $1 at time $T - 1$, then the outcome from this investment can be described as X_T, where X_T is a random variable.[5] If instead, the investor had k dollars at $T - 1$, then the outcome from this investment would be

$$W_T = kX_T \tag{8}$$

If the utility of an investment plan is to be independent of starting wealth, then the utility of kX_T must be a linear transformation of the utility of X_T, or

$$u(kX_T) = a + bu(X_T) \tag{9}$$

where a and b may depend on k but are independent of X_T.

The utility functions for which equation (9) holds are easy to derive. Taking the derivative of equation (9) with respect to W_T, we get

$$u'(W_T) = b \frac{\partial u(X_T)}{\partial X_T} \frac{\partial X_T}{\partial W_T} \tag{10}$$

where $W_T = kX_T$ from equation (8) and $u'(W_T)$ denotes the derivative of the utility of final wealth with respect to wealth.

From equation (8)

$$\frac{\partial X_T}{\partial W_T} = \frac{1}{k}$$

Substituting into equation (10),

$$ku'(W_T) = b \frac{\partial u(X_T)}{\partial X_T} \tag{11}$$

Taking the derivative of equation (11) with respect to k,

$$ku''(W_T) \frac{\partial W_T}{\partial k} + u'(W_T) = \frac{\partial b}{\partial k} \frac{\partial u(X_T)}{\partial X_T} \tag{12}$$

---

[4] This analysis closely parallels Mossin [21]. The major difference is that we take the derivative with respect to W_T. This is necessary for the independence argument used later.

[5] In this case, X_T represents the wealth relatives (1 plus the rate of return) for period $T - 1$ through T.

Solving equation (11) for $\partial u(X_T)/\partial X_T$ and substituting into equation (12) along with $\partial W_T/\partial k$ from equation (8) yield

$$kX_T u''(W_T) + u'(W_T) = \frac{\partial b}{\partial k}\frac{k}{b}u'(W_T)$$

or

$$-\frac{W_T u''(W_T)}{u'(W_T)} = 1 - \frac{\partial b}{\partial k}\frac{k}{b} \tag{13}$$

Since we have taken derivatives with respect to both W_T and k, this equality must hold for independent variations in W_T and k. For it to hold for independent variations in W_T and k, both sides of the above expression must equal a constant. The right-hand side of this expression is called the coefficient of relative risk aversion.[6] Therefore, in order that the optimum portfolio be independent of wealth, the coefficient of relative risk aversion must be constant. Setting equation (13) equal to a constant γ and rearranging yields

$$Wu''(W) + \gamma u'(W) = 0$$

The required utility functions are solutions to this differential equation. The differential equation has four solutions:

1. $u(W) = \ln(W)$ if $\gamma = 1$.
2. $u(W) = -\ln(W)$ if $\gamma = 1$.
3. $u(W) = W^{1-\gamma}$, all $\gamma \neq 1$.
4. $u(W) = -W^{1-\gamma}$, all $\gamma \neq 1$.

If the investor's utility function has any of these forms, the multiperiod portfolio problem is significantly simplified.[7]

Most economists would further restrict these functions in order to ensure increasing utility of wealth and risk avoidance [i.e., $u'(W) > 0$ and $u''(W) < 0$]. If we assume these criteria, then function 2 can be eliminated, since for it $u'(W) < 0$. Applying these criteria to functions 3 and 4 limits the range of γ. For example, for function 4

$$u'(W) = -(1 - \gamma)W^{-\gamma} > 0$$
$$u''(W) = \gamma(1 - \gamma)W^{-\gamma-1} < 0$$

These inequalities hold if γ is greater than 1. Therefore, the utility functions of interest are

$$u(W) = \ln(W) \qquad \text{if } \gamma = 1 \qquad\qquad \text{function A}$$
$$u(W) = -W^{1-\gamma} \qquad \text{if } \gamma > 1 \qquad\qquad \text{function B}$$
$$u(W) = W^{1-\gamma} \qquad \text{if } 0 < \gamma < 1 \qquad \text{function C}$$

---

[6] As defined by Pratt [23] and Arrow [1].

[7] More explicitly: if the investor's utility function has any of these functional forms or is a linear transform of any of these functions.

An example can be used to illustrate how these utility functions lead to a significant simplification of the multiperiod portfolio problem and in particular make the selection of portfolios independent of wealth. Assume that the investor's decision problem can be characterized as the maximization of the utility function $u(W) = W^{1-\gamma}$. Further assume that the investor is evaluating three possible investments, each of which can be purchased separately in any amount, although they cannot be purchased in combination. Letting Π_i be the probability of the ith outcome, the expected utility from each of the three investments can be depicted as one of the three elements in the following vector:

$$\left[\left(\sum_i u(W_i)\, \Pi_i \right),\ \left(\sum_j u(W_j)\Pi_j \right),\ \left(\sum_l u(W_l)\Pi_l \right) \right]$$

Since $u(W) = W^{1-\gamma}$, we have

$$\left[\left(\sum_i W_i^{1-\gamma}\Pi_i \right),\ \left(\sum_j W_j^{1-\gamma}\Pi_j \right),\ \left(\sum_l W_l^{1-\gamma}\Pi_l \right) \right]$$

If the investor had started with k times as many dollars as assumed above, his decision problem would be to select between

$$\left[\left(\sum_i (kW_i)^{1-\gamma}\Pi_i \right),\ \left(\sum_j (kW_j)^{1-\gamma}\Pi_j \right),\ \left(\sum_l (kW_l)^{1-\gamma}\Pi_l \right) \right] \quad \text{or}$$

$$\left[\left(k^{1-\gamma} \sum_i (W_i)^{1-\gamma}\Pi_i \right),\ \left(k^{1-\gamma} \sum_j (W_j)^{1-\gamma}\Pi_j \right),\ \left(k^{1-\gamma} \sum_l (W_l)^{1-\gamma}\Pi_l \right) \right]$$

Each of the elements in the vector has been increased by $k^{1-\gamma}$. If the the constant $k^{1-\gamma}$ is factored out of the vector, we have

$$(k^{1-\gamma})\left[\left(\sum_i (W_i)^{1-\gamma}\Pi_i \right),\ \left(\sum_j (W_j)^{1-\gamma}\Pi_j \right),\ \left(\sum_l (W_l)^{1-\gamma}\Pi_l \right) \right]$$

The three elements in this vector are identical to the three elements in the initial decision problem. Each vector will have the same maximum. This implies that for $u(W) = W^{1-\gamma}$ a solution to the first decision problem provides a solution to the decision problem when a different amount of money is available. That is, there is a unique ranking of investments for each period that is independent of the amount of funds available for the investment. Consequently, the solution to one portfolio in each period is sufficient if investors can be characterized as maximizing the utility function $u(W) = W^{1-\gamma}$. The same analysis holds for $u(W) = -W^{1-\gamma}$.

A similar conclusion can be reached when the log utility function is used. Again assume that an investor is choosing between three possible investments purchasable in any amount. The investor can be depicted as choosing the investment with the highest utility from the following vector:

$$\left[\left(\sum_i u(W_i)\Pi_i\right), \left(\sum_j u(W_j)\Pi_j\right), \left(\sum_l u(W_l)\Pi_l\right)\right] \quad \text{or}$$

$$\left[\left(\sum_i \ln (W_i)\Pi_i\right), \left(\sum_j \ln (W_j)\Pi_j\right), \left(\sum_l \ln (W_l)\Pi_l\right)\right]$$

If instead the investor had started with k times as many dollars to invest, his decision problem would be to select between

$$\left[\left(\sum_i \ln (kW_i)\Pi_i\right), \left(\sum_j \ln (kW_j)\Pi_j\right), \left(\sum_l \ln (kW_l)\Pi_l\right)\right] \quad \text{or}$$

$$\left[\left(\sum_i (\ln (W_i)\Pi_i + \ln (k)\Pi_i)\right), \left(\sum_j (\ln (W_j)\Pi_j + \ln (k)\Pi_j)\right),\right.$$
$$\left.\left(\sum_l (\ln (W_l)\Pi_l + \ln (k)\Pi_l)\right)\right]$$

Since $\sum_i \Pi_i = \sum_j \Pi_j = \sum_l \Pi_l = 1$ and since $\ln k$ is constant, we have

$$\left[\left(\sum_i \ln (W_i)\Pi_i + \ln k\right), \left(\sum_j \ln (W_j)\Pi_j + \ln k\right),\right.$$
$$\left.\left(\sum_l \ln (W_l)\Pi_l + \ln k\right)\right]$$

The three elements in this vector are identical to the three elements in the initial decision problem except a constant has been added to each. Consequently, both vectors will have the same maximum. Once again with the log utility function the investor's decision problem is independent of the amount available for investment, and the solution to a single portfolio problem is sufficient in any one period. With this background we can now turn to an analysis of the original decision problem.

2. Solution to the Recursive Relationship for the Log and Power Functions

As discussed above, if the utility function is of the log or power form, then the optimum portfolio to hold or the optimum proportions of funds to invest in any security is independent of the amount available for investment. This property not only simplifies computations but allows the derivation of an explicit solution. Let g_t be the expected utility in t from the *optimum* investment of a dollar in period $t - 1$, or

$$g_t = E\left[u\left[\sum_i (\beta_{it-1} - r_{t-1})z^*_{it-1} + r_{t-1}\right]\right] \tag{14}$$

where

1. z_{it-1}^{*} is the optimum amount to invest in the ith security in period $t-1$ if one dollar is the sum available for investment.
2. Other symbols as before.

For period $T-1$ we have, utilizing equations (5), (4), and (3) and assuming that the investor's utility function is of the log form,

$$f_{T-1}(W_{T-1}) = \max_{z_{iT-1}} E(f_T(W_T)) = \max_{z_{iT-1}} E[\ln W_T]$$

$$= \max_{z_{iT-1}} E\left[\ln \sum_i (\beta_{iT-1} - r_{T-1})z_{iT-1} + W_{T-1}r_{T-1}\right]$$

Factoring out W_{T-1} (the dollars available for investment at $T-1$) yields

$$f_{T-1}(W_{T-1}) = \max_{z_{iT-1}} E \ln \left\{ W_{T-1}\left[\sum_i (\beta_{iT-1} - r_{T-1}) \frac{z_{iT-1}}{W_{T-1}} + r_{T-1}\right]\right\}$$

As shown in the previous section, if the investor's utility is of the log form, the optimum proportions to invest in any asset are independent of the dollar amount invested. Consequently, the decision problem which utilizes z_{iT-1}/W_{T-1} as the decision variable will lead to the same proportion of funds invested in each asset as the decision problem with z_{iT-1} as the decision variables.[8] For these reasons, and since $\ln xy = \ln x + \ln y$, we have

$$f_{T-1}(W_{T-1}) = \ln W_{T-1} + \max_{z_{iT-1}/W_{T-1}} E \ln \left[\sum_i (\beta_{iT-1} - r_{T-1}) \frac{z_{iT-1}}{W_{T-1}} + r_{T-1}\right] \tag{15}$$

But by the definition of z_{iT-1}^{*}, z_{iT-1}^{*} is that value of z_{iT-1}/W_{T-1} which maximizes the right-hand side of equation (15). Therefore from equation (14) we have

$$f_{T-1}(W_{T-1}) = \ln W_{T-1} + g_T$$

For $T-2$ the recursive relationship is

$$f_{T-2}(W_{T-2}) = \max_{z_{iT-2}} E[f_{T-1}(W_{T-1})]$$

$$= \max_{z_{iT-2}} E[\ln W_{T-1} + g_T]$$

$$= \max_{z_{iT-2}} E\left[\ln \left(\sum_i (\beta_{iT-2} - r_{T-2})z_{iT-2} + W_{T-2}r_{T-2}\right) \right.$$

$$\left. + g_T\right]$$

[8] To change a solution in terms of z_{iT-1}/W_{T-1} to the solution in terms of dollar investment in each security, one simply multiplies by W_{T-1}.

Factoring W_{T-2} we have

$$f_{T-2}(W_{T-2}) = \max_{z_{iT-2}} E\left[\ln\left[W_{T-2}\right.\right.$$

$$\left.\left.\times \left(\sum_i (\beta_{iT-2} - r_{T-2}) \frac{z_{iT-2}}{W_{T-2}} + r_{T-2}\right)\right] + g_T\right]$$

Then by reasoning analogous to that employed above,

$$f_{T-2}(W_{T-2}) = \ln W_{T-2} + \max_{z_{iT-2}/W_{T-2}}\left[E\left(\ln \sum_i (\beta_{iT-2} - r_{T-2}) \frac{z_{iT-2}}{W_{T-2}}\right.\right.$$

$$\left.\left.+ r_{T-2}\right) + g_T\right] = \ln W_{T-2} + g_{T-1} + g_T$$

The generalization is now obvious, and for the tth period we have

$$f_t(W_t) = \ln W_t + \sum_{i=t+1}^{T} g_i \tag{16}$$

The power function also leads to a simple solution. For period $T - 1$ the recursive relationship is

$$f_{T-1}(W_{T-1}) = \max_{z_{iT-1}} E[f_T(W_T)] = \max_{z_{iT-1}} E[W_T]^{1-\gamma}$$

Using the definition of W_T [i.e., equation (3)],

$$f_{T-1}(W_{T-1}) = \max_{z_{iT-1}} E[\sum (\beta_{iT-1} - r_{T-1})z_{iT-1} + W_{T-1}r_{T-1}]^{1-\gamma}$$

Factoring out W_{T-1}, we have

$$f_{T-1}(W_{T-1}) = \max_{z_{iT-1}} (W_{T-1})^{1-\gamma}E\left[\sum_i (\beta_{iT-1} - r_{T-1}) \frac{z_{iT-1}}{W_{T-1}} + r_{T-1}\right]^{1-\gamma}$$

Once again for this utility function the decision problem utilizing z_{iT-1}/W_{T-1} as the decision parameters leads to the same asset proportions as the decision problem utilizing the z_{iT-1}. Because of this and since $W_{T-1}^{1-\gamma}$ is a constant, we have

$$f_{T-1}(W_{T-1}) = (W_{T-1})^{1-\gamma} \max_{z_{iT-1}/W_{T-1}}$$

$$E\left[\sum_i (\beta_{iT-1} - r_{T-1}) \frac{z_{iT-1}}{W_{T-1}} + r_{T-1}\right]^{1-\gamma} \tag{17}$$

By the definition of z_{iT-1}^{*}, z_{iT-1}^{*} is the value of z_{iT-1}/W_{T-1} which maximizes the right-hand side of equation (17). Therefore from equation (14)

$$f_{T-1}(W_{T-1}) = (W_{T-1})^{1-\gamma}g_T$$

For $T - 2$ we have

$$
\begin{aligned}
f_{T-2}(W_{T-2}) &= \max_{z_{iT-2}} E[f_{T-1}(W_{T-1})] \\
&= \max_{z_{iT-2}} E[(W_{T-1})^{1-\gamma}g_T] \\
&= \max_{z_{iT-2}} E\left[\left(\sum_i (\beta_{iT-2} - r_{T-2})z_{iT-2} - W_{T-2}r_{T-2}\right)^{1-\gamma}g_T\right]
\end{aligned}
$$

By now familiar reasoning,

$$
\begin{aligned}
f_{T-2}(W_{T-2}) &= \max_{z_{iT-2}} E\left[(W_{T-2})^{1-\gamma}\left(\sum_i (\beta_{iT-2} - r_{T-2})\frac{z_{iT-2}}{W_{T-2}} - r_{T-2}\right)^{1-\gamma}g_T\right] \\
&= (W_{T-2})^{1-\gamma} \max_{z_{iT-2}/W_{T-2}} E\left[\left(\sum_i (\beta_{iT-2} - r_{T-2})\right.\right. \\
&\qquad\qquad \left.\left. \times \frac{z_{iT-2}}{W_{T-2}} - r_{T-2}\right)^{1-\gamma}g_T\right] \\
&= W_{T-2}^{1-\gamma}g_{T-1}g_T
\end{aligned}
$$

The generalization for arbitrary t is straightforward:

$$f_t(W_t) = W_t^{1-\gamma}\left(\prod_{i=t+1}^{T} g_i\right) \tag{18}$$

3. Myopic Decision Making

An investor who behaves as if each period is the last decision period is said to behave myopically. In the context of this problem, myopia means that the investor uses the utility function for terminal wealth directly in solving the one-period portfolio problem rather than deriving one from a dynamic programming problem. Myopia implies that it is optimum for the investor to neglect all information about future periods as well as to neglect the fact that the one-period utility function which is appropriate must in general be derived from a recursive relationship.

If such behavior were consistent with maximizing the utility of terminal wealth, the investor's decision problem would be greatly simplified and the analysis derived for one-period decision making would be applicable. Since most analysis has been concerned with the one-period decision problem, the optimality of myopic decision making would be an exceedingly pleasant result.

It is easy to show that for the log and power functions, myopic behavior is optimal.[9] If the utility function is log, then for any time t, equation (16) can be written as

$$f_t(W_t) = \ln W_t + g_{t+1} + \sum_{i=t+2}^{T} g_i$$

Substituting the expression for g_{t+1} from equation (14) and rearranging yield

$$f_t(W_t) = \ln W_t + E \ln \left(\sum (\beta_{it} - r_t)z_{it}^* + r_t \right) + \sum_{i=t+2}^{T} g_i$$

$$= \max_{z_{it}} E[\ln \left(\sum (\beta_{it} - r_t)z_{it} + W_t r_t \right)] + \sum_{i=t+2}^{T} g_i$$

This is identical to the decision problem of an investor maximizing the expected utility of the first period's terminal wealth except for the term $\sum_{i=t+2}^{T} g_i$. However, since the ranking produced by a utility function is unchanged by a linear transform and since $\sum_{i=t+2}^{T} g_i$ is a constant, the presence of $\sum_{i=t+2}^{T} g_i$ will not affect the ranking, and the log function is myopic.

If the utility function is a power function, then for any time t, equation (18) can be rewritten as

$$f_t(W_t) = W_t^{1-\gamma} g_{t+1} \left(\prod_{i=t+2}^{T} g_i \right)$$

Substituting for g_{t+1} and rearranging yield

$$f_t(W_t) = W_t^{1-\gamma} E[(\beta_{it} - r_t)z_{it}^* + r_t]^{1-\gamma} \left(\prod_{i=t+2}^{T} g_i \right)$$

or

$$f_t(W_t) = \max_{z_{iT}} [\sum (\beta_{it} - r_t)z_{it} + W_t r_t]^{1-\gamma} \left(\prod_{i=t+2}^{T} g_i \right)$$

Once again this decision problem is identical to the one faced by an investor maximizing the expected utility of the first period's terminal wealth except for the constant $\prod_{i=t+2}^{T} g_i$. Since utility functions are unique

---

[9] Mossin [21] states that other functions are myopic when the r_t are zero and partially myopic when the $r_t \neq 0$. In this case, partially myopic means that only the future interest rates need be known to solve the decision problem. Hakansson [15] has shown that these results depend critically on the assumption of unlimited borrowing and short sales. If realistic limits are placed on the amount of borrowing and short sales, these functions are no longer in general myopic or partially myopic. Therefore, the only functions which are generally myopic are the log and power functions.

up to a linear transform, both formulations will have the same solution, and the power function is myopic.

4. Conclusion to Section A

In Section A the multiperiod portfolio problem was examined, under the assumption that the investor's objective function was the maximization of the expected utility of terminal wealth. A general dynamic programming formulation of the problem was presented. This formulation was used to show that a *derived* utility function could be found which led to behavior on the part of the investor which was indistinguishable from that of a one-period utility of wealth maximizer. However, the functional form of the derived utility function might differ from both the form of the utility function for terminal wealth and the forms considered appropriate for a one-period decision maker. Furthermore, if the utility of terminal wealth is concave and exhibits increasing utility of wealth, the derived utility function for each period will have these same properties. Finally, if the utility function for terminal wealth is of the log or power form, the derived utility function for each period will be identical to the utility function for terminal wealth.

B. Multiperiod Portfolio Analysis with the Following Criterion: Maximize the Utility of Multiperiod Consumption

In the previous section we studied the properties of multiperiod portfolio problems when the following criteria was applied: Maximize the expected utility of terminal wealth. In this section a more broadly applicable objective function, maximize the expected utility of multiperiod consumption, will be examined. The implications of various forms of this objective function have been studied by Fama [9], Hakansson [11, 12, 13, 14], Merton [19, 20], Phelps [22], Samuelson [24], and Sandmo [25]. Initially, a dynamic programming model of this problem will be constructed under the least restrictive assumption about multiperiod utility functions. The implications of this model for investment and consumption will then be analyzed. Finally, the additional implications which can be drawn from a dynamic programming approach when more restrictive assumptions are made about the form of the utility function will be examined.

1. The Analysis with General Utility Functions

For the most general case, let us postulate a utility function for lifetime consumption as[10]

$$U(c_1, c_2, \ldots, c_k, \ldots, c_{T-1}, c_T \mid \phi_1, \phi_2, \ldots, \phi_k, \ldots, \phi_{T-1}, \phi_T)$$

---

[10] Fama [9] has analyzed this problem extensively. The analysis in this section draws on his work.

1. c_t is consumption in period t, where t goes from 1 (birth), the time at which the initial consumption decision is made, to the time at which a bequest is left upon death, T. Time period $T - 1$ is the time in which the last portfolio decision is made. Time period k is the time period in which the investor currently faces a decision.
2. ϕ_t is the new information that becomes available between period $t - 1$ and t. More explicitly, ϕ_1 through ϕ_t is the information available at the time that the consumption decision c_t is made.

Notice that this is a completely general utility function. The utility of consumption at any point in time t is allowed to be a function of consumption in other periods. For example, the utility of a particular dollar amount of consumption in any period can be a function of the dollar amount consumed in other periods and the size of any bequest. Furthermore, the utility of any level of consumption can be a function of the state of the world (all information available to the investor).

For compactness it is convenient to define the vector ϕ_t as all information available at time t:

$$\phi_t = (\phi_1, \phi_2, \ldots, \phi_t)$$

Using this notation, the utility function becomes

$$u(c_1, c_2, \ldots, c_{T-1}, c_T \mid \phi_T)$$

In subsequent discussions we shall use the more compact notation unless it obscures the issues being discussed.

The problem situation is defined as follows. At each point in time the decision maker must decide on how much to consume and on the composition of his investment portfolio. His investment provides the wealth at the next period, which is then consumed or invested.[11] This continues until death at which time the remaining wealth is consumed in the form of a bequest.[12] Transaction costs and taxes are assumed to be zero.

The utility function given earlier is the end condition, that is,

$$f_T(c_1, c_2, \ldots, c_{T-1}, W_T \mid \phi_T) = u(c_1, c_2, \ldots, c_{T-1}, c_T \mid \phi_T)$$

for all c_i, $i = 1, \ldots, T - 1$, all W_T, and all elements of the vector ϕ_T. This expression gives the utility of lifetime consumption for all possible consumption patterns and states of the world.[13] To derive the recursive relationship at $T - 1$, we need to derive a relationship between wealth in adjacent time periods (i.e., t and $t + 1$).

---

[11] The introduction of a certain income stream from human capital is straightforward; see Section B, #2.

[12] Generalizations to incorporate uncertainty concerning death are trivial, involving only notational changes. See Fama [9].

[13] Obviously since the investor is in period k, c_1 to c_{k-1} would not be varied but rather fixed at their previous actual level.

The wealth at time $t + 1$ is the value at $t + 1$ of the investment portfolio selected at t, or

$$W_{t+1} = \sum_{i=2}^{m} \beta_{it}(\phi_{t+1})z_{it} + r_t z_{1t}$$

where

1. $\beta_{it}(\phi_{t+1})$ is 1 plus the return on a dollar invested in asset i for period t. It is a function of all information which will exist at time $t + 1$. Since at time t this information set is a random variable, β_{it} itself is a random variable.
2. z_{it} is the dollar amount invested in asset i in period t.
3. r_t is the return on a riskless investment.

The dollar amount invested at any time (t) is limited to wealth less consumption at time t, or $\sum_{i=1}^{m} z_{it} = W_t - c_t$. Substituting this into the previous equation, we can derive an expression for wealth in $t + 1$ as a function of wealth and consumption in t:

$$W_{t+1} = \sum_{i=2}^{m} [\beta_{it}(\phi_{t+1}) - r_t]z_{it} + (W_t - c_t)r_t \qquad (19)$$

For period T the utility of lifetime consumption of being in state $[c_1, c_2, \ldots, c_{T-1}, W_T \mid \phi_T]$ is $f_T(c_1, c_2, \ldots, c_{T-1}, W_T \mid \phi_T)$. The terminal recursive relationship can now be stated as

$$f_{T-1}(c_1, c_2, \ldots, c_{T-2}, W_{T-1} \mid \phi_{T-1})$$
$$= \max_{z_{iT-1}c_{T-1}} E[f_T(c_1, c_2, \ldots, c_{T-1}, W_T \mid \phi_T)$$

where the expected value is taken over all levels of ϕ_T.

A value of f_{T-1} is computed for all values of c_i, where $i = 1, \ldots, T - 2$, all W_{T-1}, and all values of each element of the vector ϕ_{T-1}. From equation (19) W_T is

$$W_T = \sum_{i=2}^{m} [\beta_{iT-1}(\phi_T) - r_{T-1}]z_{iT-1} + r_{T-1}[W_{T-1} - c_{T-1}]$$

To see that z_{iT-1} and c_{T-1} are the variables over which the maximum is taken, examine the expression for W_T. $\beta_{iT-1}(\phi_T)$ has a known probability distribution, while r_{T-1} is a known (deterministic) variable. W_{T-1} is also known since it is a state variable. Therefore, the decision variables are z_{iT-1} and c_{T-1}. For an arbitrary t the recursive relationship becomes

$$f_t(c_1, c_2, \ldots, c_{t-1}, W_t \mid \phi_t)$$
$$= \max_{z_{it}c_t} E[f_{t+1}(c_1, c_2, \ldots, c_t, W_{t+1} \mid \phi_{t+1})] \qquad (20)$$

subject to equation (19), for all c_i, $i = 1, \ldots, t - 2$, all W_t, and all elements of the vector ϕ_t. To understand this equation, examine the meaning of $f_{t+1}(c_1, c_2, \ldots, c_t, W_{t+1} \mid \phi_{t+1})$. This function gives the maximum expected utility from period $t + 1$ to the horizon, given

1. Any particular consumption pattern in periods 1 to t.
2. Any particular level of investor's wealth in $t + 1$.
3. Any particular pattern of information about the world ϕ_{t+1}.
4. An optimum consumption plan and portfolio strategy from $t + 1$ to the horizon.

Equation (20) allows us to move back in time by repetitively selecting the optimum consumption and investment mix at t, so that for any consumption level from 1 to $t - 1$ and for any wealth level at t, the expected utility of lifetime consumption is maximized.

Equation (20) together with equation (19) represents the generalized dynamic programming formulation of the multiperiod portfolio problem when the objective function is to maximize the expected utility of multiperiod consumption. All that is necessary to fully specify the model is to develop the expression for starting conditions. If the investor currently faces the investment-consumption decision as of the start of period k (he has made consumption decisions for $k - 1$ periods), then his initial decision can be characterized as

$$f_k(c_1, c_2, \ldots, c_{k-1}, W_k \mid \phi_k)$$
$$= \max_{z_{ik}, c_k} E[f_{k+1}(c_1, c_2, \ldots, c_{k-1}, c_k, W_{k+1} \mid \phi_{k+1})]$$

But in period k, $c_1, c_2, \ldots, c_{k-1}$ are known quantities. Therefore, the right-hand side is just a function of c_k and W_{k+1}. If we define

$$f^*_{k+1}(c_k, W_{k+1} \mid \phi_{k+1}) = f_{k+1}(\hat{c}_1, \hat{c}_2, \hat{c}_3, \ldots, \hat{c}_{k-1}, c_k, W_{k+1} \mid \phi_{k+1})$$

where the caret over the variable represents the actual previous level of consumption, then the starting equation can be written as

$$f_k(\hat{c}_1, \hat{c}_2, \ldots, \hat{c}_{k-1}, W_k \mid \phi_k) = \max_{z_{ik}, c_k} E[f^*_{k+1}(c_k, W_{k+1} \mid \phi_{k+1})] \quad (21)$$

Now we have formally defined the recursive relationship for all relevant periods. In theory, this formulation can be used to solve any multiperiod problem of the type under study. In practice, the amount of computation involved makes a recursive solution to the problem infeasible.[14]

---

[14] This infeasibility can easily be illustrated. Assume that we are in period k; then there are $T - k$ periods left in which portfolio decisions need to be made. Assume that there are N possible levels of consumption in each period and that the informational variable ϕ_i can take on M different values in any period $T - 1$. In this case, $N^{T-k}M^{T-k}$ portfolio problems would have to be solved. N^{T-k} of these are necessary because of the various possible levels of consumption in each period. M^{T-k} are necessary because of the possible levels of information. In the period $T - 2$, N^{T-k-1}, M^{T-k-1} portfolio problems would have to be solved. In total, there are $N^{T-k}M^{T-k} + N^{T-k-1}M^{T-k-1} + \cdots + NM + 1$ portfolio problems to solve. Even for a small number of periods and small values for N and M, this is a prohibitively large problem.

The solution to this problem could be simplified and meaningful implications could be drawn if the problem could be made analogous to a one-period problem. Equation (21) resembles a one-period portfolio problem except for the dependency of utilities on information (the state dependency). Fama [9] argues that the utility function would not be state-dependent if the following conditions hold:

1. The consumer's tastes for particular consumption goods and services are independent of the state of the world.
2. The consumer acts as if consumption opportunities in terms of goods and their prices are known at the beginning of any previous period.
3. The consumer acts as if the distribution of one-period returns on all assets is known at the beginning of any previous period.

If these conditions hold, then equation (21) can be written as

$$f_k(\hat{c}_1, \hat{c}_2, \ldots, \hat{c}_{k-1}, W_k) = \max_{z_{ik}, c_k} E[f_{k+1}^*(c_k, W_{k+1})] \qquad (22)$$

This equation is formally equivalent to the one-period problem. If we call the functional relationship $f_{k+1}(\ )$ a utility function, then in both the one-period problem and the equation above, the decision maker maximizes the expected value of the utility of current consumption and terminal wealth. Thus, although the decision maker has derived the utility function via dynamic programming (employing information concerning future investment opportunities and a multiperiod utility function), each period's decision is identical in form to that engaged in by a one-period expected utility maximizer.

This in itself says very little, since without further assumptions the previous equation provides no insight into the functional form of the one-period utility function. In particular, without further assumptions the utility function derived by dynamic programming need not bear any resemblance to a utility function that is considered reasonable in a one-period case. Its derivatives could have any sign; its functional form cannot be specified.

However, if we assume that the utility function for multiperiod consumption is monotonically increasing and strictly concave in the c_t, then as Fama has shown, the derived one-period utility function has these same properties. The essential reason is that the expected value function involves taking a weighted average of concave functions, and the sum of concave functions is concave. Monotonicity is easy to understand since if any extra dollar is available for current wealth, it can be consumed leaving the same decisions in future periods feasible. Since we have assumed that the multiperiod functions are monotonically increasing, this must yield higher utility.

Although for many purposes the knowledge that the decision maker should maximize the expected utility of a concave monotonically increasing function is sufficient, for other decisions some knowledge concerning the possible functional form of the utility function is necessary.

Without further assumptions no stronger statements can be made about the form of the derived single-period utility function. In particular, there is no reason to believe that the derived utility function of equation (22) bears any resemblance to functions that can be justified in one-period decisions. However, the introduction of separable utility functions allows stronger conclusions to be drawn.

2. The Analysis with Separable Utility Functions

The multiperiod portfolio problem with intermediate consumption becomes much more tractable if we continue to assume that utility is independent of the information set (state of the world) and if in addition we accept the assumption that utility functions are separable.[15] Under the assumption of separable utilities, the utility of a level of consumption in any period is unrelated to the past or future level of consumption. Thus, the utility of consumption from period t onward (until death in year T) can be defined as[16]

$$u_t(c_t, c_{t+1}, \ldots, c_{T-1}, W_T) = u(c_t) + \alpha_t u(c_{t+1})$$
$$+ \alpha_t \alpha_{t+1} u(c_{t+2}) + \cdots + \alpha_t \alpha_{t+1} \cdots \alpha_{T-2} u(c_{T-1})$$
$$+ \alpha_t \alpha_{t+1} \cdots \alpha_{T-1} u(W_T) \quad (23)$$

where

α_t = the appropriate discount factor for period t

W_T = terminal wealth in the form of a bequest

The problem situation facing the investor is defined as follows. In each period the investor must decide on how much to consume and how to allocate the remaining funds among alternative investment opportunities. These investment opportunities consist of securities whose return is a random variable and a safe investment earning a known rate of interest. Furthermore, the investor has a known income stream that will be available over time.[17] This income stream can be thought of as return

---

[15] This is the assumption that is implicitly or explicitly made in the work of Samuelson [24], Merton [19, 20], Hakansson [11, 12, 13, 14] and Phelps [22]. The limitations of the assumption of separable utility functions are well known and need no further elaboration here.

[16] Once again the introduction of uncertainty of death is trivial. It simply involves defining α as the discount factor times 1 minus the probability of death.

[17] We have added an exogenous deterministic income stream. The addition of such a variable to the previous analysis is trivial but would complicate the analysis and obscure the main issues without adding anything of substance. We have made the addition at this point since it adds few complications and is illustrative of an addition made by some authors. If the reader wishes to delete it from the analysis in this section, he merely has to set all income terms (y_t terms) equal to zero. This analysis could also be performed with a stochastic exogenous income stream rather than a deterministic one. However, the computational implications of such a model are quite complex.

from employment. The investment and consumption decisions are made in each period until a known horizon, at which time all remaining wealth in the form of a bequest is consumed. Taxes and transaction costs are assumed to be zero.[18]

If we can let W_t (the state variable) be the cash available in t for consumption or investment, then we can link t and $t+1$ as follows:

$$W_{t+1} = \sum_{i=2}^{m} \beta_{it} z_{it} + r_t z_{1t} + y_t \qquad (24)$$

Equation (24) shows that the cash available at $t+1$ is equal to the value of the investment portfolio of risky securities $\sum_{i=2}^{m} \beta_{it} z_{it}$, plus the value of the safe investment $r_t z_{1t}$, plus the known income from other opportunities y_t, which becomes available at time $t+1$. The value of an individual security at $t+1$ is equal to the value of a dollar invested at t (which is β_{it}) times the number of dollars invested in that security at t, (z_{it}) in the above formulation.

The relationship between $t+1$ and t can be further clarified by solving for the dollars placed in the risk-free investment. The dollars invested in the safe investment z_{1t} are equal to the dollars available in t, less consumption, less the dollars invested in risky securities, or

$$z_{1t} = W_t - c_t - \sum_{i=2}^{m} z_{it} \qquad (25)$$

Substituting equation (25) into equation (24) and rearranging yield

$$W_{t+1} = \sum_{i=2}^{m} (\beta_{it} - r_t) z_{it} + r_t(W_t - c_t) + y_t$$

We are now ready to derive the recursive relationship. Let $f_t(W_t)$ be the expected utility of consumption from period t to the horizon if W_t dollars in wealth are available at t. Then from equation (23) $f_t(W_t)$ is equal to

$$f_t(W_t) = \max E[u(c_t) + \alpha_t u(c_{t+1}) + \alpha_t \alpha_{t+1} u(c_{t+2})$$
$$+ \alpha_t \alpha_{t+1} \cdots \alpha_{T-1} u(W_T)] \qquad (26)$$

If we assume that the β_{it} are independently distributed over time (the random walk assumption), then using the principle of optimality,

---

[18] Some authors (e.g., Hakansson [11], p .445) argue that taxes and transaction costs can be proportional to the dollar amount invested and still be included in β_{it}. For this to be true the taxes and transaction costs would have to be incurred irrespective of previous or future investments. In other words, the same taxes and transaction costs would have to be incurred irrespective of whether the security was held in the previous period or would be held in future periods. Such an assumption adds no realism. See footnote 3 for a discussion of the inclusion of transaction costs and taxes.

equation (26) can be written as

$$f_t(W_t) = \max_{c_t z_{it}} [u(c_t) + \alpha_t E[f_{t+1}(W_{t+1})]] \qquad (27)$$

subject to

$$W_{t+1} = \sum_{i=2}^{m} (\beta_{it} - r_t)z_{it} + r_t(W_t - c_t) + y_t$$

An examination of equation (27) shows that the only decision variables are consumption c_t and the dollar amount placed in the assets z_{it} since r_t, W_t, y_t, and β_{it} are either known quantities or have known probability distributions. Therefore, the maximum is over the variables that are indicated in the recursive relationship. The right-hand side of equation (27) is composed of two terms. The first term is the utility of consuming c_t dollars in period t, and the second term is the expected utility of consumption from $t + 1$ to the horizon if W_{t+1} dollars are available in $t + 1$.

To solve equation (27) the decision maker must solve a problem with the same decision variables and format as the one-period problem.[19] In both cases, the decision maker is selecting a portfolio to maximize the utility of current consumption plus future wealth. This should not be surprising, since this decision problem is simply a special case of the decision problem presented earlier. However, this simplified decision model yields more results. The right-hand side of equation (27) involves linear operations. The expected value operator is a linear average of $f_{t+1}(W_{t+1})$, and this is added to the utility of current consumption. Since $f_T(W_T)$ is a linear average of the terminal utility, all earlier $f_t(W_t)$ are also linear averages of utility functions. The following conclusion can now be stated.

The investor described above will face a series of single-period portfolio problems which has an objective function of the same functional form as the utility function for consumption in each future period if a linear combination of these individual utility functions preserves the form. However, the portfolio problem is still complex if the optimum z_{it} depend on the amount of wealth available. In this case a different set of z_{it} would have to be determined for each level of wealth. Since this usually involves the solution of a mathematical programming problem, the calculations would be prohibitive.

However, if the optimum proportions to invest in the assets are independent of the amount invested, the decision problem is vastly simplified. In this case, z_{it} above could be replaced by $k_t z_{it}^*$, where the z_{it}^* are independent of the amount available for investment and k_t is a constant of proportionality. This would greatly facilitate the computations since only

---

[19] Note that the solution to a dynamic programming problem employing information about future investment opportunities is still necessary in order to derive $f_{t+1}(W_{t+1})$ in equation (27).

one portfolio problem would need to be solved, independent of the values of W_t and c_t. As discussed earlier the log and power functions have properties which require the solution to only one portfolio problem in any period. For these utility functions we can derive a simplified recursive relationship.

3. Solution to the Recursive Relationship with Log and Power Utility Functions

Recall that the recursive relationship is

$$f_t(W_t) = \max_{c_t z_t} [u(c_t) + \alpha_t E f_{t+1}(W_{t+1})]$$

where

$$W_{t+1} = \sum_{i=2}^{m} (\beta_{it} - r_t) z_{it} + r_t(W_t - c_t) + y_t$$

Employing either the log or power utility functions not only makes the multiperiod portfolio problem computationally feasible but also means that a simple analytical solution for both consumption and utility of wealth can be derived. For utility functions of the log and power form this solution has been shown by Hakansson [11] to be[20]

$$f_t(W_t) = K_t u(W_t + Y_t) + L_t \tag{28}$$

$$c_t(W_t) = N_t(W_t + Y_t) \tag{29}$$

where

$$Y_t = \frac{y_t}{r_t} + \frac{y_{t+1}}{r_t r_{t+1}} + \cdots + \frac{y_T}{r_t r_{t+1} \cdots r_T}$$

$$g_t = E\left[u\left(\sum_{i=2}^{m} \beta_{it} - r_t \right) z_{it}^* + r_t \right]$$

and N_t, K_t, and L_t for the various utility functions are given by

1. For $u(c) = \ln c$

$K_t = 1 + \alpha_t + \alpha_t \alpha_{t+1} + \alpha_t \alpha_{t+1} \alpha_{t+2} + \cdots + \alpha_t \alpha_{t+1} \alpha_{t+2} \cdots \alpha_{T-1}$

$L_t = -K_t \log K_t$
$\qquad + (\alpha_t + \alpha_t \alpha_{t+1} + \alpha_t \alpha_{t+1} \alpha_{t+2} + \cdots + \alpha_t \alpha_{t+1} \alpha_{t+2} \cdots \alpha_{T-1})(g_t + \ln \alpha_t)$
$\qquad + (\quad\ \ \alpha_t \alpha_{t+1} + \alpha_t \alpha_{t+1} \alpha_{t+2} + \cdots + \alpha_t \alpha_{t+1} \alpha_{t+2} \cdots \alpha_{T-1})(g_{t+1} + \ln \alpha_{t+1})$
$\qquad + (\qquad\qquad\ \ \alpha_t \alpha_{t+1} \alpha_{t+2} + \cdots + \alpha_t \alpha_{t+1} \alpha_{t+2} \cdots \alpha_{T-1})(g_{t+2} + \ln \alpha_{t+2})$
$\qquad + \qquad \cdots$
$\qquad + \qquad\qquad\qquad\qquad\qquad\quad (\alpha_t \alpha_{t+1} \alpha_{t+2} \cdots \alpha_{T-1})(g_{t-1} + \ln \alpha_{T-1})$

$N_t = K_t^{-1}$

---

[20] See Appendix I for the proof for the log case.

2. For $u(c) = -c^{1-\gamma}$ $\qquad \gamma > 1,$

$$K_t = [1 + [\alpha_t(-g_t)]^{1/\gamma} + [\alpha_t\alpha_{t+1}(-g_t)(-g_{t+1})]^{1/\gamma} + \cdots$$
$$+ [\alpha_t\alpha_{t+1} \cdots \alpha_{T-1}(-g_t)(-g_{t+1}) \cdots (-g_{T-1})]^{1/\gamma}]^\gamma$$

$$L_t = 0$$

$$N_t = K_t^{-1/\gamma}.$$

3. For $u(c) = c^{1-\gamma}$ $\qquad 0 < \gamma < 1,$

$$K_t = [1 + (\alpha_t g_t)^{1/\gamma} + (\alpha_t\alpha_{t+1}g_t g_{t+1})^{1/\gamma}$$
$$+ (\alpha_t\alpha_{t+1}\alpha_{t+2}g_t g_{t+1}g_{t+2})^{1/\gamma} + \cdots$$
$$+ (\alpha_t\alpha_{t+1}\alpha_{t+2} \cdots \alpha_{T-1}g_t g_{t+1}g_{t+2} \cdots g_{T-1})^{1/\gamma}]^\gamma$$

$$L_t = 0$$

$$N_t = K_t^{-1/\gamma}$$

Several conclusions can now be drawn.

a. THE PORTFOLIO MIX

For utility functions of the log or power form, the composition of the optimum portfolio in any one period depends only on the specific type of utility function selected and the opportunities available in that period.[21] The optimum portfolio is that portfolio which maximizes the expected utility of the one-period utility function $u(c_t)$. This means that the analysis derived for one-period models is equally applicative for the multiperiod case. In particular, the functional form of the portfolio problem is the same in every period and depends only on the utility function assumed. Solution procedures to portfolio problems, such as the ones discussed in this section, do exist for important distributional assumptions concerning stock price movements. For example, Elton and Gruber [8] prove that the optimum portfolios lie on the exterior of all portfolios plotted in a mean variance space when stock price returns are log normally distributed. Furthermore, they show which exterior points are optimum given various utility functions. For the log utility function, the optimum is particularly easy to determine. Elton and Gruber [7] have shown that for the log utility function, maximization of expected utility is equivalent to maximizing the geometric mean. If the distribution of returns is log normal, Elton and Gruber [8] have developed a specific formula for determining the exterior point which maximizes the geometric mean. Solving the portfolio problem would involve a solution to the standard quadratic programming problem and the application of a simple formula.

---

[21] However, the optimum one-period distribution of wealth between consumption and investment is not independent of future investment opportunities, so this decision cannot be made employing single-period data. The relationship between consumption and future investment opportunities is analyzed below.

b. DETERMINING THE OPTIMUM AMOUNT OF CONSUMPTION

While utility functions of the log or power form allow the composition of each period's optimum investment portfolio to be determined on the basis of only information in that period, the optimum dollar split between consumption and investment in each period is a function of information from many periods.[22] An examination of equation (29) shows that consumption in any period t is a percentage of current wealth (W_t) plus the present value of the future certain income stream at t, (y_t). The sum of these two terms may be thought of as total certain wealth. In the case of the log utility function, the percentage of total certain wealth consumed in any period depends only on the discount factor and is not affected by the profitability of future investment opportunities. If the discount factor is constant over time, then the percentage of total certain wealth consumed increases with time. With other patterns of discount rates, the time path of the percentage of certain total wealth consumed is unclear.[23] Increases in the size of α_t lead to decreases in the fraction consumed (i.e., $\partial N_t/\partial \alpha_t < 0$ for all α_t).

Examination of equation (29) and the values for N_t shows that for both power functions the fraction of wealth consumed in any period depends on the discount factors and available investment opportunities for all future periods. For utility functions of type B and C, $\partial N_t/\partial \alpha_t$ is negative, implying a decrease in consumption with an increase in the discount rate. An increase in the profitability of investment opportunities will increase present consumption for utility function B $(\partial N_t/\partial g_t > 0)$, while it decreases present consumption for utility function C.

4. Conclusion to Section B

In this section we have constructed a general dynamic programming model of the multiperiod portfolio problem when the investor is assumed to act so as to maximize the expected utility of lifetime consumption. Even under the most general assumptions about utility functions, a one-period utility function can be *derived* under which the investor will act

---

[22] Conclusions similar to those found in this section are contained in Hakansson [11].

[23] Hakansson [11], p. 455, argues that the percentage increases with time. It is easy to demonstrate that this statement is not true in general:

$$K_t = 1 + \alpha_t + \alpha_t\alpha_{t+1} + \cdots + \alpha_t\alpha_{t+1}\cdots\alpha_{T-1}$$
$$= 1 + \alpha_t + \alpha_t[S] \tag{1}$$

where $[S] = \alpha_{t+1} + \alpha_{t+1}\alpha_{t+2} + \cdots + \alpha_{t+1}\alpha_{t+2}\cdots\alpha_{T-1}$

$$K_{t+1} = 1 + \alpha_{t+1} + \alpha_{t+1}\alpha_{t+2} + \cdots + \alpha_{t+1}\alpha_{t+2}\cdots\alpha_{T-1}$$
$$= 1 + [S] \tag{2}$$

The question is the relationship of $\alpha_t + \alpha_t[S]$ to $[S]$. If $\alpha_j \neq \alpha_{j+1}$, then $[S]$ has limits 0 to ∞. If $[S]$ is zero, then equation (1) $>$ equation (2). As $[S] \to \infty$, equation (2) $>$ equation (1). For example, if $[S] = 10$ and $\alpha_t = .8$, then equation (2) $>$ equation (1).

in a manner indistinguishable from a one-period decision maker. However, the form of the derived one-period utility function might differ from both the form of the utility function for multiperiod consumption and any utility function that is considered appropriate for single-period decision makers. However, if the multiperiod consumption function is concave and monotonically increasing with wealth, the derived single-period function will have these same properties.

To derive additional conclusions from the model, it was necessary to assume that the multiperiod consumption function was separable. Under this assumption, the derived utility function for any single period will have the same form as the utility function for consumption in any period if taking linear combinations of these utility functions preserves the form. Furthermore, if the investor's utility function for consumption in each period is of the log or power form, then the composition of each period's portfolio can be selected on the basis of single-period information about securities. However, to reach a decision about the split between consumption and investment for each period, the investor still has to consider information from all future periods.

Appendix I: Derivation of the Optimum Values for K_t and N_t and L_t in the Log Case

The method of proof consists of showing that if the solution holds for $t + 1$, then the solutions are as stated for t. Once the relationships are shown to hold for the horizon, the proof is complete. Substituting the solution of equation (28) for $t + 1$ into equation (27) stated in Section B and employing the log utility function, we have

$$f_t(W_t) = \max_{c_t z_t} [\ln c_t + \alpha_t E[K_{t+1} \ln (W_{t+1} + Y_{t+1}) + L_{t+1}]]$$

Substituting in for W_{t+1} and noting that $y_t + Y_{t+1}$ is equal to $r_t Y_t$, we have

$$f_t(W_t) = \max_{c_t z_t} [\ln c_t + \alpha_t E[K_{t+1} \ln (\sum (\beta_{it} - r_t) z_{it}$$
$$+ r_t(W_t - c_t + Y_t)) + L_{t+1}]]$$

Factoring out $W_t - c_t + Y_t$ and defining z_{it}^* as $z_{it}/(W_t - c_t + Y_t)$, we have

$$f_t(W_t) = \max_{c_t z_t} [\ln c_t + \alpha_t E[K_{t+1} \ln ((W_t - c_t + Y_t)(\sum (\beta_{it} - r_t) z_{it}^*$$
$$+ r_t)) + L_{t+1}]]$$

This factoring does not change the solution to the portfolio problem since from the discussion in Section B we know the solution is independent of the dollars available for investment. In short, the portfolio problem will have the same solution whether the z_{it} are determined or the z_{it}^* are determined and the dollars allocated are z_{it}^* times $W_t - c_t + Y_t$. Letting $g_t = E[u(\sum (\beta_{it} - r_t)z_{it}^* + r_t)]$ and noting that $\ln xy = \ln x + \ln y$, we have

$$f_t(W_t) = \max_{c_t} [\ln c_t + \alpha_t[K_{t+1}(g_t + \ln (W_t - c_t + Y_t)) + L_{t+1}]] \quad \text{(I-1)}$$

To determine the optimum consumption, we take the derivative with respect to c_t:

$$\frac{df_t(W_t)}{dc_t} = \frac{1}{c_t} + \frac{\alpha_t K_{t+1}(-1)}{W_t - c_t + Y_t} = 0$$

Solving for c_t, we have

$$c_t = (W_t + Y_t)\left(\frac{1}{1 + \alpha_t K_{t+1}}\right) = K_t^{-1}(W_t + Y_t)$$

The latter step comes directly from the definition of K_t given in Section B. Substituting this expression into equation (I-1), we have

$$f_t(W_t) = \left[\ln \frac{W_t + Y_t}{K_t} + \alpha_t K_{t+1} g_t \right.$$
$$\left. + \alpha_t K_{t+1} \ln \left(W_t - \frac{W_t + Y_t}{K_t} + Y_t\right) + \alpha_t L_{t+1}\right]$$

Rearranging yields

$$f_t(W_t) = \ln \left(\frac{W_t + Y_t}{K_t}\right) + \alpha_t K_{t+1} g_t$$
$$+ \alpha_t K_{t+1} \ln (W_t + Y_t) \left(\frac{K_t - 1}{K_t}\right) + \alpha_t L_{t+1}$$

Simplifying by noting that $\ln (W/y) = \ln W - \ln y$, $\ln WY = \ln W + \ln Y$, and $\alpha_t K_{t+1} = K_t - 1$, we have

$$f_t(W_t) = [\ln (W_t + Y_t) - \ln K_t + \alpha_t K_{t+1} g_t$$
$$+ \alpha_t K_{t+1} \ln (K_t - 1) - K_t \ln K_t + \ln K_t$$
$$+ K_t \ln (W_t + Y_t) - \ln (W_t + Y_t) + \alpha_t L_{t+1}]$$

Simplifying,

$$f_t(W_t) = [K_t \ln (W_t + Y_t) + \alpha_t K_{t+1} g_t + \alpha_t K_{t+1} \ln (\alpha_t K_{t+1})$$
$$- K_t \ln K_t + \alpha_t L_{t+1}]$$

By examining the equation (in Section B) for L_t and the equation for L_{t+1},

$$f_t(W_t) = K_t \ln (W_t + Y_t) + L_t$$

The above expression is the solution stated for t in Section B. To complete the proof we must show that they hold for the horizon. Using the definitions of K_t, L_t, N_t at the horizon, we have $K_t = 1$, $L_t = 0$, and $N_t = 1$. This implies that all dollars are consumed. From the utility function this is obviously the optimum, and the proof is complete.

Bibliography

[1] Arrow, Kenneth, "Aspects of the Theory of Risk Bearing," *Yrjö Jahnsson Lectures* (The Yrjö Jahnsson Foundation, Helsinki), 1965.

[2] Chen, Andrew, Frank Jen, and Stanley Zionts, "The Optimal Portfolio Revision Policy," *Journal of Business*, 64, No. 1, Jan. 1971, pp. 51–61.

[3] Dreze, J. H., and F. Modigliani, *Consumption Decisions Under Uncertainty*, CORE Discussion Paper No. 6906 (Université Catholique de Louvain), 1969.

[4] Elton, Edwin J., and Martin J. Gruber, "The Multiperiod Consumption Investment Problem and Single Period Analysis," *Oxford Economic Papers*, Sept. 1974.

[5] Elton, Edwin J., and Martin J. Gruber, *Security Evaluation and Portfolio Analysis* (Prentice-Hall, Inc., Englewood Cliffs, N.J.), 1972.

[6] Elton, Edwin J., and Martin J. Gruber, "On the Maximization of the Geometric Mean when Returns are Lognormally Distributed," forthcoming *Management Science*.

[7] Elton, Edwin J., and Martin J. Gruber, "On the Optimality of Some Multiperiod Portfolio Selection Criteria," *Journal of Business*, April 1974.

[8] Elton, Edwin J., and Martin J. Gruber, "Portfolio Theory when Investment Relatives Are Lognormally Distributed," *Journal of Finance*, June 1974.

[9] Fama, Eugene, "Multi-period Consumption–Investment Decisions," *American Economic Review*, 60, March 1970, pp. 163–174.

[10] Hagen, Käre, "On the Problem of Optimal Consumption and Investment Policies Over Time," *The Swedish Journal of Economics*, 74, No. 2, June 1972, pp. 201–220.

[11] Hakansson, Nil, "Optimal Investment and Consumption Under Risk, an Uncertain Lifetime and Insurance," *International Economic Review*, 10, No. 3, Oct. 1969, pp. 443–466.

[12] Hakansson, Nils, "Risk Disposition and the Separation Property in Portfolio Selection," *Journal of Financial and Quantitative Analysis*, 4, No. 4, Dec. 1969, pp. 401–416.

[13] Hakansson, Nils, "An Induced Theory of the Firm Under Risk: the Pure Mutual Fund," *Journal of Financial and Quantitative Analysis*, 3, No. 2, June 1970, pp. 155–178.

[14] Hakansson, Nils, "Optimal Investment and Consumption Strategies Under Risk for a Class of Utility Functions," *Econometrica*, 38, Sept. 1970, pp. 587–607.

[15] Hakansson, Nils, "On Optimal Myopic Portfolio Policies with and without Serial Correlation of Yields," *Journal of Business*, 44, No. 3, July 1971, pp. 324–335.

[16] Hirshleifer, Jack, *Investment Interest Capital* (Prentice-Hall, Inc., Englewood Cliffs, N.J.), 1970.

[17] Latane, Henry, "Criteria for Choice Among Risky Ventures," *Journal of Political Economy*, 67, April 1959, pp. 144–155.

[18] Leland, H., "Saving and Uncertainty: The Precautionary Demand for Saving," *Quarterly Journal of Economics*, 82, No. 3, Aug. 1968, pp. 465–472.

[19] Merton, Robert, "Lifetime Portfolio Selection Under Uncertainty: The Continuous Time Case," *Review of Economics and Statistics*, 50, Aug. 1969, pp. 247–257.

[20] Merton, Robert, "Optimal Consumption and Portfolio Rules in a Continuous Time Model," *Journal of Economic Theory*, 3, No. 4 Dec. 1971, pp. 373–413.

[21] Mossin, Jan, "Optimal Multi-period Portfolio Policies," *Journal of Business*, 41, April 1968, pp. 215–229.

[22] Phelps, Edmund, "The Accumulation of Risky Capital: A Sequential Utility Analysis," *Econometrica*, 30, Oct. 1962, pp. 729–743.

[23] Pratt, John, "Risk Aversion in the Small and in the Large," *Econometrica*, 32, 1–2, Jan.–April 1964, pp. 122–136.

[24] Samuelson, Paul, "Lifetime Portfolio Selection by Dynamic Stochastic Programming," *Review of Economics and Statistics*, 50, Aug. 1969, pp. 239–246.

[25] Sandmo, A., "Portfolio Choice in a Theory of Savings," *Swedish Journal of Economics*, 70, No. 2, June 1968, pp. 106–122.

[26] Sandmo, A., "Capital Risk, Consumption and Portfolio Choice," *Econometrica*, forthcoming.

[27] Sandmo, A., "The Effect of Uncertainty on Savings Decisions," *The Review of Economic Studies*, forthcoming.

[28] Tobin, James, "Liquidity Preference as a Behavior Towards Risk," *Review of Economic Studies*, 25, No. 67, Feb. 1958, pp. 65–87.

```
66666666666666666666666666666666666666666666666666666666666666666666666666666666666
66666666666666666666666666666666666666666666666666666666666666666666666666666666666
6666666666666666666666666666666    6666666666    666    66666666666666666666666666666
6666666666666666666666666666666    6666666666    6666    6666666666666666666666666666
6666666666666666666666666666666    666666666    66666    6666666666666666666666666666
6666666666666666666666666666666    6666666    666666    66666666666666666666666666666
66666666666666666666666666666666    66666    6666666    66666666666666666666666666666
666666666666666666666666666666666    666    66666666    66666666666666666666666666666
6666666666666666666666666666666666    6    666666666    66666666666666666666666666666
66666666666666666666666666666666666        6666666666    6666666666666666666666666666
666666666666666666666666666666666666    6666666666    6666666666666666666666666666666
66666666666666666666666666666666666666666666666666666666666666666666666666666666666
66666666666666666666666666666666666666666666666666666666666666666666666666666666666
```

The Valuation of Warrants and Other Contingent Claim Assets

In this chapter we shall be concerned with a technique for valuing an asset that derives its value at least in part from the price action of a second asset. We shall call such an asset a contingency claim asset. Contingency claim assets include warrants, convertible bonds, convertible preferred stocks, preemptive rights, and options (puts, calls, straddles, spreads, strips, and straps). These contingency claim assets differ in

1. The source of origination. For example, warrants, convertible securities, and preemptive rights are issued by corporations, while options are issued by individuals.
2. The sources of potential income to the contingency claim holder. For example, warrants and convertible bonds both represent a contingency claim on common stock, but during the time the contingency claim is held (before it is executed or sold) convertible bondholders receive income in the form of interest payments on the bond, while warrant holders receive no income.
3. The payments that must be made to acquire the contingency claim. Preemptive rights are originally issued (free of cost) to a firm's stockholders, while later they may be bought on the open market at some price. Other contingency claims are purchased at some market price.

4. The cost of executing the contingency claim. All the contingency claims listed above allow shares of a security (usually common stock) to be sold or bought at a stated price. With convertible bonds and convertible preferred stock this price is usually zero. However, with these securities execution means foregoing future interest payments which would have been received had conversion not taken place.

The similarities between these instruments are much more important than the differences that exist. Each contingency claim can be exchanged for a second instrument in a stated ratio or a second instrument can be bought or sold at a stated price during a stated period of time. The rate of exchange or the price of execution can change over the life of the contingency claim, but any such changes are known at the time the instrument is created. It is this common element that causes us to refer to these instruments as contingency claims, and it is through this common element that they receive most of their value.

Rather than attempting to construct models to represent the valuation of each of the contingency claims, one, claim warrants, will be singled out for special treatment. The methodology developed in studying warrants is applicable to all contingency claims. The modifications that must be made in the warrant model to fit other types of contingency claims are reasonably straightforward.

A warrant is an option which gives the holder the right to buy a specified number of shares of common stock at a stated price either at or during a stated period of time. The price at which a share of stock can be purchased is referred to as the exercise price. In this chapter we shall be concerned with two types of warrants: the European and the American warrant. The European warrant can be exercised only at a particular moment of time. The American warrant can generally be exercised anytime during its stated life; however, the price at which it can be exercised may change at one or more dates.

A. European Warrants

The valuation process for European warrants is straightforward. Since European warrants can be executed only as of a certain date, their value is equal to the present value of the expected value that the European warrant will have on its exercise date. Its value on the exercise date will be either zero (if the stock is selling below the exercise price) or the difference between the market value of the stock it can be converted into and the sum of money that must be paid to execute it (if the price of the stock is higher than the exercise price). Thus, the value of the European warrant is

$$F_0(X_0) = e^{-\beta T} \int_Y^\infty (X_T - Y) \, P(X_T \mid X_0) \, dX_T \tag{1}$$

where

T = the number of periods until the warrant can be executed
β = the discount rate (required rate of return) on the warrant[1]
X_0 = the market value of the common stock commanded by the warrant at the time the warrant is valued
X_T = the market value of the common stock commanded by the warrant at the time the warrant can be executed; X_T is a stochastic variable
$P(X_T|X_0)$ = the probability distribution of X_T given X_0
Y = the sum of money which must be paid to execute the warrant; this is equal to the exercise price times the number of shares the warrant commands
$F_0(X_0)$ = the value of the warrant as of time 0

In the above equation the lower limit of integration is Y, since if the market value of the stock is lower than the price which must be paid to execute the warrant, the warrant will not be executed and thus its value will be zero.

The expression for valuing a European warrant is of interest for several reasons. As we shall see below, it serves as a starting point for the valuation of the more familiar American warrant. In addition, some recent literature has argued that under several alternative sets of assumptions it will not pay to execute an American warrant before its terminal execution date and therefore equation (1) is also the appropriate valuation equation for American warrants.[2]

B. The American Warrant

It is obvious that the price of an American warrant can never be lower than the price of a European warrant, for the American warrant can be thought of as a European warrant with added decision possibilities. That is, in addition to converting the option at some date T, it can be converted at any time up to and including T. Having extra courses of action available can never lower the value of a security, for these courses of action can always be ignored. The question remains as to how to value these extra courses of action.

---

[1] In earlier applications, we assumed discrete discounting. Here we have assumed continuous discounting. This was done since growth in stock prices is usually treated as a continuous phenomenon and it is convenient to treat both the compounding and discounting phenomena in the same manner. We, like most authors, have incorporated risk considerations into the discount rate.

[2] Three sets of conditions have been put forth under which an American warrant will be treated by the market as a European warrant. The three approaches involve utility theory (see Samuelson and Merton [12]), general equilibrium theory (see Black and Scholes [3]), and arbitrage positions (see Merton [9]). The detailed assumptions inherent in each of these approaches are presented in the respective articles.

Early attempts at valuing American warrants treated the value of a warrant at any moment in time t as

$$VW_t = \int_{Y_t}^{\infty} (X_t - Y_t) \, P(X_t \mid X_0) \, dX_t \tag{2}$$

where a subscript has been added to Y to recognize the fact that the exercise price can change over the life of the warrant.[3]

The value of the American warrant was then asserted to be

$$f_0(X_0) = \max_t \, [e^{-\beta t} VW_t] \tag{3}$$

In other words, a warrant was valued by assuming that it was executed at that time in which execution produced the highest expected present value.

The problem with this solution is that it imputes a value to warrants as if the decision on when to execute the security has to be made on the basis of expected values, a course of action which we saw was inappropriate in Chapter 1. Better decisions may be reached by making the course of action taken in the future conditional upon the state (stock price) that occurs in the future. That is, even if equation (3) shows that we expect it to be optimal to execute in period t, we do not in fact have to execute in period t. The warrant may be executed earlier if a particular fortuitous event occurs, or it may not be executed until later if the stock prices up through time t are lower than expected. This can be illustrated with a simple example. See Figure 6-1. Assume that the values for stock prices

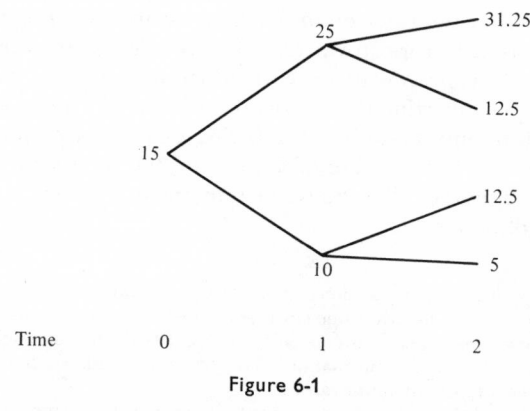

| Time | 0 | 1 | 2 |

Figure 6-1

---

[3] Variations of this procedure have been advocated by Sprenkle [15] and Ayres [1] for warrants, by Boness [4] for puts and calls, and by Baumol et al. [2] for convertible securities.

with outcomes in any period are equally likely. Furthermore, assume that the required rate of return on the warrant equals zero, each warrant commands one share of the stock, and the execution price is \$10. Then the possible values of the warrant from equation (2) are

$$VW_0 = (15 - 10) = 5$$

$$VW_1 = \frac{1}{2}(25 - 10) + \frac{1}{2}(10 - 10) = \frac{15}{2} = 7.5$$

$$VW_2 = \frac{1}{4}(31.25 - 10) + \frac{1}{4}(12.5 - 10) + \frac{1}{4}(12.5 - 10)$$

$$+ \frac{1}{4}(0) = \frac{26.25}{4} = 6.56$$

From equation (3) we see that the traditional analysis calls for us to plan to execute in period 1 and that the value of the warrant is \$7.50.

However, there are more complex strategies open to the investor. One such strategy is to execute the warrant in period 1 if the stock price is \$25 but otherwise to wait for expiration. The expected value under this strategy is

$$\frac{1}{2}(25 - 10) + \frac{1}{4}(12.5 - 10) + \frac{1}{4}(0) = \$8.125$$

The investor will reach a higher value for the warrant if he examines the entire distribution of possible stock prices and formulates a strategy based on possible outcomes in each period rather than on expected values.

As we have seen in Chapter 1, stochastic dynamic programming is ideally suited to solving such a problem.

1. The Dynamic Programming Solution

Chen [5] was the first person to formulate the warrant valuation problem as a dynamic programming problem, and much of the discussion in this section is based on his work.

At the time an American warrant expires (time T) one must either execute it or let it expire. If the market price of the stock is greater than the exercise price, it should be executed; otherwise it should be allowed to expire. The value of a warrant at T can be stated as

$$f_T(X_T) = \max \begin{bmatrix} \text{Execute} & X_T - Y_T \\ \text{Do not execute} & 0 \end{bmatrix} \quad (4)$$

At period $T - 1$ the investor can again be envisioned as facing a choice between executing and not executing the warrant. If the investor executes at some price X_{T-1}, then he receives a sum of money $(X_{T-1} - Y_{T-1})$.

On the other hand, if he refrains from executing, he receives the present value of the expected value of the warrant at T. The value of the warrant at $T - 1$ is the maximum of these two options. Thus,

$$f_{T-1}(X_{T-1}) = \max \begin{bmatrix} \text{Execute} & X_{T-1} - Y_{T-1} \\ \text{Do not execute} & e^{-\beta} \int_0^\infty f_T(X_T)\, P(X_T \mid X_{T-1})\, dX_T \end{bmatrix}$$

where

1. $f_{T-1}(X_{T-1})$ is the value of the warrant at time $T - 1$ given that the price at time $T - 1$ is X_{T-1} and an optimum policy is followed from time $T - 1$ on with respect to the timing of the execution of the warrant.
2. All other terms as before.

This expression can easily be generalized for all $t < T$ as

$$f_t(X_t) = \max \begin{bmatrix} \text{Execute} & X_t - Y_t \\ \text{Do not execute} & e^{-\beta} \int_0^\infty f_{t+1}(X_{t+1})\, P(X_{t+1} \mid X_t)\, dX_{t+1} \end{bmatrix}$$

$$(5)$$

Equations (4) and (5) represent a general model that can be used to solve any warrant valuation problem. However, to implement the solution one needs to know the conditional distribution of stock prices.

2. The Form of an Optimum Policy

Once again the special structure of the recursive relationship can often be used to determine an optimal policy. In particular, we shall show that for each period there exists at most one critical stock price (C_t). If actual stock prices above this critical value occur, the investor should always execute the warrant. For stock prices below this critical value it is never optimal for the investor to execute.[4] Let us assume that the sum of money which must be paid to execute a warrant is constant over the life of the warrant. We shall define this value as Y. The existence of a critical value for period T is obvious. As long as the stock price is above the execution price it pays to execute; otherwise the warrant should be allowed to expire. Therefore, Y is the critical value for the stock price at time T.

The value of the optimal policy for period T can be stated as

$$f_T(X_T) = \begin{bmatrix} X_T - Y & \text{if } X_T > Y \\ 0 & \text{if } X_T \leq Y \end{bmatrix}$$

---

[4] The derivation assumes that the expected rate of return on the warrant is not a function of the level of stock prices.

Note that $\partial f_T(X_T)/\partial X_T$ is less than or equal to 1 for all values of X_T. Now if we look at the decision process one period earlier, we have

$$f_{T-1}(X_{T-1}) = \max \begin{bmatrix} \text{Execute} & X_{T-1} - Y \\ \text{Do not execute} & e^{-\beta} \int_0^\infty f_T(X_T)\, P(X_T \mid X_{T-1})\, dX_T \end{bmatrix}$$

(6)

To prove that not more than one critical value can exist for earlier periods it is sufficient to show that the increase in the value of the "do not execute" option with a change in X_{T-1} is always less then the increase in value of the "execute" option. In this case, once a critical value is reached (the execute option is superior) it will continue to be superior for all higher values of X_{T-1}. The change in the execute option with a change in X_{T-1} is given by

$$\frac{\partial(X_{T-1} - Y)}{\partial X_{T-1}} = 1$$

To see the size of the change in the do not execute option with respect to a change in X_{T-1} define the value of the do not execute option as of time $T - 1$ as

$$g(X_{T-1}) = e^{-\beta} \int_0^\infty f_T(X_T)\, P(X_T \mid X_{T-1})\, dX_T$$

Adding and subtracting $f_T(0)$ to the right-hand side of the equation,

$$g(X_{T-1}) = e^{-\beta} \int_0^\infty [f_T(X_T) - f_T(0)]\, P(X_T \mid X_{T-1})\, dX_T + e^{-\beta} f_T(0)$$

Taking the derivative with respect to X_{T-1},

$$\frac{\partial g(X_{T-1})}{\partial X_{T-1}} = e^{-\beta} \int_0^\infty [f_T(X_T) - f_T(0)]\, \frac{\partial P(X_T \mid X_{T-1})}{\partial X_{T-1}}\, dX_T \qquad (7)$$

But we know that $\partial f_T(X_T)/\partial X_T \leq 1$. This means that

$$f_T(0) + X_T \geq f_T(X_T) \qquad (8)$$

Substituting equation (8) into equation (7) yields

$$\frac{\partial g(X_{T-1})}{\partial X_{T-1}} \leq e^{-\beta} \int_0^\infty [f_T(0) + X_T - f_T(0)]\, \frac{\partial P(X_T \mid X_{T-1})}{\partial X_{T-1}}\, dX_T$$

or

$$\frac{\partial g(X_{T-1})}{\partial X_{T-1}} \leq e^{-\beta} \int_0^\infty X_T\, \frac{\partial P(X_T \mid X_{T-1})}{\partial X_{T-1}}\, dX_T$$

But the expression on the right-hand side of the above equation is identical to $e^{-\beta}$ times the derivative of the expected value of X_T, or

$$\frac{\partial g(X_{T-1})}{\partial X_{T-1}} \leq e^{-\beta} \frac{\partial E(X_T \mid X_{T-1})}{\partial X_{T-1}} \tag{9}$$

This equation can be further simplified by drawing on the theoretical and empirical work that has been done on the distribution of stock price changes. There is general agreement that price movements follow geometric Brownian motion or that[5]

$$E(X_T \mid X_{T-1}) = X_{T-1}e^{\alpha} \tag{10}$$

In this expression α is the expected growth in stock prices per unit of time and is independent of the level of X_{T-1}. Taking the derivative of equation (10) and substituting into equation (9), we have

$$\frac{\partial g(X_{T-1})}{\partial X_{T-1}} \leq e^{\alpha-\beta}$$

A sufficient condition for the existence of at most one critical value is that the rate of change in the execute option with a change in X_{T-1} is larger than the rate of change in the do not execute option, or in terms of the above analysis that

$$e^{\alpha-\beta} < 1$$

Thus, we have established the existence of *at most* one critical point for time period $T-1$ if $\beta > \alpha$. Having shown that $\beta > \alpha$ is a sufficient condition for the existence of *at most* one critical point, we shall now show that if $\beta > \alpha$ a critical point will in fact always exist.[6] This will be shown for $T-1$; an analogous demonstration will hold for earlier periods. From equation (6) in period $T-1$, we shall execute the warrant only if

$$X_{T-1} - Y > e^{-\beta} \int_0^{\infty} f_T(X_T) \, P(X_T \mid X_{T-1}) \, dX_T$$

---

[5] While geometric Brownian motion is widely accepted in the financial literature, a controversy still rages over the form of the distribution of price relatives. Most authors believe that the log of price relatives either follows a normal distribution [7, 10, 11] or a nonnormal stable paretian distribution [6, 8].

[6] This proof rests on some very strong assumptions. In particular, we are assuming that the investor is attempting to maximize the present value of expected income and that at the time when execution becomes the preferred option the market value of the warrant will equal its execution value. Alternative formulations of this problem involving market equilibria, arbitrage positions, and expected utility criteria have been put forth [4, 9, 12]. These show that under alternative sets of assumptions it will not pay to execute an American warrant until it expires and that the valuation of an American warrant is identical to a European warrant.

But we know that $f_T(X_T)$ is zero for X_T less than Y and is equal to $X_T - Y$ for X_T greater than Y. Therefore, the right-hand side of the above expression can be written as

$$e^{-\beta} \int_Y^\infty (X_T - Y)\, P(X_T \mid X_{T-1})\, dX_T$$

or

$$e^{-\beta} E(X_T - Y) + e^{-\beta} \int_0^Y (Y - X_T)\, P(X_T \mid X_{T-1})\, dX_T$$

The inequality can now be written as

$$X_{T-1} - Y > e^{-\beta} E(X_T - Y) + e^{-\beta} \int_0^Y (Y - X_T)\, P(X_T \mid X_{T-1})\, dX_T$$

Substituting the expression $E(X_T) = X_{T-1} e^\alpha$ into this equation yields

$$X_{T-1} - Y = e^{-\beta}(X_{T-1} e^\alpha - Y) + e^{-\beta} \int_0^Y (Y - X_T)\, P(X_T \mid X_{T-1})\, dX_T$$

or

$$X_{T-1}(1 - e^{\alpha-\beta}) = Y(1 - e^{-\beta}) + e^{-\beta} \int_0^Y (Y - X_T)\, P(X_T \mid X_{T-1})\, dX_T \tag{11}$$

At the value $X_{T-1} = Y$ the inequality cannot hold since the last term is positive and $Y(1 - e^{\alpha-\beta}) < Y(1 - e^{-\beta})$. Thus, at some value of X_{T-1} the do not execute option is preferable. However, from previous analysis we know that as long as $\beta > \alpha$ the value of the execute option increases faster than the value of the do not execute option. Therefore, at some X_{T-1} it pays to execute the warrant, and we have one and only one critical value. Furthermore, it can be shown that the critical values decrease with time, or $c_t \geq c_{t+1}$. A diagrammatic presentation of this policy is presented in Figure 6-2.

An extension of the above proof shows that if the execution price of the warrant increases over the life of the warrant (a not uncommon feature), the effect is to increase the critical value above which execution will take place in all periods prior to the change in execution price.

Having established that for $\beta > \alpha$ we have one and only one critical value, we shall now show that for $\alpha \geq \beta$ no critical values can exist or, equivalently, it never pays to execute the warrant before the date the warrant expires. We shall show this for period $T - 1$. The proof in earlier periods is analogous. From equation (11) we have

$$X_{T-1}(1 - e^{\alpha-\beta}) > Y(1 - e^{-\beta}) + e^{-\beta} \int_0^Y (Y - X_T)\, P(X_T \mid X_{T-1})\, dX_T$$

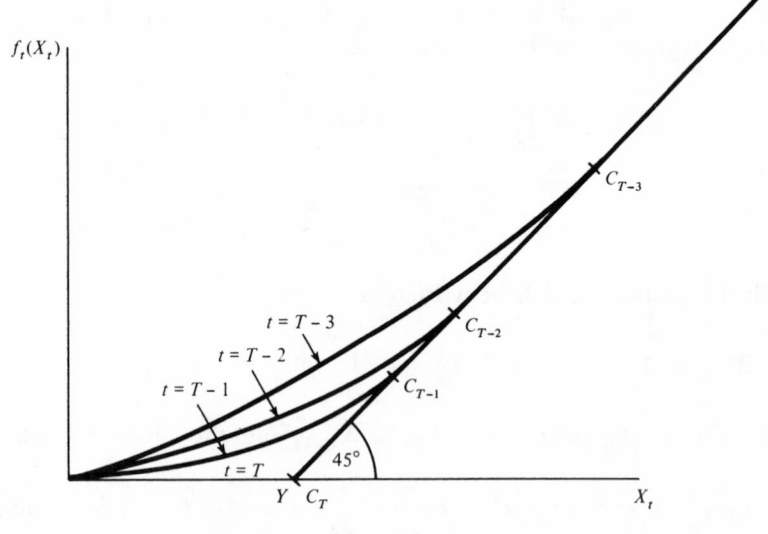

Figure 6-2

The limits of the integration assure that this last term is always positive. Therefore, ignoring it makes the inequality even easier to meet. The inequality can now be written as

$$X_{T-1}(1 - e^{\alpha-\beta}) > Y(1 - e^{-\beta})$$

For $\alpha > \beta$ the left-hand side of this inequality is negative, while for $\alpha = \beta$ it is equal to zero. Since the right-hand side is positive, the inequality can never hold. Thus, it will not pay to execute a warrant if $\alpha \geq \beta$. As long as the growth rate in stock prices is equal to or greater than the required rate of return from holding the warrant, the investor should not execute a warrant until the horizon and the additional conversion privileges provided by an American warrant have no value. An American warrant can then be valued by the simple equation (1) developed for the valuation of European warrants.

Conclusion

In this chapter we have discussed the nature of contingency claim assets. Rather than constructing a series of models for each type of contingency claim asset, one type, warrants, has been studied in great detail. A general model for warrant valuation was first constructed, and then the properties of this model were employed to derive an optimum policy with respect to the execution of warrants over time.

Bibliography

[1] Ayres, H., "Risk Aversion in the Warrant Markets," in *The Random Character of Stock Market Prices*, Paul Cootner, ed., rev. ed. (The M.I.T. Press, Cambridge, Mass.), 1964, pp. 497–505.

[2] Baumol W., B. Malkiel and R. Quandt, "The Valuation of Convertible Securities," *Quarterly Journal of Economics*, 80, Feb. 1966, pp. 48–59.

[3] Black, F., and M. Scholes, "Capital Market Equilibrium and the Pricing of Corporate Liabilities," *Journal of Political Economy*, 71, No. 3, May/June 1973, pp. 637–655.

[4] Boness, A., "Elements of a Theory of Stock-Option Value," *Journal of Political Economy*, 72, April 1964, pp. 163–175.

[5] Chen, A., "A Model of Warrant Pricing in a Dynamic Market," *Journal of Finance*, 25, No. 5, Dec. 1970, pp. 1041–1059.

[6] Fama, Eugene F., "The Behavior of Stock Prices," *Journal of Business*, 38, No. 1, July 1965, pp. 34–105.

[7] Kendall, M.G., "The Analysis of Economic Time Series," *Journal of the Royal Statistical Society* (series A), *XCVI*, 1953, pp. 11–25.

[8] Mandelbrot, Benoit, The Variation of Certain Speculative Prices," *Journal of Business*, 36, No. 4, Oct. 1963, pp. 394–419.

[9] Merton, R., "Theory of Rational Option Pricing," *Bell Journal of Economics and Management Science*, 4, No. 1, Spring 1973, pp. 141–184.

[10] Moore, Arnold, "A Statistical Analysis of Common Stock Prices," unpublished doctoral dissertation (Graduate School of Business, University of Chicago, Chicago), 1962.

[11] Osborne, M. F. M., "Brownian Motion in the Stock Market," *Operations Research*, *VII*, March-April 1959, pp. 145–173.

[12] Samuelson, P., and R. Merton, "A Complete Model of Warrant Pricing that Maximizes Utility," *Industrial Management Review*, 10, No. 2, (Winter, 1969) pp. 17–46.

[13] Shelton, John P., "The Relation of the Price of a Warrant to the Price of its Associated Stock," Part I, *Financial Analysts Journal*, 23, No. 3, May–June 1967, pp. 134–151.

[14] Shelton, John, P., "The Relation of the Price of a Warrant to the Price of its Associated Stock," Part II, *Financial Analysts Journal*, 23, No. 4, July–August 1967, pp. 80–100.

[15] Sprenkle, L., "Warrant Prices as Indicators of Expectations and Preferences," in *The Random Character of Stock Market Prices*, Paul Cootner, ed., rev. ed (The M.I.T. Press, Cambridge, Mass.), 1964 pp. 412–474.

The Equipment Replacement Decision

ONE of the first finance problems which was recognized and solved as a multiperiod problem is the equipment replacement problem. The equipment replacement problem is determining when current equipment should be replaced given that successive replacements over a specified period of time are feasible. The multiperiod formulation of this problem explicitly takes consideration of the effect of potential future replacements on earlier replacement decisions. In this chapter we shall provide a synthesis of the very extensive literature in which this problem has been analyzed.[1]

Equipment replacement models can conveniently be categorized according to the assumptions made about cash flows and the time horizon. Cash flows can be assumed to be either deterministic or random. The time horizon is either finite or infinite. In the first section we shall consider deterministic models, and in the second section, models under risk.

A. Deterministic Models

The equipment replacement problem involves the following variables.

I_t = the capital costs of new equipment in period t
B_{tj} = the revenue stream associated with equipment purchased in year t and j years old

---

[1] See the Bibliography for a list of references.

C_{tj} = the operating costs of equipment purchased in period t and j years old.

S_{tj} = the scrap value of equipment purchased in year t and j years old; alternatively, the value of the equipment if converted to a secondary less profitable use (perhaps as backup equipment or for spare parts)

α_t = the discount factor in t (i.e., 1 over 1 plus the relevant discount rate) which is used to find the present value as of t of a cash flow which occurs at $t + 1$.

A number of concepts usually discussed in the equipment replacement literature are incorporated in the above definitions. The first is obsolescence. Obsolescence has a number of meanings. First, it can incorporate technological improvement or the idea that new equipment is functionally superior to the old. Some models assume that new equipment is obtainable only at a capital cost related to the amount of improvement (reduction in operating cost), while in other models no change in capital cost is assumed. Obsolescence is also used to mean that equipment deteriorates (operating costs go up) as it ages. The usual procedure is to separately define obsolescence and then assume that the operating costs or capital costs or both are constant except for obsolescence. Given the variety of definitions of obsolescence, we prefer to incorporate these considerations directly in terms of capital cost and operating cost.

Maintenance is a second concept often discussed in the equipment replacement literature. We shall not explicitly consider maintenance, although we shall implicitly incorporate it in the operating cost function. The models which deal with maintenance expenses explicitly either allow its inclusion in operating costs or are so complex and specialized that they are beyond the scope of this chapter.

Two formulations of the equipment model are possible. First, one can maximize the net present value of inflows less outflows. Second, one could minimize the present value of the cost of providing the service performed by the machine. This second formulation is equivalent to the first if the function performed by the machine is to be provided over the horizon under study (its desirability cannot be determined by the second formulation) and if revenue changes are incorporated in costs. Operating costs must include not only the increased cost caused by deteriorating quality or overtime due to inefficiency but also changes in the revenue stream. The present value of the revenue received in each future period can change because of deterioration in the quality of products, seasonality, or simply because receipts in the far future are more heavily discounted than receipts in the near future.[2] Because it seems simpler not to worry about incorporating all these changes in the operating costs, we shall work with maximization of net present value in this chapter. The readers should be very careful to keep these considerations in mind when they read the literature using cost minimization as an objective.

---

[2] The problems in employing a cost formulation will become clearer in footnote 4.

1. Finite Horizon

Let us assume that I_t, B_{tj}, C_{tj}, and S_{tj} are defined as above and that the firm has a finite horizon after which the function performed by the equipment will no longer be necessary. Then the recursive relationship is

$$f_T = 0$$

for $0 \leq t < T$

$$f_t = \max_{j=1,\ldots,T-t} \sum_{k=1}^{j} d_{t+k}B_{tk} - I_t - \sum_{k=1}^{j} d_{t+k}C_{tk} + d_{t+j}S_{tj} + d_{t+j}f_{t+j} \quad (1)$$

where $d_{t+k} = \prod_{i=t}^{t+k-1}$ and α_i is the discount factor. f_t is the maximum profit from t to the horizon given that a new machine is purchased at t and an optimum policy is followed from t to the horizon.

If new equipment is purchased in t, then the firm receives discounted revenues of $\sum_{k=1}^{j} d_{t+k}B_{tk}$, incurs capital costs of I_t, incurs discounted operating costs until the next replacement of $\sum_{k=1}^{j} d_{t+k}C_{tk}$, has an inflow at the next replacement equal to the salvage value, and receives the benefit of providing the service performed by the equipment from the time of the next replacement until the horizon given that an optimal policy is followed.

The logic underlying this recursive solution to the problem is directly parallel to that encountered in studying the bond-refunding problem. Working backward from the horizon, the decision maker determines the optimum time to replace equipment purchased at any time t given that an optimum replacement policy is followed from the time this equipment is replaced. Part of this calculation involves the use of f_{t+j} for all values of j. But since the decision maker is working backward, he already knows all f_{t+j} (the maximum benefit of providing the services of a machine from period $t + j$ to the horizon). Working backward recursively, the decision maker arrives at f_0. If the firm currently does not have existing equipment, then f_0 is the maximum benefit from providing the service of the machine over the decision horizon and the replacement policy associated with f_0 is the optimum policy.

If the firm has equipment, then the possibility of continuing to use the initial equipment must be considered, and the initial recursive relationship should be defined as

$$f_{\text{decision}} = \max \begin{bmatrix} S_{.0} + f_0 \\ \max_{j=1,..,T} \left[\sum_{k=1}^{j} d_k B_{.k} - \sum_{k=1}^{j} d_k C_{.k} + d_j S_{.j} + d_j f_j \right] \end{bmatrix}$$

where

d_j = the discount factor, $\prod_{i=0}^{j-1} \alpha_i$
$B_{.j}$ = the revenue in period j associated with the existing equipment
$C_{.j}$ = the operating cost of the existing equipment for period j
$S_{.j}$ = the salvage value of the existing equipment for period j

2. Infinite Horizon

Under several alternative sets of assumptions about the changes in cash flows with respect to time, a stationary replacement policy (one involving replacement at equal intervals) can be shown to be optimum. In these cases, the calculation of the optimal policy and associated benefits is vastly simplified. Consequently, a large amount of attention has been focused on this problem, and we shall devote the remainder of this section to analyzing it. We shall first examine the case where the discount rate, revenues, investment costs, and salvage values do not depend on time. We shall later examine the formulation under one widely accepted assumption about technological change.

If the discount factor, revenues, investment cost, operating cost, and salvage value do not depend on time, then the time subscripts can be deleted from these variables and equation (1) can be rewritten as

$$f_t = \max_j \left[\sum_{k=1}^{j} \alpha^k B_k - I - \sum_{k=1}^{j} \alpha^k C_k + \alpha^j S_j + \alpha^j f_{t+j} \right] \qquad (2)$$

If these costs are constant over time, then the firm will face a series of identical decisions over time and a policy involving replacement at equal intervals is optimum.[3]

When a stationary policy is optimal in an infinite horizon problem, it can be shown that the present value of the cost of following an optimal policy from year t to the horizon (given a new machine at t) is identical to the present value of the cost of following the same policy from year $t+j$ to the horizon given a new machine at $t+j$, that is, $f_t = f_{t+j}$. The reason for this is easy to understand. The present value at year 3 of an infinite sequence of 10-year investments beginning at year 3 is the same as the present value at year 7 of the same sequence of 10-year investments beginning at year 7, since the same pattern of costs ensues. The equality of f_t and f_{t+j} will now be shown analytically.

We can represent the present value (at the time a machine is purchased) of the benefits associated with the life of any machine kept for j years as

$$Z_j = \sum_{k=1}^{j} \alpha^k B_k - I - \sum_{k=1}^{j} \alpha^k C_k + \alpha^j S_j$$

For the stationary replacement policy, equation (2) can be written as the sum of an infinite series of identical machines, or

$$f_t = \max_j \left[Z_j + \alpha^j Z_j + \alpha^{2j} Z_j + \cdots \right]$$

$$= \max_j \left[Z_j + Z_j \sum_{i=1}^{\infty} \alpha^{ij} \right] \qquad (3)$$

[3] For a rigorous proof that a stationary policy is optimum in this case, see Bibliography Reference [3].

Let j^* equal the value of j which maximizes equation (3). Then

$$f_t = Z_{j*} + Z_{j*} \sum_{i=1}^{\infty} \alpha^{ij*} \tag{4}$$

But from equation (2)

$$f_t = Z_{j*} + \alpha^{j*} f_{t+j*} \tag{5}$$

By substituting equation (4) into equation (5) and solving for f_{t+j*},

$$f_{t+j*} = \frac{1}{\alpha^{j*}} Z_{j*} \sum_{i=1}^{\infty} \alpha^{ij*} = Z_{j*} \sum_{i=1}^{\infty} \alpha^{ij*} = f_t$$

By analogous reasoning $f_t = f_{t+j*} = f_{t+2j*} = f$. Substituting this relationship into equation (2) yields

$$f = \max_j \left[\sum_{k=1}^{j} \alpha^k B_k - I - \sum_{k=1}^{j} \alpha^k C_k + \alpha^j S_j + \alpha^j f \right]$$

or rearranging terms

$$f = \max_j \frac{\sum_{k=1}^{j} \alpha^k B_k - I - \sum_{k=1}^{j} \alpha^k C_k + \alpha^j S_j}{1 - \alpha^j} = \max_j \left[\frac{Z_j}{1 - \alpha^j} \right]$$

The question arises as to whether the replacement decision arrived at by this recursive optimization process differs from that arrived at by simply maximizing the benefits of the first replacement.

A decision maker considering only the initial decision would maximize Z_j, while the multiperiod decision maker maximizes $Z_j[1/(1 - \alpha^j)]$. Since α is less than 1, α^j decreases as j increases and $1/(1 - \alpha^j)$ also decreases as j increases. This implies that it is optimum to keep a machine for a longer period of time if it will not be replaced than it is to keep the machine if it is the first in an infinite chain of such machines.[4]

How much earlier the decision maker would replace using multiperiod analysis depends on the specific problem being considered. As an illustration, consider the investment called A in Table 7-1. The third column shows the present value for various lives of a single machine

---

[4] The difficulty in using a formulation involving the minimization of costs, rather than the maximization of revenues, can easily be seen by an extension of this analysis. If we were minimizing costs, the equation which follows in the text would normally be written as

$$f = \min_j \frac{I + \sum_{k=1}^{j} \alpha^k C_k - \alpha^j S_j}{1 - \alpha^j}$$

But under this formulation, costs are usually minimized by never replacing. In the above equation the denominator is maximized by making α^j as small as possible. If α^j decreases faster than S_j and C_j increase, then the numerator is minimized by making α^j as small as possible. Since $\alpha^j \rightarrow 0$ as $j \rightarrow \infty$, the cost is minimized by never replacing. Formulating the problem in terms of benefits (as is done in the text) explicitly takes into consideration the effects of discounting on the benefit stream and so leads to different (and correct) results.

called *A*. The fourth column shows the present value of an infinite number of *A*s replaced at various intervals. Ignoring future replacements, the maximum present value is associated with a 21-year life, while explicitly

TABLE 7-1

Year	$\dfrac{1}{1-\alpha_j}$	Z_A	$\dfrac{Z_A}{1-\alpha_j}$	Z_B	$\dfrac{Z_B}{1-\alpha_j}$
1	10.99	1	10.99	1	10.99
2	5.75	2	11.50	2.5	14.38
3	4.02	2.95	11.86	4.0	16.08
4	3.15	3.85	12.13	5.5	17.33
5	2.64	4.70	12.41	7.0	18.48
6	2.29	5.50	12.60	7.5	17.18
7	2.05	6.25	12.81	8.0	16.40
8	1.87	6.95	13.00	8.5	15.90
9	1.74	7.60	13.22	9.0	15.66
10	1.63	8.20	13.37	9.5	15.49
11	1.54	8.75	13.48	9.6	14.78
12	1.47	9.25	13.60	9.7	14.26
13	1.41	9.70	13.69	9.8	13.82
14	1.36	10.10	13.74	9.9	13.46
15	1.31	10.45	13.69	10.0	13.10
16	1.28	10.75	13.76	10.05	12.86
17	1.25	11.00	13.75	10.10	12.63
18	1.22	11.20	13.66	10.15	12.38
19	1.20	11.35	13.62	10.20	12.24
20	1.18	11.45	13.51	10.25	12.10
21	1.16	11.50	13.34	10.25	11.89
22	1.14	11.50	13.11		

taking into account future replacements means that the firm replaces every 16 years.

Not only will the replacement interval be affected by viewing the problem as a series of replacements, but also the optimum project to select can be affected. Table 7-1 shows two projects *A* and *B*. The present value of the initial investment can be examined by comparing the third and fifth columns. Project *A* is the preferred one since it has a net present value of $11.50 over its 21-year life, as opposed to $10.25 for project B. Examination of the fourth and sixth columns shows what happens when the infinite series of replacements is included. Project *A* will be replaced every 16 years with a present value of $13.76. Project *B* will be replaced every 5 years with a present value of $18.48. When the infinite series of replacements are considered, project *B* is the preferred project. Thus, viewing the problem as a series of replacements can affect not only the frequency of replacement but also the project selected.

Up to this point we have examined one simple set of cost functions which lead to a stationary policy and therefore a simple solution. There are many other cost functions which also lead to a stationary policy.[5] The fact that certain cost patterns lead to a stationary policy has been proved by Elton and Gruber [3].

To illustrate an alternative assumption that leads to a stationary policy, assume that operating costs on a type of new machinery decrease by a constant dollar amount per unit of time. Such a change could be considered the effect of improved equipment because of technological change. If we let θ be the reduction from one period to the next in the operating costs of new machines because of technological change, then the infinite horizon model becomes

$$\max_j \left[Z_j + \alpha^j \left[Z_j - \theta j \sum_{k=0}^{j-1} \alpha^k \right] + \alpha^{2j} \left[Z_j - \theta 2j \sum_{k=0}^{j-1} \alpha^k \right] \right.$$
$$\left. + \cdots + \alpha^{nj} \left[Z_j - \theta nj \sum_{k=0}^{j-1} \alpha^k \right] + \cdots \right]$$

The term θnj represents the increase in benefits (via a decrease in costs) resulting from technological improvements that accrue each year the nth machine is used. The term $\theta nj \sum_{k=0}^{j-1} \alpha^k$ represents the present value of these benefits at the time the machine is purchased.

Collecting terms in the above expression yields

$$\max_j \left[Z_j + \alpha^j Z_j + \alpha^{2j} Z_j + \cdots + \alpha^{nj} Z_j + \cdots \right.$$
$$\left. + \left[\theta j \alpha^j \left(\sum_{k=0}^{j-1} \alpha^k + 2\alpha^j \sum_{k=0}^{j-1} \alpha^k + \cdots + n\alpha^{(n-1)j} \sum_{k=0}^{j-1} \alpha^k + \cdots \right) \right] \right]$$

or[6]

$$\max_j \left[Z_j + \alpha^j Z_j + \alpha^{2j} Z_j + \cdots + \alpha^{nj} Z_j + \cdots \right.$$
$$\left. + \left[\theta j \alpha^j \left(\sum_{k=0}^{\infty} \alpha^k + \alpha^j \sum_{k=0}^{\infty} \alpha^k + \cdots + \alpha^{(n-1)j} \sum_{k=0}^{\infty} \alpha^k + \cdots \right) \right] \right]$$

---

[5] This problem has been studied in Bibliography References [2], [8], [9], [11], [16], and [17].

[6] The terms in the parentheses can be written in an alternative way. We can write $\alpha^j \sum_{k=0}^{j-1} \alpha^k$ as $\sum_{k=j}^{2j-1} \alpha^k$, and we can write $\alpha^{2j} \sum_{k=0}^{j-1} \alpha^k$ as $\sum_{k=2j}^{3j-1} \alpha^k$. Applying this change to all terms in the parentheses, we have

$$Z_j + \alpha^j Z_j + \alpha^{2j} Z_j + \cdots + \alpha^{nj} Z_j + \cdots$$
$$- \left[\theta j \alpha^j \left(\sum_{k=0}^{j-1} \alpha^k + 2 \sum_{k=j}^{2j-1} \alpha^k + 3 \sum_{k=2j}^{3j-1} \alpha^k + \cdots \right) \right]$$

Employing the formula for the sum of a geometric progression to the terms in the brackets yields

$$Z_j + \alpha^j Z_j + \alpha^{2j} Z_j + \cdots + \alpha^{nj} Z_j + \cdots - \left[\theta j \alpha^j \left[\frac{1}{1-\alpha} + \frac{\alpha^j}{1-\alpha} + \frac{\alpha^{2j}}{1-\alpha} + \cdots \right] \right]$$

Employing the formula for the sum of a geometric progression yields the formula in the text.

Employing the formula for the sum of a geometric progression,

$$\max_j \left[\frac{Z_j}{1 - \alpha^j} + \frac{\theta j \alpha^j}{(1 - \alpha^j)(1 - \alpha)} \right]$$

The reasoning that this formulation leads to a stationary policy can be summarized as follows. The firm purchases new equipment because the new equipment has superior operating characteristics compared to the old. This operating superiority is reflected in the difference between the cost of operating the old equipment and the new. With the formulation above, this difference is a function only of the time since the last replacement and not the number of replacements that preceded it. In other words, the difference in cost between operating a 7-year-old machine and a replacement machine is constant over time. Since it is the operating superiority of the new machine that triggers the replacement, this constant relationship leads to a stationary policy.[7] A similar assumption regarding revenues would also lead to a stationary policy. For example, a stationary policy would result from the revenue function changing a constant amount with each equipment replacement resulting from, perhaps, an improved product.

Changes that lead to cost differentials (the difference in cost between an old and a new machine) being a function of the number of replacements lead to nonstationary policies. For example, if installation costs were reduced with each new installation because of, perhaps, experience, then a nonstationary policy would ensue.

B. Risk Models

Any of the variables on the right-hand side of equation (1) can be treated as a stochastic variable in analyzing the equipment replacement problem. To illustrate the incorporation of risk, we shall assume that the uncertain element is the basic level of costs. However, the analysis necessary to incorporate risk in any other variable is directly analogous to that presented below. We shall assume that once the level of costs for a particular piece of replacement equipment is specified, then the structure of costs over the life of the equipment is known. Furthermore, we shall assume that the probability of any level of costs occurring for any one replacement depends on the level that occurred in the previous period. In particular, let

1. L be a random variable equal to the level of costs.
2. L^* be the level of costs in the current decision period.
3. L_i be the ith level of costs.
4. $P(L_i/L^*)$ be the probability of costs equal to L_i when the level of costs with the previous replacement was L^*.

We are now ready to examine the models in more detail.

---

[7] For a formal proof of the stationarity of the policy, see Elton and Gruber [3].

1. Finite Horizon Model

The expression for operating costs must be modified to allow for a stochastic term. Total operating costs will be assumed to be composed of two terms, a stochastic term specifying the level of costs and a deterministic term specifying the change in costs over time. In equation form, this is

$$C_{tj} = L + c_{tj}$$

Introduction of a stochastic cost term affects not only this term but also changes the state variable (f_t). The reason for this is easy to see. The optimum course of action in any one period depends on the level of costs. A different course of action may be appropriate with different levels of costs. We shall call the new state term $f_t(L_i)$. We are now ready to state the recursive relationship:

$$\text{For } t = T, \qquad f_t(L_i) = 0, \qquad \text{all } L_i$$

$$\text{For } t < T, \qquad f_t(L^*) = \max_{j=1,\ldots,T-t} \left[\sum_{k=1}^{j} d_{t+k} B_{tk} - I_t - \sum_{k=1}^{j} d_{t+k} c_{tk} \right.$$

$$\left. - \sum_{k=1}^{j} d_{t+k} L^* + d_{t+j} S_{tj} + d_{t+j} \sum_i f_{t+j}(L_i) \, P(L_i \mid L^*) \right],$$

$$\text{all } t, \qquad \text{all } L^* \quad (6)$$

Equation (6) states that the minimum expected cost from period t to the horizon, given the purchase of a new machine in period t, is the present value of revenues, the investment cost, the present value of the operating costs less salvage value, plus the expected value of costs from period $t + j$ to the horizon. If the firm has no existing equipment, then equation (6) can also be used in the initial period. With existing equipment, the equation in the initial period is

$$f_{\text{decision}} = \min \left[\begin{array}{l} S_{.0} + \sum_i f_0(L_i) \, P(L_i \mid L^*) \\[2mm] \max_{j=1,\ldots,T} \left[\sum_{k=1}^{j} d_k B_{.k} - \sum_{k=1}^{j} d_k c_{.k} \right. \\[2mm] \left. - \sum_{k=1}^{j} d_k L^* + d_j S_{.j} + d_j \sum_i f_j(L_i) \, P(L_i \mid L^*) \right] \end{array} \right] \quad (7)$$

Equations (6) and (7) can be used to solve the equipment replacement problem with uncertain costs. Modification to encompass uncertainty in other variables can be done in a parallel manner.

2. Infinite Horizon

Let us assume that the firm is still uncertain about the basic level of costs but now has an infinite horizon. Furthermore, assume that management expects costs to follow a Markov process so that $P(L_i/L^*)$ is known and stationary over time. With a stationary policy, the time subscript can be dropped from equation (6), and we have

$$f(L^*) = \max_j \left[\sum_{k=1}^{j} \alpha^k B_k - I - \sum_{k=1}^{j} \alpha^k c_k - \sum_{k=1}^{j} \alpha^k L^* \right.$$

$$\left. + \alpha^j S_j + \alpha^j \sum_i f_{t+j}(L_i) \, P(L_i \mid L^*) \right], \quad \text{all } L_i = L^*$$

This infinite horizon model can be solved using linear programming as shown in Appendix I of Chapter 2 or Appendix I of Chapter 3. Equation (6) is the appropriate equation for the initial period if there is no equipment currently in use. If there is equipment, equation (7) is appropriate.

C. Conclusion

In this chapter we have presented models which can be used to solve the equipment replacement model for finite and infinite horizons under certainty and risk. In addition, we have shown that the equipment replacement model and the capital budgeting model can reach different decisions.

Bibliography

[1] Bellman, R., "Equipment Replacement Policy," *SIAM*, 3, Sept. 1955, pp. 133–136.

[2] Churchman, C. West, Russel Ackoff and Leonard Arnoff, *Introduction to Operations Research* (John Wiley & Sons, Inc., New York), 1957.

[3] Elton, Edwin J., and Martin J. Gruber, "On the Optimality of an Equal Life Policy for Equipment Subject to Technological Improvement," unpublished manuscript.

[4] Fetter, R. B., and G. Goodman, "An Equipment Investment Analog," *Operations Research*, 5, (1957), pp. 657–665.

[5] Hertz, David, and Roger Eddison, *Progress in Operations Research*, Vol. II (John Wiley & Sons, Inc., New York), 1964.

[6] Jorgenson, D. W., J. J. McCall and R. Radner, *Optimal Replacement Policy* (Rand McNally & Company, Skokie, Ill.), 1967.

[7] Masse, Pierre, *Optimal Investment Decisions: Rules for Action and Criteria for Choice* (Prentice-Hall, Inc., Englewood Cliffs, N.J.), 1962.

[8] Merret, A. J., "Investment in Replacement· The Optimal Replacement Method," *The Journal of Management Studies*, 2, May 1965, pp. 153–166.

[9] Merret, A. J., and A. Sykes, *Finance and the Analysis of Capital Projects* (Long-mans, Green & Co. Ltd., London), 1963.

[10] Meyer, Robert, "Equipment Replacement under Uncertainty," *Management Science*, 17, No. 11, July 1971, pp. 750–758.

[11] Preinreich, G. A., "The Economic Life of Industrial Equipment," *Econometrica, VIII*, Jan. 1940.

[12] Schweyer, Herbert, *Analytic Models for Managerial and Engineering Economics* (Van Nostrand Reinhold Company, New York), 1964.

[13] Smith, Vernon, "Economic Equipment Policies: An Evaluation," *Management Science*, 20, Oct. 1957.

[14] Smith, Vernon, *Investment and Production* (Harvard University Press, Cambridge, Mass.), 1961.

[15] Stapleton, Richard, David Hemmings and Harry Scholefield, "Technical Change and the Optimal Life of Assets," *Operations Research Quarterly*, *23*, No. 1, pp. 46–59.

[16] Terborgh, George, *Dynamic Equipment Policy* (McGraw-Hill Book Company, New York), 1949.

[17] Terborgh, George, *Business Equipment Policy* (Machine and Allied Products Institute, Washington, D.C.), 1958.

```
8888888888888888888888888888888888888888888888888888888888888888888888888888888888888
8888888888888888888888888888888888888888888888888888888888888888888888888888888888888
88888888888888888888888888      8888888888888    888    888    888    88888888888888888888888888
8888888888888888888888888888      88888888888    8888    888    888    88888888888888888888888888
88888888888888888888888888888      888888888    88888    888    888    88888888888888888888888888
888888888888888888888888888888      8888888    888888    888    888    88888888888888888888888888
8888888888888888888888888888888      88888    8888888    888    888    88888888888888888888888888
88888888888888888888888888888888      888    88888888    888    888    88888888888888888888888888
888888888888888888888888888888888      8    888888888    888    888    88888888888888888888888888
8888888888888888888888888888888888          8888888888    888    888    88888888888888888888888888
888888888888888888888888888888888888      8888888888    888    888    88888888888888888888888888
8888888888888888888888888888888888888888888888888888888888888888888888888888888888888
8888888888888888888888888888888888888888888888888888888888888888888888888888888888888
```

Asset Selection Under Cash Constraints

Up to this point all the problems examined have involved multiperiod decisions. The type of analysis used to solve these problems has other applications in finance. Although this book is concerned with multiperiod models, it seems appropriate to briefly review other types of financial problems where recursive optimization has been applied. Dynamic programming can be used to solve multistage problems where the recursive element is not time. These classes of problems are usually referred to as *distribution of effort* problems, and asset selection under cash constraints is one such problem. In this chapter we shall first introduce the distribution of effort dynamic programming model. Then the problem of asset selection under cash constraints will be described and a dynamic programming solution presented.

A. The Distribution of Effort Model

Let us start off with a simple example to illustrate the distribution of effort model. Let us propose that management faces a problem involving the allocation of some new equipment among existing plants. Let

C = the number of machines available for distribution
X_i = the number of machines given to the ith plant
N = the total number of plants among which machines can be distributed
$b_i(X_i)$ = the profit from assigning X_i machines to the ith plant

The problem is to allocate the machines among the plants so as to maximize profit, or maximize

$$\sum_{i=1}^{N} b_i(X_i)$$

subject to

$$\sum_{i=1}^{N} X_i \leq C, \qquad X_i = 1, 2, \ldots, C \text{ for each } i$$

This problem can be solved as a dynamic programming problem. To do so, let

C' = an arbitrary number of machines $C' \leq C$
$f_i(C')$ = the maximum profit when C' machines are distributed optimally to plant, $1, \ldots, N$

The dynamic programming formulation can then be stated as

$$f_0(C') = 0$$
$$_i(C') = \max f(b_i(X_i) + f_{i-1}(C' - X_i)) \qquad (1)$$

for $i = 1, 2, \ldots, N$ and $X_i \leq C'$, where $C' = 1, \ldots, C$.

In previous problems optimization was obtained by arriving at an optimal decision at a moment in time and then deriving the optimal decision sequentially for earlier periods. In the distribution of efforts problem an optimum is reached by finding the optimum allocation of the scarce resource (machines) when one use (plant) is considered and then adding uses (plants) sequentially. For this problem the decision maker first calculates the profit for all possible numbers of machines used at the first plant. He then determines the profit from the optimum allocation for all possible numbers of machines with two plants. He continues adding one plant at a time until all plants are considered. The order in which uses (plants) are added makes no conceptual difference in the solution to the problem.[1]

To illustrate the use of the distribution of effort dynamic programming model let us solve a simple example. Let us assume that management is facing a decision on the allocation of three machines among its four operating plants. The present value of the cash flow from placing alternative numbers of machines in each plant is given in Table 8-1.

One can easily solve this problem by using the recursive relationship presented in equation (1). The value of $f_1(C')$ is simply the value of placing alternative numbers of machines in plant 1 or $f_1(0) = 0$, $f_1(1) = 100, f_1(2) = 180, f_1(3) = 180$. If we consider $f_2(3)$, we see that

---

[1] It can make a computational difference. For a discussion of these computational differences, see Weingartner and Ness [4] and Nemhauser and Ullman [1].

TABLE 8-1   Number of Units C_i Placed in Plant i

Plant	Index (i)	$X_i = 0$	$X_i = 1$	$X_i = 2$	$X_i = 3$
A	1	0	100	180	180
B	2	0	90	185	185
C	3	0	110	160	200
D	4	0	90	200	300

we have a choice of placing 0, 1, 2, or 3 machines in plant 2. We want to find

$$f_2(3) = \max \begin{bmatrix} b_2(3) + f_1(0) = 185 + 0 \\ b_2(2) + f_1(1) = 185 + 100 \\ b_2(1) + f_1(2) = 90 + 180 \\ b_2(0) + f_1(3) = 0 + 180 \end{bmatrix} = 285$$

The extension of the recursive relationship to all plants is shown in Table 8-2. The optimal solution is to place two machines in plant 4 and one machine in plant 3.

Before leaving this section let us illustrate the form of equation (1) that is appropriate for the solution of allocation problems involving more than one constraint. In particular, let us assume that there is a restriction on the amount of labor needed to install machines of the form

$$\sum_{i=1}^{N} c_i(X_i) \leq C_L$$

where

$c_i(X_i)$ = the amount of labor needed to install X_i machines in plant i
C_L = the maximum amount of labor available

Then the dynamic programming model becomes

$$f_i(C', C'_L) = \max_{X_i} \left(b_i(X_i) + f_{i-1}(C' - X_i, C'_L - c_i(X_i)) \right)$$

for $i = 1, \ldots, N$, where $C'_L \leq C_L$ and $C' \leq C$.

Models of this type can be used to solve problems involving the allocation of scarce resources to competitive uses. Many such problems arise in finance. For example, the optimal location of lock boxes by a bank can be solved by this procedure. In the rest of this chapter we shall be concerned with one such allocation problem—the allocation of a limited amount of funds to competing capital assets (asset selection under capital rationing).

TABLE 8-2

$$f_i(1) = \max(b_i(X_i) + f_{i-1}(1 - X_i))$$

i	$f_i(0)$	$X_i = 1$	$X_i = 0$	$f_i(1)$
1	0	100	0	100
2	0	$90 + 0$ $= 90$	$0 + 100$ $= 100$	100
3	0	$\boxed{110 + 0 \atop = 110}$	$0 + 100$ $= 100$	110

$$f_i(2) = \max(b_i(X_i) + f_{i-1}(2 - X_i))$$

i	$X_i = 2$	$X_i = 1$	$X_i = 0$	$f_i(2)$
1	180	100	0	180
2	$185 + 0$ $= 185$	$90 + 100$ $= 190$	$0 + 180$ $= 180$	190
3	$160 + 0$ $= 160$	$110 + 100$ $= 210$	$0 + 190$ $= 190$	210

$$f_i(3) = \max(b_i(X_i) + f_{i-1}(3 - X_i))$$

i	$X_i = 3$	$X_i = 2$	$X_i = 1$	$X_i = 0$	$f_i(3)$
1	180	180	100	0	180
2	$185 + 0$ $= 185$	$185 + 100$ $= 285$	$90 + 180$ $= 270$	$0 + 180$ $= 180$	285
3	$200 + 0$ $= 200$	$160 + 100$ $= 260$	$110 + 190$ $= 300$	$0 + 285$ $= 285$	300
4[a]	$300 + 0$ $= 300$	$\boxed{200 + 110 \atop = 310}$	$90 + 210$ $= 300$	$0 + 300$ $= 300$	310

◯ indicates an optimum path.

[a] Since the return from using a machine is never less than zero, solutions involving the allocation of less than the total number of machines can be neglected when all plants are considered.

B. Capital Budgeting Under Capital Rationing

The problem of the optimal selection of assets given an upper level on the amount of funds which can be invested in one or more periods has received a great deal of attention in the finance literature. While there are many alternative formulations of this problem, we shall adopt that put forth by Weingartner ([3], Chapter 3).[2] In particular, let us define the following terms:

b_i = the net present value of project i [3]
c_{ti} = the cash outflow required by the ith project in the tth period
C_t = the maximum amount of funds that can be invested in period t
X_i = an integer with a value of 1 if the project i is accepted and a value of 0 if project i is rejected
i = a subscript representing a particular project, $i = 1, \ldots, N$
t = a subscript representing a particular period of time, $t = 1, \ldots, T$

To maximize the present value of cash flows over the horizon T one has to find that combination of projects which has the highest present value and does not violate any budget constraint. The solution to this problem was first formulated as an integer programming model by Weingartner [2].

One statement of the problem is[4] maximize

$$\sum_{i=1}^{N} b_i X_i$$

subject to

$$\sum_{i=1}^{N} c_{ti} X_i \leq C_t \qquad \text{for } t = 1, \ldots, T$$

$$X_i = 0 \text{ or } 1 \qquad \text{for } i = 1, \ldots, N$$

Weingartner [3] reported computational difficulty in reaching a solution in a feasible amount of time when he used the integer programming algorithms which existed at that time. Consequently in a subsequent article [2] he applied dynamic programming in order to obtain a solution to this problem. The dynamic programming solution given below is based on his contribution in this area.

---

[2] Dynamic programming techniques similar to those employed in this chapter can be applied to alternative formulations of this problem.

[3] The appropriate discount rate for defining net present value has been subject to a great deal of controversy.

[4] This is one form of the capital rationing problem and is the one discussed by Weingartner [2] and Nemhauser and Ullman [1]. Normally the problem would be modified to allow transfer of funds between periods and interdependencies between projects. In addition controversy exists concerning the appropriate objective function, and a number of alternative formulations incorporating these different objective functions can be found in the literature.

C. The Dynamic Programming Solution

The allocation of scarce funds among competing projects is directly analogous to the distribution of machines among competing plants.

To construct this recursive relationship define C'_t as an arbitrary budget level for the tth period, where $C'_t \leq C_t$:

$$f_i(C'_1, C'_2, \ldots, C'_T) = \text{Present value of cash flow from an optimal}$$
allocation of funds among the first i projects where the amount of funds available in each period is defined by the appropriate C'_t

Then the recursive relationship is simply

$$f_0(C'_1, C'_2, \ldots, C'_T) = 0$$

$$f_i(C'_1, C'_2, \ldots, C'_T) = \max_{X_i=0 \text{ or } 1} (b_i X_i + f_{i-1}(C'_1 - c_{1i}X_i,$$

$$C'_2 - c_{2i}X_i, \ldots, C'_T - c_{Ti}X_i))$$

$$\text{for } i = 1, 2, \ldots, N$$

where $C'_t = 1, 2, \ldots, C_t$ for each $t = 1, 2, \ldots, T$.

The firm first calculates for all possible budget levels the value obtained from investing in the first project, then the value obtained from the optimum combinations of the first and second projects for all possible budget levels, then the value from the best combination of the first three projects, and so forth.[5]

Though the dynamic programming formulation is a solution to the linear integer programming problem initially presented by Weingartner, a straightforward application of the recursive relationship would lead to a prohibitively large number of calculations. For example, if budget constraints of $100 existed for each of seven periods and calculations were done in units of $1, we would have 100^7 possible budget levels to consider. In general we would have $\prod_{t=1}^{T} C_t$ budgets to examine. Clearly, for any realistic capital budgeting problem we would have to perform a prohibitively large number of calculations.[6] The dynamic program solution is made feasible by the fact that the projects are discrete and hence budget levels with slack need not be considered.

For example, if the first two projects involved outlays of $3 and $7

---

[5] Since all feasible combinations of projects are examined, the order in which projects are examined does not affect the solution.

[6] In general the potential calculations involved are greater than the product of the budget levels since the possibility of cash throw-off from investments raises the effective budget limit.

in period 1, then the only values of C_1 that would have to be considered in computing $f_2(C_1, C_2, \ldots, C_N)$ are \$3, \$7, and \$10.[7]

Nevertheless, for realistic capital budgeting problems the calculations involved are still enormous. A discussion of the different techniques which can be used to reduce the computations necessary to solve the dynamic programming formulation of this asset selection problem are contained in Bibliography References [1], [2], and [4].

Bibliography

[1] Nemhauser, G., and R. Ullman, "Discrete Dynamic Programming and Capital Allocation," *Management Science*, 15, No. 9, May 1969, pp. 494–505.

[2] Weingartner, H. Martin, "Capital Budgeting of Interrelated Projects: Survey and Synthesis," *Management Science*, 12, No. 7, March 1966, pp. 485–516.

[3] Weingartner, H. Martin, *Mathematical Programming and the Analysis of Capital Budgeting Problems* (Markham Publishing Company, Chicago), 1967.

[4] Weingartner, H. Martin, and David Ness, "Methods for the Solution of the Multidimensional 0/1 Knapsack Problem," *Operations Research*, 15, No. 1, Jan.–Feb. 1967, pp. 83–103.

---

[7] See Weingartner and Ness [4] and Nemhauser and Ullman [1] for a discussion of algorithms utilizing this insight.

The Optimum Cost of Capital, Financing, and Valuation of the Firm[*]

THE finance literature contains a large number of articles dealing with the determination of the firm's optimum cost of capital, financing patterns, and valuation. Two types of models have been developed. The first analyzes the problem using single-period analysis. The second uses a multiperiod valuation model where the parameters are fixed exogenously or are fixed in solution at a constant level for all time.[1] In this chapter we shall apply multiperiod techniques to the solution of a simple version of this problem.[2] The distinguishing characteristic of this analysis is that in contrast to other approaches, decision parameters are free to vary over time.

In addition to presenting a model for the optimal cost of capital, financing, and valuation of the firm, we shall present an introduction to control theory as one possible tool for intertemporal analysis. Control theory can be thought of as the continuous time analog to dynamic

---

[*] This chapter is based on the first section of an article [4] which the authors of this monograph jointly authored with Zvi Lieber.

[1] Sometimes the parameters themselves are not fixed but rather their growth rate.

[2] For the application of control theory to other formulations of this problem, see Elton *et al.* [4] and Krouse [7, 8]. For applications to regulated industries see Elton, Gruber and Lieber [3] and Elton and Gruber [1].

programming. Applications of control theory are starting to appear in the finance literature, and indeed aspects of some of the problems discussed in previous chapters have been analyzed via control theory.[3]

We have restricted the application of control theory to one chapter, since there are fewer applications of control theory than of dynamic programming, since the problems analyzed using control theory can often be analyzed more easily using dynamic programming, and since dynamic programming is a more general modeling structure.[4] The mathematics employed in this chapter are of necessity more difficult than that used in previous chapters.

The model we shall analyze in this chapter is based on a set of simplifying assumptions. Modigliani and Miller's definition [12, 14] of the value of stockholder wealth is assumed to hold at each moment in time. Investment opportunities are taken as exogenously determined. Earnings are generated from the accumulation of past investments. Book depreciation equals real depreciation. Finally, the market value of debt is limited to a fraction of the market value of the firm's stock. Employing these assumptions plus the criteria of maximizing the wealth of initial stockholders, we shall derive the optimal time path of dividends, external equity, and additions to debt, as well as optimum rates of capital accumulation and rates of earnings growth. In addition, Modigliani and Miller's proposition regarding the null effects of dividend policy and the tax-induced benefits of debt financing are demonstrated to hold in the continuous time infinite horizon framework. However, the cost of new debt and equity and the firm's financing pattern are different from the results indicated by a one-period model.

A. The Basic Structure

To construct an intertemporal model of the firm's cost of capital, financing, and valuation decision, we must define some symbols. Let

$S(t)$ = the market value of common equity at time t

$s_N(t)$ = the dollar amount of new flotation of common stock occurring at time t; new common stock is assumed to be issued ex-dividend[5]

i = the interest rate on debt; it is assumed constant over time

$b_N(t)$ = the dollar value of bonds issued at time t

$B(t)$ = the market value of bonds outstanding at time t; for bonds, market value and book value are the same, since interest rates are assumed constant over time

---

[3] See, for example, Merton [10, 11] and Samuelson [16] for applications to portfolio theory and Sethi and Thompson [17] for an application in the cash management area.

[4] Control theory is usually inapplicable for problems containing fixed charges because the first derivative of the cost function is not continuous at all points. In addition, the mathematics of control theory for the risk case are extremely complex and not fully developed.

[5] $s_N(t)$ and $b_N(t)$ are really rates of new security flotation in the continuous time formulation of the problem.

$r(I)$ = the rate of return on new investment of amount I
$D(t)$ = the total dividends paid at time t
τ = the corporate income tax rate
$E(t)$ = the total earnings of the firm at time t net of economic depreciation. $E(t)$ is the earnings after taxes that the firm would earn if it had only equity financing.
ρ^τ = the rate of return to equity holders of an all-equity firm in a particular risk class
$k(t)$ = the rate of return to equity holders at time t; when debt equals zero, $k(t) = \rho^\tau$
r^* = the average rate of return when an optimum amount of new investment is undertaken

In the rest of the chapter we shall drop the time subscript except where it might lead to confusion, and dots will be used to indicate derivatives (i.e., $\dot{S}$ is the change in S).

The fundamental valuation equation of Miller and Modigliani is[6]

$$S(t) = \frac{1}{1 + k(t)} (D(t) + S(t + 1) - s_N(t))$$

where $k(t)$ is a function of $B(t)$ and $S(t)$. Stockholder wealth at time t consists of the present value of the dividends paid to stockholders at the end of the period, plus the market value of the firm at the end of the period, minus the market value of the firm sold during the period.

In continuous time

$$\dot{S} = kS - D + s_N \tag{1}$$

This equation is the standard valuation equation used in most of the economic literature.[7] The behavioral assumption underlying it is that future policies of the firm are fully anticipated and capitalized. For example, this implies that new investments at time 0 do not lead to a readjustment of the value of the firm at time 1, since the value of this investment is already fully reflected in the current price. Integrating equation (1) yields

$$S(0) = \int_0^\infty [D(w) - s_N(w)] e^{\int_0^w -k(u)\,du}\,dw$$

where w and u are variables of integration. Notice that if k is a constant over time, the above equation becomes

$$S(0) = \int_0^\infty [D(w) - s_N(w)] e^{-kw}\,dw$$

---

[6] Miller and Modigliani [12], equation (3). This is a standard valuation equation used in most analysis. A recent example is Krouse [8]. Krouse's equation is identical except that he allows the issuance of stock at other than market prices.

[7] To be consistent with the original Modigliani and Miller analysis, we shall ignore transaction costs throughout.

Thus equation (1) is the differential equation underlying a valuation equation which equates the wealth of the current stockholders $S(0)$ with the present value of future dividends to the current stockholders. This valuation equation has been shown to be equivalent to valuation equations utilizing earnings and cash flow.[8]

Modigliani and Miller [14], under the assumption of perfect capital markets, have shown that arbitrage will cause the single-period after-tax yield on common stocks to be[9]

$$\rho^\tau + (1 - \tau)(\rho^\tau - i)\frac{B}{S}.$$

In the continuous time analog of the Modigliani and Miller problem, this expression will still represent the after-tax yield at any point in time, so the expression for after-tax yield can be written as

$$k(t) = \rho^\tau + (1 - \tau)(\rho^\tau - i)\frac{B(t)}{S(t)} \tag{2}$$

where the tax yield on equity at time t is seen to depend on the market value of debt and equity at time t.[10]

Three other equations are needed to complete the basic model: one relating the change in earnings to investment, one (an accounting identity) equating sources and uses of funds, and one adjusting total debt for new additions. The change in earnings is assumed to be equal to the product of new investment (I) and the return on the investment $[r(I)]$. The after-tax change in earnings is

$$\dot{E} = r(I)I(1 - \tau) \tag{3}$$

The only restrictions placed on the return function is that it is a continuous decreasing function in I. This assumption is consistent with projects being ranked in order of decreasing return.

The firm is assumed to have three sources of funds: earnings, new equity, and new debt. These funds can be used to pay interest, to invest, and to pay dividends.[11] In an optimal feasible solution, the sources must equal the uses, or[12]

$$E + s_N + b_N = D + I + iB(1 - \tau)$$

---

[8] See Miller and Modigliani [12].

[9] A number of alternative proofs of this are available. Hamada [5] and Hirshlaefer [6] are two examples.

[10] The assumption is being made that the basic level of interest rates and required yield on stock (under any given debt to equity ratio) are constant over time.

[11] The assumption being made here is that book and economic depreciation are equal.

[12] A feasible solution requires only that sources exceed uses. Inspection easily shows that surplus funds are nonoptimal, since their use (for example, as dividends) increases the objective function. Thus, cash is nonoptimal, and the inequality can be stated as an equality.

Rearranging to solve for D yields

$$D = E + s_N + b_N - I - iB(1 - \tau) \qquad (4)$$

The final equation needed is to relate the change in debt to new debt:

$$\dot{B} = b \qquad (5)$$

These five equations are the multiperiod analog of the Modigliani and Miller system. As they pointed out, in this situation the value of the firm increases linearly with the addition of debt, because interest is tax deductible and the addition of debt increases the amount of the tax subsidy on interest. Since the addition of debt increases the tax subsidy, the optimal course of action for the firm is to immediately add an infinite amount of debt. Modigliani and Miller [13, 14] argued that what prevented the firm from adding an unlimited amount of debt was an institutional constraint on the market value of the debt equity ratio.[13] In equation form this is

$$\theta \geq \frac{B(t)}{S(t)} \qquad (6)$$

The optimal behavior of a firm over time can now be studied as a control problem with states S, E, and B and control variables s_N, b_N, and I. The terminology of control theory is very descriptive of the analysis to be performed. Management makes a set of decisions about the level at each point in time of the control variables in order to change the state of the system (state variables) over time so as to maximize an objective function. The appropriate objective function for this problem is

$$\max [B(0) - B'] + S(0) \qquad (7)$$

where B' is the initial value of debt in the firm's capital structure. The amount $B(0) - B'$ is an instantaneous adjustment of the initial level of debt. The proceeds from this adjustment are instantaneously paid out to initial stockholders and thus contribute immediately to their wealth. $S(0)$ is the present value of the stream of future dividends to the initial stockholders. The equations governing the system are

1. Differential equations:

$$\dot{S} = kS - D + s_N \qquad (1)$$

$$\dot{E} = r(I)I(1 - \tau) \qquad (3)$$

$$\dot{B} = b \qquad (5)$$

---

[13] Krouse [7] incorporates debt financing in a dynamic model, but in doing so he makes the unrealistic assumptions that book rather than market valuation of the firm's capital structure is important and that the firm faces unlimited investments at a fixed rate.

2. Equalities:

$$k = \rho^\tau + (1 - \tau)(\rho^\tau - i)\frac{B}{S} \qquad (2)$$

$$D = E + s_N + b_N - I - iB(1 - \tau) \qquad (4)$$

3. Constraints:

$$\theta S - B \geq 0 \qquad (6)$$

$$D \geq 0$$

$$s_N \geq 0$$

We have added the last two equations to those discussed earlier in order to ensure that the firm never pays negative dividends or sells negative amounts of new stock. Later these constraints will be shown to be redundant and will be dropped.

B. The Solution

We have seen that the problem under study involves a set of decision or control variables $s_N(t)$, $b_N(t)$, and $I(t)$ which determine (changes in) the level of state variables S, E, and B. What we want to do is to set these control variables so as to maximize the objective function given by equation (7). To do this let us define a new set of variables (called costate variables), one for each state variable:

$\psi_B(t)$ = the value (in terms of the objective function) of an added dollar of debt at time t

$\psi_S(t)$ = the value of an added dollar of equity at time t

$\psi_E(t)$ = the value of an added dollar of earnings at time t

To maximize the objective function, we should at any moment in time change the state variable so that the amount of each state variable added times the marginal value of adding a dollar to that state is maximized. In other words, we should seek to maximize

$$\psi_S(t)\dot{S}(t) + \psi_B(t)\dot{B}(t) + \psi_E(t)\dot{E}(t)$$

This expression is usually referred to in control theory as the Hamiltonian. In maximizing this function, we have to stay within the limits defined by the constraints on debt to equity ratios, dividends, and new equity sales. We can adjoin these constraints to the Hamiltonian with Lagrangian multipliers to form what is generally called, in the control theory literature, the Lagrangian function:

$$L(t) = \psi_S(t)\dot{S}(t) + \psi_B(t)\dot{B}(t) + \psi_E(t)\dot{E}(t) + \gamma_1(t)D(t)$$
$$+ \gamma_2(t)s_N(t) + \lambda(t)[\theta S(t) - B(t)]$$

where γ_1, γ_2, and λ are Lagrangian multipliers and thus for any t are each always greater than or equal to zero.

Dropping the time subscript for compactness, substituting in equations (1), (2), (3), (4), and (5) for the appropriate variables, and simplifying yield

$$
\begin{aligned}
L = {} & \psi_S[\rho^r S + \rho^r(1 - \tau)B - E - b_N + I] \\
& + \psi_B b_N + \psi_E[r(I)I(1 - \tau)] \\
& + \gamma_1[E + s_N + b_N - I - iB(1 - \tau)] + \gamma_2 s_N + \lambda(\theta S - B) \quad (8)
\end{aligned}
$$

Having developed the appropriate Lagrangian function for our problem, we can now apply the maximum principle to obtain a set of conditions that must be met at the optimum.[14] These conditions allow us to determine the optimum time path for our variables and derive implications for optimal management behavior.

First we shall present the general form of the maximum principle. Define

1. $C_i(t)$ as a control (decision) variable, $i = 1, \ldots, I$.
2. $S_j(t)$ as a state variable, $j = 1, \ldots, J$.
3. $\psi_j(t)$ as the costate variable associated with state j.

The maximum principle has two parts. The first part states that each control variable should be chosen at each moment in time, so that the Lagrangian function is maximized. In the case of convex functions, this means that[15]

$$
\frac{\partial L(t)}{\partial C_i(t)} = 0 \qquad \text{for all } i = 1, \ldots, I \text{ and all } t
$$

The second part of the maximum principle requires that the rate of change with respect to time of each costate variable be equal to the negative of the partial derivative of the Lagrangian function with respect to the corresponding state variable. In analytical terms

$$
\dot{\psi}_j(t) = -\frac{\partial L(t)}{\partial S_j(t)} \qquad \text{for all } j = 1, \ldots, J \text{ and all } t
$$

Applying the second part of the maximum principle will result in a series of differential equations. To solve these differential equations,

---

[14] We shall not derive the maximum principle. For the reader who wishes to explore the development of the maximum principle, see Pontryagin [15] and Mangasarian [9]. They prove that the necessary conditions of the maximum principle are also sufficient whenever the problem is convex. Clearly, Mangasarian's results hold in our problem, and his formulation of the maximum principle is used in the text.

[15] This condition is exactly what one would expect from basic calculus. In basic calculus, the first derivative is zero at a maximum for convex functions.

one needs either starting conditions $\psi_j(0)$ or ending conditions $\psi_j(\infty)$ for each costate variable.[16]

We can now apply the maximum principle to our problem. Recalling that the problem involves three control variables s_N, b_N, and I we can apply the first part of the maximum principle:

$$\frac{\partial L}{\partial s_N} = \gamma_1 + \gamma_2 = 0 \tag{9}$$

$$\frac{\partial L}{\partial b_N} = -\psi_S + \psi_B + \gamma_1 = 0 \tag{10}$$

$$\frac{\partial L}{\partial I} = \psi_S + \psi_E \left(\frac{\partial r(I)}{\partial I} I + r(I) \right)(1 - \tau) - \gamma_1 = 0 \tag{11}$$

Recalling that our problem contains three state variables S, B, and E and applying the second part of the maximum principle yield

$$\dot{\psi}_S = -\frac{\partial L}{\partial S} = -\rho^r \psi_S - \lambda\theta \tag{12}$$

$$\dot{\psi}_B = -\frac{\partial L}{\partial B} = -(1 - \tau)\rho^r \psi_S + \lambda + i(1 - \tau)\gamma_1 \tag{13}$$

$$\dot{\psi}_E = -\frac{\partial L}{\partial E} = \psi_S - \gamma_1 \tag{14}$$

To start the analysis, examine equation (9). γ_1 and γ_2 are the Lagrangians associated, respectively, with the constraint that dividends and new equity cannot be negative. As Lagrangians, they measure the cost of the constraint. If the constraint is not binding, their value is zero since the constraint does not restrict the maximum obtainable. If the constraint were binding, then they would be positive and their magnitude would measure, on the margin, the cost of the constraint in terms of how much it restricts the maximum value of the multiperiod problem. Equation (9) states that the sum of γ_1 and γ_2 is zero. Since neither γ_1 nor γ_2 can be negative, for their sum to be zero both γ_1 and γ_2 must equal zero. γ_1 and γ_2 equal to zero implies that the constraints on dividends and new equity sales are not binding and are therefore redundant. Consequently, in the rest of the analysis they will be ignored and γ_1 and γ_2 will be eliminated.

Notice that $\dot{\psi}_S$ and $\dot{\psi}_B$ are functions of λ. To proceed further with our analysis, it is necessary to get an explicit solution for λ. From equation (10), we know that $\psi_S = \psi_B$ and therefore $\dot{\psi}_S = \dot{\psi}_B$ for all t. Substituting from equations (12) and (13) yields

$$-\rho^r \psi_S - \lambda\theta = -(1 - \tau)\rho^r \psi_S + \lambda$$

---

[16] If the problem has a finite horizon T rather than an infinite horizon, one must either know $\psi_j(0)$ or $\psi_j(T)$ for each costate variable.

Solving for λ, we get

$$\lambda = \frac{-\tau \rho^\tau}{1 + \theta} \psi_S \qquad (15)$$

Substituting for λ in equations (12), (13), and (14) and recognizing that γ_1 and γ_2 both equal zero yield

$$\dot{\psi}_S = -m\psi_S$$

$$\dot{\psi}_B = -m\psi_S$$

$$\dot{\psi}_E = \psi_S$$

where

$$m = \rho^\tau \left(1 - \tau \frac{\theta}{1 + \theta} \right)$$

To solve this set of differential equations, one needs either a starting or ending value for each of the costate variables. The appropriate values for the costate variables in our problem are $\psi_S(\infty) = 0$, $\psi_B(\infty) = 0$, and $\psi_E(\infty) = 0$.[17]

Employing the beginning and ending conditions, the differential equations can be solved, yielding[18]

$$\psi_S = -e^{-mt} \qquad (16)$$

$$\psi_B = -e^{-mt} \qquad (17)$$

$$\psi_E = \frac{1}{m} e^{-mt} \qquad (18)$$

---

[17] The starting or ending conditions for costate variables can usually be deduced logically from the structure of a problem. For example, the present value of a dollar of earnings received in the infinite future is zero. Hence, $\psi_E(\infty) = 0$.

[18] The solution to these differential equations can easily be illustrated. Substituting equation (16) into the expression for ψ_B yields

$$\psi_B = -m\psi_S = me^{-mt}$$

The value of ψ_B at infinity equals the value at zero, plus the change in value between zero and infinity or

$$\psi_B(\infty) = \psi_B(0) + \int_0^\infty me^{-m\tau} \, d\tau = 0$$

Thus

$$\psi_B(0) = -1$$

Since the value of ψ_B at any moment of time t is equal to its value at time 0, plus the change in its value between 0 and t, we have

$$\psi_B(t) = \psi_B(0) + \int_0^t me^{-m\tau} \, d\tau = -1 - e^{-mt} + 1 = -e^{mt}$$

where

$$m = \rho^r\left(1 - \tau\frac{\theta}{1 + \theta}\right) \tag{19}$$

Since ψ_S is negative, equation (15) shows that $\lambda > 0$ for all t. λ is the Lagrangian associated with the debt equity constraint. Since it is always positive (binding), the optimum solution requires that the firm always operate with maximum allowable debt in its capital structure. If we let asterisks designate values at the optimum, then $B^*/S^* = \theta$. Thus, $\theta/(1 + \theta) = B^*/(B^* + S^*)$ and equation (19) becomes

$$m = \rho^r\left(1 - \tau\frac{B^*}{B^* + S^*}\right) \tag{20}$$

Substituting the expressions for ψ_S and ψ_E into equation (11) and solving for the marginal rate of return which must be earned on new investment yield

$$\left[r(I) + \frac{\partial r(I)}{\partial I}I\right](1 - \tau) = m = \rho^r\left(1 - \tau\frac{B^*}{B^* + S^*}\right) \tag{21}$$

The optimum cutoff rate for new investment (in terms of posttax cash flows) is equal to the cost of capital for an all-equity firm minus the product of this rate, the firm's tax rate, and its maximum allowable debt to debt plus equity ratio. Several conclusions can now be drawn.

First, note that ρ^r, τ, and θ are constant over time: Thus, m is also a constant over time. Since m is constant over time, the cutoff rate for new investment is constant over time. Furthermore, since the firm faces the same investment schedule at all instants of time, the amount of investment taken I^* and the average rate of return earned on that investment r^* must be constant over time.[19] Since m is the cutoff rate for new investment, $r^* \geq m$.

Second, note that this equation is identical to Modigliani and Miller's equation (8) [14] in footnote 16. Their one-period formulation of the cutoff rate for new investment is equally valid in the continuous time growth analog to their no growth static analysis. Note, however, that the cost of debt and equity funds given by equations (16) and (17) are different from those proposed by Modigliani and Miller. Specifically, the cost of debt and equity funds are both equal to $\rho^r\{1 - \tau[B^*/(B^* + S^*)]\}$.[20] In the Modigliani and Miller formulation, the cost of debt funds is always less than the cost of equity funds.[21] As they have pointed out, this

---

[19] Note that r^* remaining constant is a result of our analysis, not an assumption. In standard valuation literature, r^* is set as a constant by assumption.

[20] $\psi_S = \psi_B = -e^{-mt}$. Note that e^{-mt} is the continuous analog to the discrete static discount rate of m.

[21] This is not a criticism of Modigliani and Miller. They computed the cost of debt and equity funds before they introduced the concept of a constraint on debt funds.

calls for a firm to be composed of 100 % debt financing. They recognize that a constraint exists on the amount of debt funds that can be used. Once this constraint is imposed, then (as we have shown above) the firm should always operate so that the constraint is binding. Given that the firm operates at its maximum debt to equity ratio, an increase in debt is more costly than the unconstrained case would suggest because an increase in debt must be accompanied by an increase in equity. Similarly, an increase in equity loosens the constraint and allows the firm to employ more debt. Funds should always be added in the proportion set by θ. Thus, the costs are identical and are equal to m. The necessity for the cost of debt to equal the cost of equity can be seen elsewhere in the analysis. As a condition for an optimum, debt should be added until the change in L with a change in debt equals zero. Examination of equation (10) shows that debt should be added until the cost of debt equals the cost of equity.

The initial value of the firm and the value of initial stockholder wealth are easy to derive. Since the debt constraint is always binding,

$$\dot{S} = \frac{b_N}{\theta} \qquad (22)$$

Substituting for $\dot{S}$ from equation (1), we get

$$\frac{b_N}{\theta} = kS - D + s_N$$

Substituting equation (2) for k and equation (4) for D and noting that $\theta S = B$, we have

$$\frac{b_N}{\theta} = \rho^r S + (\rho^r - i)(1 - \tau)\theta S - (E(0) + r*I*(1 - \tau)t)$$
$$+ I* - s_N - b_N + i\theta S(1 - \tau) + s_N$$

Solving for b_N and substituting the expression for b_N into equation (22) yields

$$\dot{S} = \left(\rho^r - \frac{\tau\rho^r\theta}{1 + \theta}\right)S - \frac{E(0) + r*I*(1 - \tau)t - I*}{1 + \theta}$$

Solving this differential equation yields

$$S(0) = \left[\frac{E(0)}{m} - \frac{I*}{m} + \frac{r*I*(1 - \tau)}{m^2}\right]\frac{1}{1 + \theta} \qquad (23)$$

$$S(0) + B(0) = \frac{E(0)}{m} - \frac{I*}{m} + \frac{r*I*(1 - \tau)}{m^2}$$

Note that the value of stockholder wealth (and the value of the firm) is not a function of the dividend policy followed by the firm. The value of stockholder wealth depends on the initial level of earnings, the investment schedule facing the firm, and θ. All these variables are independent of the level of dividends in any period. Thus, the null effect of dividend policy first analyzed in a static, no debt model has been reaffirmed in the continuous time model incorporating debt financing. This is true even though the value of the stockholder's wealth was defined to be the present value of all future dividends.

As we shall now show, the fact that dividend policy does not matter does not imply that new equity financing does not matter. We have already discussed the fact that γ_1 always equals zero. For γ_1 to equal zero, enough new equity must be sold so that the dividend constraint is not binding. However, since $\partial L/\partial s_N$ is zero for all levels of equity sales above this minimum, equity sales above the minimum have no effect on the value of the firm. From equation (23), the rate of change in the value of the firm and the rate of growth in earnings are

$$\dot{S} = \frac{r^*I^*(1-\tau)}{m}\frac{1}{1+\theta}$$

$$\dot{E} = r^*I^*(1-\tau)$$

Substituting these equations into the expression for dividends (4) and utilizing the fact that the debt constant is always binding yield

$$D(t) = E(0) + r^*I^*(1-\tau)t + s_N(t) + \frac{r^*I^*(1-\tau)}{m}\frac{\theta}{1+\theta} - I^*$$
$$- i(1-\tau)\frac{\theta}{1+\theta}\left[\frac{E(0)}{m} + \frac{r^*I^*(1-\tau)t}{m} - \frac{I^*}{m} + \frac{r^*I^*(1-\tau)}{m^2}\right]$$

$D(t)$ can be divided into two sets of terms; one set is constant while the other grows over time. Define C as the constant part of $D(t)$; then

$$C = E(0) + \frac{r^*I^*(1-\tau)}{m}\frac{\theta}{1+\theta} - I^*$$
$$- i(1-\tau)\frac{\theta}{1+\theta}\left[\frac{E(0)}{m} - \frac{I^*}{m} + \frac{r^*I^*(1-\tau)}{m^2}\right]$$
$$D(t) = s_N(t) + C + r^*I^*(1-\tau)t - \frac{i(1-\tau)\theta}{m(1+\theta)}(r^*I^*(1-\tau)t)$$

The minimum dividend that can be paid is zero. The right-hand side must be greater than or equal to zero. Thus,

$$s_N(t) \geq -C + \frac{i(1-\tau)\theta}{m(1+\theta)}r^*I^*(1-\tau)t - r^*I^*(1-\tau)t \qquad (24)$$

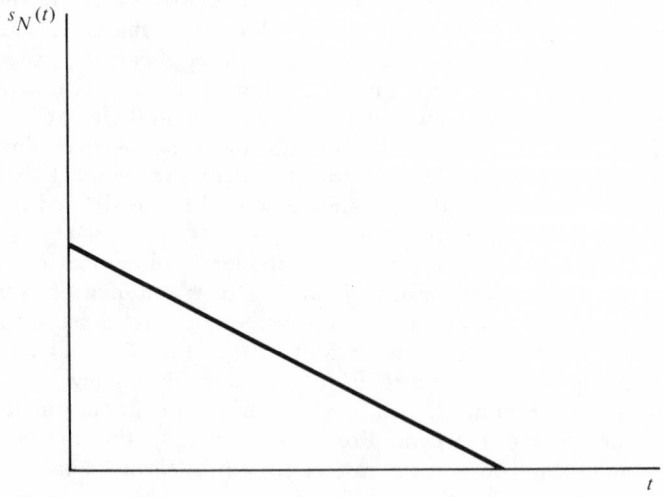

Figure 9-1

$s_N(t)$ is also restricted to being larger than zero. Thus, the minimum new equity financing is zero or determined by the right-hand side of equation (24).

The minimum pattern of new equity sales is depicted in Figure 9-1 under the assumption that, initially, investment opportunities are sufficiently abundant so that inequality (24) is the binding constraint. The intercept is given by the right-hand side of this inequality at time 0. As long as this inequality is binding, the change in the amount of new equity is given by the derivative of the right-hand side, or

$$\frac{\partial s_N(t)}{\partial t} = r^* I^* (1 - \tau) \left(\frac{i(1 - \tau)}{m} \frac{\theta}{1 + \theta} - 1 \right)$$

The minimum amount of new equity sales over time will decrease until internal funds plus the cash flow from new debt are sufficient to finance new investment. Thus, although dividend policy does not matter, a minimal level exists for new equity flotation at any moment in time. Any new equity flotation above the minimum level leaves the wealth of initial stockholders unchanged.

Conclusion

In this chapter we have introduced control theory in the context of a model which explicitly incorporates the intertemporal interdependencies between financing and investment decisions. The model provides insight into optimum firm behavior over time. The optimum cost of capital for debt and equity funds, cutoff rate for new investment, and financing pattern have been developed. In addition, the value of the firm which follows this optimum course of action is derived. In performing this analysis, the M and M postulates concerning the null effects of dividends and the appropriate cutoff rate for new investment, which were developed assuming a discrete single-period world, have been shown to hold in a continuous time horizon problem.

Bibliography

[1] Elton, Edwin, Martin Gruber and Zvi Lieber, "Valuation Optimal Investment and Financing for the Firm Subject to Regulation," *Journal of Finance*, May 1975.

[2] Elton, Edwin J., and Martin J. Gruber, "Valuation and the Cost of Capital for Regulated Industries," *Journal of Finance*, 26, No. 3, June 1971, pp. 661–670.

[3] Elton, Edwin and Martin Gruber, "Optimal Investment and Financing Patterns under Alternative Methods of Regulation," Conference on Regulated Utilities at Dartmouth College, Aug. 1974.

[4] Elton, Edwin J., Martin J. Gruber and Zvi Lieber, "The Optimal Investment, Financing, and Valuation of the Firm: An Intertemporal Analysis," working paper.

[5] Hamada, Robert, "Portfolio Analysis Market Equilibrium and Corporate Finance," *Journal of Finance*, 24, No. 1, March 1969, pp. 13–31.

[6] Hirshlaefer, Jack, "Investment Decisions Under Uncertainty: Choice Theoretic Approaches," *Quarterly Journal of Economics*, 79, Nov. 1965, pp. 509–536.

[7] Krouse, Clement, "Optimal Financing and Capital Structure Programs for the Firm," *Journal of Finance*, XXVIII, June 1958, pp. 1057–1071.

[8] Krouse, Clement, "On the Theory of Optimal Investment Dividends and Growth in the Firm," *American Economic Review*, LXIII, No. 3, June 1973. pp. 269–280.

[9] Mangasarian, O. L., "Sufficient Conditions for the Optimal Control of Non-linear Systems," *SIAM Journal of Control*, IV, 1966, pp. 139–152.

[10] Merton, Robert, "Lifetime Portfolio Selection Under Uncertainty: The Continuous Time Case," *Review of Economics and Statistics*, 50, Aug. 1969, pp. 247–257.

[11] Merton, Robert, "Optimal Consumption and Portfolio Rules in a Continuous Time Model," *Journal of Economic Theory*, 3, No. 4, Dec. 1971, pp. 373–413.

[12] Miller, Merton and Franco Modigliani, "Dividend Policy Growth and the Valuation of Shares," *Journal of Business*, 34, Oct. 1961, pp. 411–433.

[13] Modigliani, Franco, and Merton Miller, "The Cost of Capital Corporation Finance, and the Theory of Investments," *American Economic Review*, XLVIII, June 1958, pp. 261–297.

[14] Modigliani, Franco, and Merton Miller, "Corporate Income Taxes and the Cost of Capital: A Correction," *American Economic Review*, 53, June 1963, pp. 433–443.

[15] Pontryagin, L. S., V. G. Boltyanskii, R. V. Gamkrelidze and E. F. Mishchenko, *The Mathematical Theory of Optimal Processes* (John Wiley & Sons, Inc., New York), 1962.

[16] Samuelson, Paul, "Lifetime Portfolio Selection by Dynamic Stochastic Programming," *Review of Economics and Statistics*, 50, Aug. 1969, pp. 239–246.

[17] Sethi, Suresh, and Gerald Thompson, "Applications of Mathematical Control Theory to Finance: Modeling Simple Dynamic Cash Balance Problems," *Journal of Financial and Quantitative Analysis*, 5, 1970, pp. 381–394.

```
101010101010101010101010101010101010101010101010101010101010101010101010101010
101010101010101010101010101010101010101010101010101010101010101010101010101010
101010101010101010101010101010101010101   10101   1010101010101010101010101010101010
101010101010101010101010101010101010101010   010   0101010101010101010101010101010101010
101010101010101010101010101010101010101010101   1   10101010101010101010101010101010101010
101010101010101010101010101010101010101010101010      01010101010101010101010101010101010
101010101010101010101010101010101010101010101   10101010101010101010101010101010101010
101010101010101010101010101010101010101010101010   0101010101010101010101010101010101010
101010101010101010101010101010101010101010101   1   10101010101010101010101010101010101010
101010101010101010101010101010101010101010   010   0101010101010101010101010101010101010
101010101010101010101010101010101010101   10101   1010101010101010101010101010101010
101010101010101010101010101010101010101010101010101010101010101010101010101010101010
101010101010101010101010101010101010101010101010101010101010101010101010101010101010
```

Conclusions

In this book we have attempted to synthesize and extend the application of multiperiod decision models to financial problems. We believe that this book is just a beginning—that over time more and more multiperiod solution techniques will be brought to bear on more and more aspects of the finance function. It seems appropriate at this point to bring forth our crystal ball and speculate concerning potential application and modeling techniques.

Decisions involving the timing of financing are multiperiod decisions for which optimum solutions may be changed if the single-period framework is removed. One example of this was presented in Chapter 2 when the bond-refunding problem was discussed. Another example was presented in Chapter 9 in an attempt to analyze the optimum financing and cost of capital for the firm. The analysis in Chapter 2 was realistic in the sense of incorporating transaction costs and uncertainty; however, simplifying assumptions had to be made about the amount of debt that was optimum for the firm—the problem involved suboptimization. On the other hand, to solve the entire optimum financing pattern for the firm (in Chapter 9), simplifying assumptions had to be made to make the problem tractable. In particular the model developed ignored uncertainty as well as taxes and transaction costs and made particular assumptions about the way common stock was valued at each moment in time.

157

In the future increased work should be done on full-scale multiperiod models to determine the optimum investment, financing, and valuation of the firm. The development of such models will depend on increased knowledge of both the valuation process and multiperiod solution techniques.

Repetitive decisions are also made in the management of short-term assets, such as inventory, accounts receivable, accounts payable, and cash. Aspects of all these areas have already been studied through multiperiod solution techniques, but further applications should prove profitable. For example, Bierman and Hausman [2] studied one aspect of accounts receivable management as a recursive process. However, their findings also strongly suggest that credit evaluation techniques (e.g., discriminate analysis) and collection techniques have been incorrectly evaluated, for the effect on future returns has been ignored. Finally, the ability of dynamic programming to decompose a complex process which takes place over time into a series of simpler or shorter processes suggests that it should prove a useful tool in both forecasting and control, two areas with which the financial executive is deeply concerned. While some work has been done in the forecasting area, this field is still largely unexplored.[1]

Accompanying the application of multiperiod techniques to new financial problems will be advanced development of the tools of analysis themselves. Dynamic programming is a very useful technique for analyzing and understanding problems. Often, however, it is computationally infeasible to use it as a solution technique. We have already seen examples of the use of linear programming techniques to solve dynamic programming problems. In the future we should see the development of other improved solution techniques to dynamic programming models. We have seen that control theory is limited in its ability to analyze problems where fixed charges and/or risk are important. Work has already begun on the development of control theory formulations which can handle these problems and thus be more applicable to finance.[2] A promising alternative technique, not often used in finance, is differential or difference equation systems. While such systems have been widely used elsewhere in economics, they have rarely been used in finance.

In the recent past, economists have turned more and more from one-period static equilibrium models to dynamic processes. It is only recently that researchers have realized that financial decisions must also be viewed in a dynamic context. As this realization grows, the application of recursive optimization to financial problems should increase markedly. We hope that this monograph will play a role in speeding this process.

---

[1] See Beckmann [1].
[2] For an example, see Merton [3].

Bibliography

[1] Beckmann, M. J. *Dynamic Programming of Economic Decisions* (Springer-Verlag, New York, Inc., New York), 1968.

[2] Bierman, Harold, and Warren Hausman, "The Credit Granting Decision," *Management Science*, 16, No. 8, April 1970, pp. B519–B532.

[3] Merton, Robert, "Optimal Consumption and Portfolio Rules in a Continuous Time Model," *Journal of Economic Theory*, 3, No. 4, Dec. 1971, pp. 373–413.